A PANTHER
IS A BLACK CAT

A PANTHER IS A BLACK CAT

Reginald Major

BLACK CLASSIC PRESS
Baltimore, MD

A PANTHER IS A BLACK CAT

Published 2006
by Black Classic Press
All Rights Reserved.

Library of Congress Card Catalog Number: 2004107094

ISBN 13: 9781574780376
ISBN 10: 1574780379

Cover design by Nathaniel Taintor

Printed by BCP Digital Printing, Inc.,
an affiliate company of Black Classic Press

Founded in 1978, Black Classic Press specializes in bringing to light obscure and significant works by and about people of African descent. If our books are not available in your area, ask your local bookseller to order them.

Visit www.blackclassicbooks.com for a full list of our titles.

You may also obtain a list of our current titles by writing to:
Black Classic Press
c/o List
P.O. Box 13414
Baltimore, MD 21203

To Katara, B.J., Pamela and Ameer.
May your generation experience freedom
as a way of life rather than
know it only as a goal.

Contents

A Panther
Is A Black Cat

1

The Jungle

OAKLAND IS A CRACKER TOWN, a 44 percent black urban plantation, a center of bigotry, a segregated dead end for people of color, and the birthplace of the Black Panther Party. To understand Oakland is perhaps to comprehend why an escalation of the tactics of black revolution, in the form of a political orientation dedicated to the overthrow of American institutions, began in these ghetto streets. But these insights are available only to those who are willing to empathize (if not identify) with the human condition that led a Huey P. Newton to insist that black political power must proceed from the barrel of a gun.

The black condition in Oakland is not really separate from that of whites. In reality, the fact of blackness only serves to concentrate disproportionately within a physical minority the effects of a generalized disregard for human worth. Panthers refer to themselves as the vanguard, an assertion that compels them to adopt the role of being that minority among blacks which demonstrates some of the political realities of black existence. They maintain that the vanguard position automatically results in their attracting a concentration of the repressive reflexes of those who maintain law and order through racism.

Similarly, blacks can be considered that group which can best display to whites the kinds of injustices endemic to the society as a whole. For racism does not create new brands of injustice; it only blunts the sensitivities of the majority group to the inequities it tolerates as normal. One aspect of Panther unhappiness with whites, therefore, issues from the fact that whites are not moving to eliminate the injustices they visit upon each other. Under these conditions, they are skeptical about the ability of whites to discover the necessity of treating blacks with the humanity and justice they deny themselves.

In a sense, Oakland was founded on a garbage dump. Sometime before the building of the Egyptian pyramids, Indians who normally lived hundreds of miles away from the Bay made annual pilgrimages there. They fished for salmon, mussels and oysters, and hunted the migrant birds that stopped off near what was to become Oakland. These Indians camped in the same spots year after year, discarded their broken pottery, the emptied mussel shells, bird bones, animal leavings, and an occasional departed brave, in the area surrounding their temporary settlements. After thousands of years these discards resulted in huge mounds. One of the largest, the Emeryville Mound, was located immediately north of Oakland in what is now the almost completely industrial city of Emeryville. The mound began fifteen feet below present sea level, rose to a height of fifty feet over the Bay, and covered more than seventy acres of ground. It was leveled in the 1930's in order to make room for the expansion of Emeryville.

Ironically, the ancient Indian leavings were almost immediately replaced with the detritus of modern existence. The mud flats bordering Oakland's western boundary, San Francisco Bay, are almost completely covered with garbage in the form of discarded tires, cast-off building materials, and useless pieces of metal. A nearby sewage-disposal plant contributes to the pollution of the Bay by daily dumping thousands of gallons of barely treated sewage into the water. And, on the precise site of the Emeryville Mound, there now stands a mountain of partially crushed castaway autos, waiting for rust, future archaeologists, or present industrial geniuses to give them an ultimate purpose.

Oakland was the site of the first known industrial plant on the West Coast. In 1840, a sawmill was established in what is now East Oakland. The land was then covered with redwood trees that were cleared in order to provide lumber to build houses in San Francisco. The sawmill was the beginning of the industrial development that was to separate Oakland residents from the city's southern shoreline just as effectively as the combination of industry and garbage keeps Oaklanders from enjoying its western shores.

This city itself was founded as the result of a land grab in which armed squatters took over a tract of West Oakland land, then known as the Peralta Grant. Once the land was secured, Oakland became a transportation center, providing supplies for prospectors headed for the goldfields some hundred miles or more away. Farm products were directed toward San Francisco, across the Bay. The coming of the railroad produced a shantytown composed primarily of Chinese who had been imported to lay track and to work in the goldfields.

A number of prominent businessmen, who had survived a vicious and sometimes deadly battle to control the numerous ferries that traveled between Oakland and San Francisco, discovered what they considered to be the unfair competition of itinerant Chinese peddlers. The Oakland Board of Trade, later to become the Oakland Chamber of Commerce, was formed in order to keep the "Celestial Bucket Brigade" from trading in what these white businessmen considered their markets. This brigade, consisting of hundreds of Chinese, each carrying his wares in buckets suspended from the ends of long poles, dominated the produce market. The Oakland

Board of Trade restricted commercial use of the ferries to their own members, and Chinese were not eligible to join.

Oakland did not have a significant non-white population until the 1940's. The census of 1860 reported a population of 1500, including 86 Indians, 75 Orientals and 15 colored. By 1968, there were 400,000 Oaklanders, including an estimated 3000 Indians, 20,000 Orientals and 175,000 blacks. The somewhat prophetic-sounding year of 1983 has been projected as the time that blacks will constitute a majority of the city's population. Panthers are insisting by their actions that the history of Oakland, indeed of most American cities, is a preparation for 1984, and much of their experience confirms this. For, if Oakland has proved nothing else, it has demonstrated that non-white political power does not grow along with the non-white population.

Huey Newton, his parents, three brothers, and two sisters were eight of the approximately 50,000 Negroes who migrated from Louisiana to Oakland during the war years. They were attracted to the Bay Area by the existence of jobs in a war industry that theoretically offered equal jobs for equal pay. Racism in Louisiana was so effective that it took precedence over the most vital of American interests—namely, the war effort. White workers in a Louisiana-based shipyard managed to strike successfully for better working conditions at the height of the war. This was a plant that outfitted LST's, the flat-bottomed landing craft that transported a tremendous number of invading American troops to the beaches of their choice. The shipyard, in fact, was the only place where LST's, most of which were floated down the Mississippi, could be fitted and pressed into war service.

The shortage of war workers there was so acute that even the upgrading of Negro workers to craftsmen did not produce enough trained crews to get the necessary work done. Crews were segregated, but additional crews could be formed by integrating those workers who were in a labor pool formed of black and white craftsmen. White workers objected to this common-sense solution to a national problem, and closed down this essential shipyard until the federal government agreed to allow the war against Nazi racism to proceed on a racially segregated basis.

Oakland, of course, had no signs indicating the geography of race, nor did it have an announced policy of racial segregation. Blacks simply settled in West Oakland because there was no other section of town available to them for living purposes.

The rapid influx of black people—most of whom not only were employed, but even fit the classification of middle-class working people—did not bring with it the power to influence city government, or significantly to affect the forces which shaped black lives.

Oakland blacks have been incapable, right up to the present moment, of electing to office Negroes who identify with black aspirations. In fact, the difficulty in getting any non-white elected or appointed to office has been enough to substantiate charges of racism in city politics.

Even Earl Warren, Alameda County District Attorney in Oakland in the 1940's, couldn't act racially liberal there. He enforced the roundup of Japanese Americans on the West Coast; 110,000 Japanese went to detention camps while 80,000 German and Italian nationals were left free.

Warren may have been a liberal then, he might have been a liberal Republican governor, and he seems to have been a liberal Chief Justice; one conclusion that should be drawn is that a liberal is capable of acting in the service of racism. Warren's credibility to black people would increase if he would publicly disavow that wartime action.

One of Warren's assistant district attorneys was J. Frank Coakley, who began in the D.A.'s office in 1926 and was appointed chief assistant D.A. in 1939. In 1943 he joined the Navy and served for twenty-nine months as a prosecutor. It was in this capacity that he prosecuted a group of fifty Negro sailors charged with mutiny for refusing to load ammunition a few days after a munitions ship had distributed parts of itself and the bodies of three hundred navy men over a considerable portion of landscape.*

When the ammunition ship exploded at Port Chicago, twenty-five miles north of Oakland on an arm of San Francisco Bay, everyone who really knew what went wrong went up with the ship. The disaster resulted in the wholesale transfer of sailors, mostly black, from other naval installations in the area to duty at Port Chicago. Crewmen who survived the disaster were aware of one fact: if they did not get next to ammunition they would reduce the possibility of experiencing a misspent youth.

The protest of the Negro sailors was based on two main points. They found it difficult to face the prospect of handling ammunition that was damaged in the explosion, and therefore potentially lethal. Also, they insisted that the order to handle the ammunition was discriminatory insofar as it was not given to any of the white troops. Coakley succeeded in obtaining sentences ranging up to fifteen years for many of the defendants.

Coakley had no postwar adjustment to make. He went into private practice and in 1947 was appointed district attorney to fill the unexpired term of his predecessor, Ralph E. Hoyt, who had been appointed judge. He proceeded to deal relentlessly with persons accused of crime. Unfortunately, at least for Negroes, a large number of defendants were black. In all fairness, Coakley prosecuted without reference to race. He was, on principle, opposed to particular categories of miscreants including holdup men, communists, sex deviates, and nonconformists. For him, the fact that a disproportionate number of Negroes were brought to court was simply unfortunate. After all, he was a prosecutor, and not a social worker.

It was Coakley who during his career as district attorney

---

* Thurgood Marshall, who was appointed to the Warren court, was an observer for the NAACP at this trial and wrote a report that severely criticized the proceedings.

wrote an annual letter to the California Adult Authority recommending the continued incarceration of Jerry Newsome, a Negro convicted of murder, who had somehow escaped the death penalty Coakley worked so hard to have delivered. It was also Coakley who near the end of his tenure maneuvered the prosecution of Huey Newton so as to guarantee an indictment on what many attorneys consider shaky evidence.*

Coakley has since retired. His job, however, was passed on to Lowell Jensen, the associate district attorney who successfully prosecuted Huey Newton. In all probability, he will continue to handle the district attorney function with little regard for the particular problems faced by black people.

The district attorney's office is neither more nor less racist than any other organized function in Alameda County. It is simply one of the parts of a network of organizations that can operate while claiming color blindness and still be oblivious to the extent to which it contributes to frustrating black desires for progress.

It makes little difference whether an individual racist is discovered, fired, recruited, neutralized, exposed, heeded, ignored, imitated, or legislated against, in or out of the D.A.'s domain. There has never been an Oakland official who would concede that racial bias had, in fact, influenced a decision, a practice, or a policy of municipal government. Similarly, there are no witnesses to an acknowledgment that past acts of racial bias

* Charles Garry has insisted throughout that Huey Newton would have never been indicted had the district attorney not included the Newton case in the fewer than 4 percent of criminal cases he sends to the Grand Jury. ". . . in a grand jury, the lawyer cannot cross-examine prosecution witnesses, as he can in the preliminary hearing when the DA proceeds by information. The district attorney has unfettered discretion, without any guidelines, to pick and choose which cases to file by information and which to bring before the grand jury. It is only a very small number that go to the grand jury where the defendant is hog tied in this way." —*Minimizing Racism in Jury Trials: The* Voir Dire *conducted by Charles R. Garry in* People of California *v.* Huey P. Newton, published by the National Lawyers Guild.

had determined a course of action by the more influential private organizations such as the Chamber of Commerce, the large manufacturing firms such as Kaiser, the very important Real Estate Board, or the mixture of private and public interest dominated by ex-Senator William Knowland, publisher of the *Oakland Tribune*, Oakland's only daily newspaper. The record demonstrates that a lot of people, mostly white, operating in and out of city government, created and maintained a set of conditions that make Oakland comparable to the most openly bigoted of southern cities.

A trickle of Negro families moved to North Oakland, Berkeley, and East Oakland after the war ended. Almost all found homes near Emeryville, the South Berkeley industrial strip, or the ten-mile-long factory, cannery and light-manufacturing concentration that stretched from West Oakland to the San Leandro border. Migration out of West Oakland was stepped up during the early 50's, spurred by massive construction projects that replaced homes with elevated freeways, rooming houses with complex traffic interchanges, apartment units with new San Francisco Bay Bridge approaches, and public housing with vacant lots.

West Oakland was a slum, characterized by ramshackle buildings, poor city services, inadequate transportation, a too high concentration of unemployed persons and an almost total disregard for the needs of the residents by official agencies of government.

Lending institutions would not invest in West Oakland on any level. Negroes who had managed to buy property could not borrow to improve it. Those Negroes seeking to buy—even those who could possibly pass stringent credit checks—found West Oakland property unfinanceable. Negroes who rented had to accept the fact that regular maintenance would be nonexistent. Negroes who simply sought to use the streets found them debris-filled, pock-marked with deteriorating pavement, and inadequately supplied with traffic-control devices.

Many West Oakland curbs are made of wood. The city, which normally maintains curbstones, has a policy which prevents it from repairing wooden curbs. This policy is non-discriminatory in wording, but it just so happens that virtually all of Oakland's wooden curbs are located in a Negro residential district. City street-cleaning equipment, geared to operate on streets equipped with conventional curbstones, does a poor job of cleaning West Oakland streets. Since Oakland prides itself on having a modern street-cleaning department, it has not made any provision for frequent manual cleaning of these blocks. As a result, debris collects.

Most lending institutions operating in cities do not habitually put money into recognized slum areas. They also have a practice of not investing in property located on unimproved city streets. Exceptions to this rule have been made in other more exclusive areas of the city, where the combination of unimproved streets and high-priced property produces a rustic flavor. But banks are not particularly interested in the country-like, shantytown appearance of a number of West Oakland streets. Their refusal to lend, moreover, has the ring of authenticity which accompanies clearly set-out regulations, and can avoid any implication of racial bias.

That means that the prospective borrower must either do without a loan or borrow from an individual or firm that specializes in slum property. The private moneylenders lean heavily toward usury, properly gimmicked to maintain an approximation of legality. They operate almost exclusively through real estate or mortgage brokers, gentlemen who often extract fees for finding private money. Private lenders demand a bonus for making the loan, an amount which approaches and often exceeds an additional 10 percent. Interest is set substantially higher than the rate charged by conventional loan sources, and the total term of the loan is usually shorter. The result, of course, is higher payments for less valuable property, made by a person whose family income is lower than that of most property-buying white families.

As can be expected, there is a fairly high rate of foreclosure on property financed in this manner, because of the marginal economic status of most black West Oakland property owners. Foreclosure, of course, means that all money invested by the borrower is lost. Nevertheless, virtually every piece of property bought by black people in West Oakland since World War II has been financed through high-priced money sources. The obvious result of these financial practices has been the almost total inability of black people in Oakland to profit from real estate transactions.

In practice, the workings of private interests and public policy have managed to further disadvantage those West Oakland property owners who managed to survive the high cost of buying. Condemnation proceedings issuing from a combination of construction projects and urban-renewal schemes have forced many property owners to sell, often at a loss. Even in those relatively rare instances where the condemning agency paid full market value (i.e., the inflated price paid for the property), excessive interest, inflated lending costs and hidden real price of the property, represented by the bonuses paid out, took care of anything resembling an equity.

There are those who are successful in maintaining West Oakland property and making it pay. Most of them are white. According to the *Wall Street Journal*, the Southern Pacific Railroad Company is one of the big owners of West Oakland property. The Oakland Planning Commission classes 64 percent of all West Oakland housing as dilapidated or deteriorating, with Enrico L. Barbera, Oakland's chief housing inspector, identifying Southern Pacific's property holdings as "collectively the worst housing in all Oakland." Southern Pacific refuses to repair their rental property, saying that to do so would be unprofitable. The city, on the other hand, refuses to condemn them on the grounds that the residents who would be evicted would have nowhere to live.

Other property throughout Oakland, some in much better condition, has been condemned, however. In fact, much of West Oakland resembles bombed-out territory because of the wholesale devastation of buildings. Much of this vacant land has stood idle for five or more years. Reportedly only seven new houses were built in West Oakland between 1960 and 1968. There have been sporadic attempts to reverse the trend in the form of small rehabilitation projects, a Model Cities program and an effort on the part of Bank of America to provide funds for the purchase and repair of West Oakland property. Most of these are paper efforts, however, and the most hopeful sounding have been stalled or abandoned in the twisted snarl that is Oakland politics.

The most ambitious rehabilitation project for West Oakland was to have been financed through the Model Cities program. This effort was scrapped when the City of Oakland failed to meet the deadline established by federal authorities. Essentially, the delay was caused by the inability of city officials, headed by the mayor, to go along with the demands of the Negro-dominated West Oakland Planning Committee that the principle of community control be respected. The committee had also demanded that the rehabilitation of the area be enlarged to include some property owned by the city.

In response to the cancellation of the project, Mayor John Reading delivered a scathing attack on Paul Cobb, secretary of the West Oakland Planning Committee. The mayor accused Cobb of being an extremist, and of spending his time leading demonstrations instead of doing the work for which he was being paid. Cobb denied the charges, but did not point out that some of the time that he could have spent working on the Model Cities program was lost because of an apparently unjustified arrest.

Mr. Cobb was one of the leaders of a boycott called by Negroes protesting the excessive use of force by police.

On April 6, 1968, two days after the assassination of Martin

Luther King, Bobby Hutton, Treasurer of the Black Panthers, was shot and killed by police. Witnesses insisted that the killing was unnecessary, that Hutton was murdered in cold blood, and that this was one more instance of an increasingly hostile posture taken by police towards black people. A committee called Blacks Strike for Justice was formed, which included Paul Cobb. The committee decided it would be futile to use the accustomed tactics of asking for a civilian review board, picketing the police station, writing angry letters to the newspaper, sending a delegation to see the mayor and the police chief, or getting petitions signed. Instead, the device of putting pressure on merchants was decided upon. The committee reasoned that businessmen had more influence on city policies than poor Negroes and that the withdrawal of customers from those establishments where Negroes shopped heavily might have the effect of causing the owners and operators to press for police reform.

The first and primary target of the boycott was the Housewives Market, a block-square downtown food emporium, which was estimated as enjoying better than 75 percent Negro patronage, and about 15 percent Mexican-American and Oriental customers. The list of establishments to be boycotted, however, included all downtown merchants, particularly those heavily shopped by minority groups.

The boycott was very effective.

Total sales for the Housewives Market fell off at least 50 percent. A downtown credit jeweler, Milen's, lost an estimated 30 percent of business volume. Other businesses suffered proportionately when thousands of black people virtually stopped doing business in downtown Oakland.

The reaction was not long in coming. Within days after the demonstration began, Mr. Cobb was arrested, ostensibly for interfering with an arrest. He reported that some of the arresting officers knew him both in his capacity with the West Oakland Planning Committee and with the Blacks Strike for Justice Committee. Further, he said that he was never aware of any arrest other than his own. Cobb insists that he was arrested after asking an officer, whom he knew slightly, why ten to fifteen police cars were parked in one block. Charges against Cobb were dismissed a few weeks later.

Other leaders of the boycott complained of police harassment in the form of being followed by officers, increasing incidence of traffic tickets, and numerous occasions of being stopped and asked for identification. The most vigorous attack on the boycott, however, was led by William Knowland, editor of the *Oakland Tribune*.

If anyone fits the description of right-wing emperor of Oakland, it is William Knowland. He seems to have inherited his attitudes, influence and newspaper from his father Joe, whose social attitudes would have qualified him as adviser to Bismark. Pappa Joe's influence, money and paper got Bill into the U.S. Senate, where he spent significant amounts of time promoting legislation that would help the Nationalist Chinese. He retired from public office in 1958, after California voters refused to elect him governor, and came back to Oakland to run a permanent campaign against unions, college activism, socialism, welfare agencies and Negroes.

Bill Knowland almost single-handedly created the Free Speech Movement in 1964. The *Oakland Tribune* was being picketed in 1964 by civil rights groups demanding increased employment opportunities for minorities. Knowland, who in the normal course of business hires private police to guard his building, called on the police and the courts to protect him. Injunctions were issued, picket leaders were arrested, and life around the Tribune Building became somewhat unbearable for blacks.

The meaning of Knowland's use of his political influence to have the courts and police attack peaceful demonstrators was not lost on students at U.C., some of whom had spent the summer in Mississippi. They decided to demonstrate that their activities could not be controlled by traditional pressure politics and proceeded to set up fund-raising tables on campus, and to organize car pools that daily brought students to down-town Oakland, parading in front of Knowland's newspaper. Knowland then put pressure on U.C., causing a flurry of official panic. First, the university tried to sell, rent, lease, or give away to the city of Berkeley the half-block area outside Sather Gate where student activists organized their campaigns. Berkeley refused to consider accepting the property under any terms, preferring not to be responsible for policing ter-ritory whose occupants' activities offended Mr. Knowland. After going through a number of other contortions to escape the wrath of Knowland, the university finally banned political activity on what they reluctantly accepted as their property.

The university exploded! White middle-class students, many of whom had managed to return from Mississippi after civil rights work with their innocence intact, suddenly found out what it was to become niggerized. Knowland experienced a drop in the number of white students picketing outside his establishment. They were demonstrating at Cal, and ulti-mately created a kind of civil rights second front.

This trauma of instant niggerization has since been trans-mitted to other colleges, and they have Bill Knowland to thank. The "senator from Formosa" taught a whole generation of college youth that people who are willing to deny oppor-tunities to blacks do not hesitate to use this same arbitrary technique with whites.

Relatively few whites were involved in actively working with the Blacks Strike for Justice boycott of downtown Oakland. Knowland was free to use every racist trick at his disposal, and he did.

The *Oakland Tribune* ran a full-page ad in which a gloved hand pointed a revolver at the reader. "What would you do in a case like this?" screamed the headline, and the text pro-ceeded to describe the boycott action as "attempted extor-tion" and "coercion." Knowland's appeal was directed toward "every citizen of Oakland, regardless of his race, creed or color." But his intended audience was white. Copies of the editorial were passed out to merchants and their almost idle employees at Housewives Market. Knowland himself, in the tradition of a general visiting troops embattled by restless natives, walked among the almost empty stalls and gave words of encouragement to the owners and their employees.

Eventually the boycott fizzled out, with no clear victory for anyone. In the last analysis, however, protesting blacks achieved a great deal. Although they did not succeed in forcing a review of police practices, they had, with relatively few resources, made a sizable dent in the profits of a number of businesses which profit from Negro business, and have never felt obliged to contribute to the success of the community. Blacks Strike for Justice showed that Negroes—who are counted upon by white politicians to be apathetic, or at least noninvolved in causes espoused by assumedly extremist blacks—could be activated. More important, blacks proved to themselves that they could, in the course of expressing a grievance, impose what Panthers call "a political consequence" on segments of the white establishment.

An argument used against boycotts such as that mounted by Blacks Strike for Justice is that those people affected are usually innocent businessmen who are themselves powerless to effect change in the lives of blacks—assuming, of course, that these businessmen would attempt to make changes if they were in a position to do so. Businessmen in Oakland, however, are far from being innocent bystanders. The business and political communities of Oakland are one and the same. City government, according to Dr. Floyd Hunter, a sociologist who conducted an extensive survey on decision-making in Oakland, has become a "coordinating effort for the business community." Oakland is not a typical political-boss-run city, although the Knowlands have traditionally wielded great amounts of power. Rather, it is a business-oriented community based on the proposition that to increase industry in Oakland is to increase the general welfare of all. In order to attract new industry it is necessary to keep the lid on, and not allow the malcontent poor—black poor in particular—to ruin the attractiveness of Oakland to prospective industrial settlers.

This power structure has not been formalized, primarily because everyone involved knows his job, the value structure within which he must work, and the type of decision-making necessary to solve a particular problem. According to Dr. Hunter, the professionals in city government "do not necessarily need to be told what to do or not to do, but through long experience in handling policy matters can anticipate, or are thoroughly convinced that they can anticipate, the reactions of the higher echelons of decision." When there are no blacks holding significant positions in either the business community or the city government it becomes obvious that they must affect this decision-making network from the outside. The boycott is perhaps only one of the methods which will be discovered.

It is almost impossible to comprehend the degree to which the Oakland power structure is committed to the business orientation. It adopted a city-manager form of government in order to put Oakland on a businesslike basis. Mayor John Houlihan, John Reading's predecessor, together with his city manager Wayne Thomson, once reported that Oakland was curbing the socialistic trend of cities by such techniques as contracting ambulance service to private industry and leasing the garbage collection to garbagemen entrepreneurs. Houlihan seriously wanted to see municipal fire departments run by insurance companies, and thought that the public library would be better handled if it were taken over by some enterprising businessman.

Houlihan held a poor opinion of Negroes, and made no secret of it. When, in 1965, a representative group of Negroes succeeded in obtaining an audience with him in order to formulate plans for preventing a Watts-type riot in Oakland, Houlihan reported to a public gathering, "Tomorrow I have to meet with the biggest bunch of kooks ever assembled in the city of Oakland."

The meeting, as could be predicted, was nonproductive of programs that would ease the life of Oakland blacks.

Houlihan never was a progressive and reform-minded mayor eager to deal with civic problems, an image he projected to the voters in 1965. In fact, he only managed to serve a little more than a year as mayor, because he was convicted of raiding the accounts of one of the clients of his law firm to the tune of $100,000. Mr. Houlihan served a little less than two years in prison as a result. At the time Houlihan was convicted, his salary as mayor was $7500 a year. Upon his release on parole, he took a job at a reported $15,000 a year as a lobbyist with World Airways, an Oakland-based firm. At the time World Airways was involved, with the blessings of Mayor John Reading, in a proposal which would have given the firm an important role in guiding the redevelopment of West Oakland.

Mayor Reading has not exactly been good news for Oakland blacks. At the time of his appointment, Mayor Reading spoke of himself as a liberal. After two terms in office, he was self-described as a moderate. The mayor opposed projected reforms brought to him by the "respectable" Negro leaders he claimed to believe in. He refused to deal with Negro delegations seeking reform in city government, claiming that only extremist programs were brought to him. According to Reading, the entire Negro community had been seized by black extremists who terrified more respectable Negroes and kept them from speaking in more moderate terms. This attitude undoubtedly explains why Mayor Reading had no difficulty in ignoring several delegations of Negroes at city council meetings, despite the fact that they had succeeded in getting a place on the agenda beforehand.

Fifty-eight ministers of all religious persuasions and racial backgrounds once directed a letter to the mayor, pointing out that both the mayor and the chief of police were directing

inflammatory statements toward the Negro community that
could only have the effect of further polarizing hostile attitudes between blacks and whites. The clergymen made specific
reference to remarks about the Black Panthers, but were trying to sensitize the mayor and Chief of Police Charles R. Gain
to the fact that many of their remarks are perceived by blacks
as anti-Negro.

The clergymen did not suggest to the mayor that perhaps
he did not have the right to specify who should represent
blacks to City Hall. The fact is that Panthers have received
a great deal of acceptance among Oakland blacks, sometimes
directly because the mayor insisted that he would never lower
himself to meeting with any representatives of the Black
Panthers.

Oakland political leaders have not lowered themselves to
meeting the legitimate needs of blacks as presented to them
time and time again by properly respectful Negroes. The
dreary housing picture is accompanied by other bleak facts.
In 1968 the Urban League reported that 13 percent of the
black labor force was unemployed, compared to 4 percent
statewide. Sixty-six percent of the city's welfare recipients and
80 percent of dependent children live in Oakland slums. According to Spencer Williams, California's former health and
welfare administrator, over one-third of Oakland's slum dwellers over twenty-five years of age have less than an eighth-
grade education. Moreover, under present conditions, there
is little hope for the younger generation through education.

Understaffed and underfinanced, Oakland schools are facing
serious difficulties because new sources of financing cannot be
found. Oakland decision-makers did manage to find two million dollars to raise the pay of police and firemen, however,
by adding a tax on utilities. If it continues at the present rate,
Oakland might well find itself in the position of Richmond,
California, a neighboring city with racial and political problems amazingly similar in detail to those being experienced in
Oakland. Richmond schools ran out of money, teachers' sala-

ries were lowered, and the school system was the object of a boycott organized by national teacher groups. Oakland might very well be next.

In reality, however, the gauge by which anyone can measure the meaning of a high-school education is rapidly disappearing. A recently passed statewide regulation established the ability to read at an eighth-grade level as a minimum requirement for the high-school diploma. In practical terms, this means that any and all youngsters who drop out of high school in Oakland, anywhere short of the diploma, will probably have received less than the equivalent of an eighth-grade education.

Life, then, in Oakland is grim. Blacks are living poorly, are educated dismally, have virtually no effective representation in the power structure, and are at the mercy of a plethora of interlocking agencies that collectively manage to maintain the status quo as it relates to Negroes.

But this is a description which could apply to other cities with large Negro populations. To a large extent, this is what urban riots are about. Nearby Richmond, with a disenfranchised black population that amounts to 30 percent of a city of 80,000, experienced two riots in as many years. Pittsburg, a small industrial city located thirty miles from Oakland, where most black residents live in a segregated housing project, erupted into violence in 1968 resulting in the near-destruction of a high school and a gun battle between blacks and police officers.

Berkeley, Oakland's immediate neighbor to the north, and reputedly a liberal city because of the presence of the University of California, has had a great deal of civic disorder, although most of it has been connected with the university. Berkeley has a black population of 40,000, who, voting in a bloc, could not overcome the white opposition to a fair-housing bill. Each of these cities can display some of the elements of social disadvantage that characterize Oakland's Negro neighborhoods.

Oakland has the Panthers, but it has not had riots—a seeming paradox in a city so overwhelmingly beset by black discontent. The explanation seems to be that Oakland has a longer and more successful history of repression due to its adopted role of enforcing its own racism along with that of its neighbors.

Most of those people important to Oakland politics do not live there. They live in San Leandro, Castro Valley, Piedmont, and Berkeley, in all-white enclaves of residential exclusivity. John Reading, the present mayor, lists his address as East Oakland, and he has publicly come out in favor of turning over law enforcement in Oakland to the National Guard.

Every morning Oakland becomes significantly whiter as the managers of Oakland commute inward. At the same time, the suburbs surrounding Oakland grow duskier, as a flood of maids, laborers, gardeners and the unemployed looking for work fans out into an area where they are good enough to work, but not to live. Their dissatisfactions are brought home with them to Oakland and are articulated by the Black Panthers, whose politics are based in the misery of Oakland's black ghetto.

The rest of the Oakland establishment cooperates with the all-white suburbs in keeping blacks bottled up in Oakland. The only significant concentration of Negro residency in southern Alameda County is in Pleasanton, where the 50 percent black-occupied county jail is located. Much of Oakland's black population has shifted from West Oakland to East Oakland, but their migration has been stopped short at the San Leandro border. San Leandro, an all-white town with a vigilante committee pledged to defend white homes against black marauders, has constantly resisted Negro encroachment. But San Leandro and cities to the south do welcome Negroes to work in their growing industrial complexes. Despite Oakland's belief in the primacy of industrial development, the truth is that Oakland has been losing industry to San Leandro and points south. Alameda County's three automobile assembly plants are located in Southern Alameda County—one in San Leandro, one in Fremont and the third in Milpitas, nearly forty miles from East Oakland.

Southern Alameda County, then, does not share the problem it helps to create. It deals only with employed blacks, who spend money in Southern Alameda when employed, and collect unemployment and welfare in Oakland when idle. In this regard, the area is supported by the barons of Oakland, who identify with all-white suburbs and are satisfied with the existence of the plantation which Oakland has become.

II

Keepers of the Peace

"The racist dog police must cease their wanton brutal murder
of black people or face the wrath of the armed people."
                                                    —Huey P. Newton

"The Black Panther Party poses a real threat to the peace and
tranquillity of the city of Oakland."
                                                    —Oakland Police Chief
                                                    Charles Gain

"PIGS WANT WAR. PANTHERS COOL"
                                                    —Headline, Black Panther Paper

OAKLAND'S POLICE CHIEF, Charles Gain con-
demns the Black Panther Party. He finds the assertion that
police do not protect and police the minority community
"ridiculous on its face." He insists the Black Panther Party
has "no practical implemental program," and he feels it is
"irrational thinking that gives rise to a movement such as the
Black Panthers." His poor opinion of the Panthers is shared
by most law enforcement officers.

Point 7 of the Black Panther platform and program, "We
want an immediate end to POLICE BRUTALITY and

MURDER of black people," is enough to uptight most police. Those officers who can maintain some sense of proportion in the face of that demand tend to lose their cool after being called "pig," a term that Panthers have made popular among a substantial number of young people of all colors.

One police officer, Terance M. Connoly, quit the Richmond, California, force. He complained of being called a "honky pig" or a white bastard at least fifteen or twenty times a day.

"For months I have answered these hollers and obscenities with a smile and a wave, hoping that I could become a mediator and that I could show that a man should not be judged by his color or his profession. . . . My efforts have been a tragic and dismal failure."

Generally, insulting a police officer is one of the surest routes to an unpleasant experience. Mayors Reading of Oakland, Daly of Chicago and Alioto of San Francisco are only three of a number of city officials who have countered charges of police brutality during demonstrations with the observation that police were goaded into club-swinging action by insults and epithets identical to those which caused Patrolman Connoly to resign.

According to the President's Commission on Law Enforcement and the Administration of Justice, Connoly was different from his fellow officers in many ways. He was twenty-seven, and the average policeman is thirty-eight. He had attended college, something outside the experience of most police officers, regardless of rank. His pay was higher than the $130 weekly average reported by the Commission. Moreover, he was recruited from a middle-class background, a status reached by most cops after they get on the force.

The Commission found that relatively few police departments (Richmond not among them) attempted to instruct new officers in the techniques of countering the hostility directed toward policemen by minority groups. As a result, rookie policemen usually adopt their superiors' indifference to blacks' attitudes and to social issues.

The average policeman is recruited from a social stratum replete with racial bias, is at an age where hardening of the attitudinal arteries can be expected, and is not at all trained to understand the facts of minority life which could result in the formation of a Black Panther Party. He certainly resents the charge that he is one of the ghetto's problems.

It should not be surprising that police reaction to the Panthers has not been characterized by brotherly love. Police have raided Panther offices, have arrested Panthers on flimsy grounds, and have seen fit to shoot at Panthers for very unsubstantial reasons.

In New York and San Francisco, raids on the Panther offices followed misdemeanor charges of illegal use of a bullhorn.

The Indianapolis Panther office was wrecked by police searching for alleged unregistered weapons. They did not find the weapons for which a warrant was issued.

In Denver, Panther headquarters were raided in a search for a large cache of guns. Four were found, after paneling had been ripped from the walls and furniture upturned and broken.

At every one of these raids, police found it necessary to tear-gas the occupants before entering.

The FBI conducted a raid on Panther headquarters in Chicago, looking for George Sams, Jr. Sams was sought on a fugitive warrant from New Haven, Connecticut, in connection with the murder for which Bobby Seale was subsequently arrested. The agents were armed with machine guns, shotguns, rifles, and pistols, and had cordoned off the area around the headquarters in preparation for trouble. They also had over thirty Chicago police officers stationed in nearby streets to prevent anticipated disturbances from Negroes reacting to the early-morning raid. Eight people were arrested. None of them was Sams, but the eight were charged with harboring a fugitive. Charges were dropped several days later. Sams was accused of murdering Alex Rackley, a member of the Harlem Chapter of the Panthers, whose mutilated body had been found in Middlefield, Connecticut. The discovery of the murder led to a post-midnight raid on the New Haven Panther office, where eight persons were arrested and charged with murder and conspiracy to commit murder. The office was also searched, resulting in considerable damage. One of those arrested was Erika Huggins, whose husband, John Huggins, Deputy Minister of Information for Southern California and one of the possible successors to Eldridge Cleaver, was murdered in Los Angeles in January, 1969.

Questionable police activities directed toward Panthers in Oakland and San Francisco have been regular occurrences. Eldridge Cleaver and his wife, along with Emory Douglas, the Black Panther Party Revolutionary Artist, were subjected to a police raid in January, 1968. Police broke into the Cleavers' San Francisco apartment and searched without a warrant.

In February, 1968, Berkeley police pushed their way into Black Panther Party Chairman Bobby Seale's house, and arrested Seale and his wife on charges of conspiracy to commit murder.

St. Augustine's Church was raided in April, 1968, when a Panther meeting was in progress, allegedly because someone was waving a gun outside.

Four known Panthers were arrested by Oakland police and charged with robbery, despite the fact that there was no evidence whatsoever linking the men with the robbery. Charges were dropped.

There have been other incidents of inappropriate police action directed against Panthers, action which did not even have the semblance of an official act. In New York, one hundred and fifty off-duty policemen, apparently members of a right-wing police organization called the Law Enforcement

Group, attacked a group of Panthers in the hallway of a Brooklyn law court.

In another incident, two Oakland policemen, Robert Farrell and Richard Williams, while on duty, shot up the National Headquarters of the Black Panther Party in Oakland, California. An eyewitness to the incident says that the officers opened fire on the storefront from a moving police car, made a U-turn, and came back to shoot some more. The building was occupied, but no one was hurt. Newspapers reported that the officers were intoxicated when arrested. The shooting occurred some twenty-four hours after Huey Newton had been convicted of voluntary manslaughter in the killing of an Oakland policeman. A number of people speculated that Williams' and Farrell's somewhat unprofessional conduct resulted from their belief that Huey deserved the gas chamber.

A San Francisco officer, Michael O'Brien, expressed his preference regarding the outcome of the Newton trial by wearing a tie clasp that read, "Gas Huey." He was transferred from duty in a predominantly Negro neighborhood after residents complained that he wore the clasp with his uniform. Some months later, off duty and under the influence of alcohol, O'Brien shot and killed a black man as the aftermath of a minor traffic accident. O'Brien was acquitted, after a lengthy trial in which he testified that he did not harbor any anti-Negro sentiments, and that the wearing of the "Gas Huey" clasp was in the nature of a joke.

Fascism, otherwise defined as a police state, is the inevitable result of allowing those dedicated to the application of force to determine politically how and when that force will be used. An evaluation of police conduct and practices is overdue, particularly in view of Panther concerns involving over-centralization, the fear of genocide, the increasing freedom of police from civilian control, and the tendency of police forces to be protective of aberrant behavior of individual police officers.

The American police establishment is something other than

the thin blue line described by police officials. A combination of coordinated police activity, a rapidly expanding police technology and a growing dependence on the back-up force of the military makes the present-day police force something of an invulnerable military operation.

The helicopter is becoming popular with police departments. In New York City, a combination of a helicopter and a super-bright floodlight has been used to spot suspected criminals fleeing from the scene of a crime. In San Francisco, a police helicopter was used to keep an auto driven by a suspected holdup man in sight, while the pilot directed pursuing police cars in effecting a capture. Airplanes have long been used by the California Highway Patrol to detect traffic offenders in the San Joaquin Valley.

Airborne surveillance of crowds, particularly at protest demonstrations, is becoming a routine matter. The next step, crowd control from the air, has already been taken. Students at Greensboro, North Carolina, and Berkeley, California, have been tear-gassed by helicopter. The gas, of course, is not selective, meaning that in both instances hundreds of innocent persons were forced to suffer the distress and inconvenience of being gassed.

Another adaptation of military ordnance is the Commando Police Vehicle. This is a twelve-man tank, designed for use in Vietnam. It is reported to be equipped with a revolving turret for machine guns, eighteen gun ports, and an array of defenses that range from armor, resistant to all but the most powerful shells, to an electrical system designed to administer a severe shock to any potential saboteur touching the vehicle. Five of these vehicles were loaned to the Detroit Police Department in 1967, which is now reported to have several of its own. Police in Cleveland have requested armored cars, as have several other jurisdictions.

Armament has also taken a dizzying leap toward giving police departments firepower greater than that once commanded by national armies. The Stoner gun, which rips through brick walls, presents a police department with an almost infinite number of lethal options. It can be purchased with a number of accessories that will convert the gun from a rifle into an automatic machine gun which can be belt or magazine fed.

The individual police officer also has available to him an array of "nonlethal" weapons. An old standby, the nightstick, has been modernized with the insertion of tear-gas or Mace dispensers, relieving officers of the need to decide whether to use Mace or a club. The Pepper Gas Fog Machine can be carried by one man, and can produce enough tear gas to control a crowd of hundreds. Berkeley police officers recently used a weapon that fires blocks of wood at velocities capable of breaking bones. Foams, lubricants, gas grenades, protective body armor, sound equipment which disables, instant barbed wire, and reportedly a nonlethal flamethrower are being introduced to police arsenals with a rapidity modified only by budgetary considerations and, occasionally, by the resistance of the public.

In the main, the new weaponry indicates an acceptance on the part of police that crowd control is becoming a routine task. This means that a significant amount of police attention is being shifted from the development of techniques and technology geared to the detection and apprehension of individual lawbreakers, to methods of controlling or containing large groups of people. Such a shift in emphasis automatically moves police departments closer to the military, and brings with it the fact that civilians are being increasingly supervised by policemen who think of themselves as military men guarding against group lawlessness, rather than as individual protectors of the law, oriented to detecting and arresting individual lawbreakers.

Nationwide meetings of police chiefs are increasingly devoting time to effecting working relationships between police jurisdictions. In October, 1968, police chiefs from forty-five American cities met to discuss problems of law enforcement during periods of riot and civil disobedience. One aspect of the military approach evident on this occasion was the almost absolute secrecy connected with all phases of the gathering, from the advance planning to the meetings themselves. No details were made public, other than the fact that the officers were concerned with the police problems accompanying civil unrest. The meeting included the nation's top law officials. Not only were police chiefs present, as were representatives of the sheriff's departments of a number of the country's more populous counties, but also Attorney General Ramsey Clark was an active participant.

California then devised a plan which divides the state into six regions for purposes of controlling large-scale disturbances. The San Francisco Bay Area is in Region Two, an area which covers a sizable portion of northern California. Under California's mutual-aid plan, police officers from a number of jurisdictions are combined under one command in time of trouble. First coordinator of the area was the San Francisco Police Chief, who, under the plan, in time of emergency commands the police resources of the area and directs as many as he deems necessary to the trouble spot. Once assigned to a city, the policemen are under the command of the local police chief. In practice, this plan has caused a great deal of police-inspired mischief.

The policemen involved in these combined operations often remove all traces of identification from their uniforms. Protected by anonymity, these officers then dish out more punishment than the situation seems to merit. Repeatedly, the victims of brutal beatings, indiscriminate use of chemical agents, unnecessary force in effecting mass arrests, and on occasion arbitrary gunfire have reported that the offending policemen have belonged to police departments from out of the area, but were otherwise unidentifiable.

Another danger in this mutual-aid approach is the amount of confusion that outside officers, unfamiliar with the city in which they are temporarily serving, bring to an already confused situation. A case in point was the ninety-minute shoot-out on April 6, 1968, in which Bobby Hutton, Black Panther Party Treasurer, was killed. An Oakland policeman, in his testimony to the grand jury, reported that he was one of the first to arrive in response to a call for assistance, and found an Emeryville policeman there, already firing into the house where the Panthers were hiding.

At the very highest level, that of the Federal government, there is a further move toward bringing military solutions to domestic problems. The Pentagon has instituted a riot-control center, which coordinates planning for civil disorder on a national scale. Reportedly all contingency plans for dealing with riots are submitted to this office. Also, the Pentagon has a role in formulating these army plans.

In August, 1969, David Hilliard called a press conference and issued copies of a Berkeley Police Department battle plan for assaulting the Panther National Headquarters. There were thirty-five elements to the plan, including provisions for a riot tank and assault squads armed with machine guns, the possible deployment of grenade launchers, extensive use of tear gas, and predetermined walls of fire. One portion of the plan states:

> 15. Front and back guard lay down fire on second floor. Assault squad (three men) armed with sub-machine guns approach building from the south. As they approach all firing cease. Squad enter building through front broken out windows and doors.
>
> a. First man cover stairs and no firing unless target is presented.
>
> b. Next two men enter and move to left and to right center of ground floor. Fire 30 rounds each up through second story floor and reload.
>
> c. By now all shutters should be blown off upper floor windows. The entire building should be flooded with

tear gas. The entire upper floor should be covered with intense fire. This should have the necessary effect. . . .
19. Assault squad will then proceed upstairs and bring down the wounded and/or dead.

The plan would go into effect if, after surrounding the building, the "offenders" did not comply with point 10 and come out of the building, "with hands up and lay on sidewalk in front of building." The copy which reached the Panthers had item 10a crossed out: "use bull horn or telephone."

Hilliard called it a plot to commit genocide. Berkeley Police Chief Bruce Baker called it good training and contingency planning. "Contingency planning is the only prudent way to protect a city," explained the chief.

This battle plan was designed to kill, pure and simple. What it makes clear is the thinking of police officers who now find it necessary to conceive of "protecting" a city by surrounding one structure within it and subjecting the building to massed firepower. At the very least, the detailed nature of this police plan indicates that local branches of the military have a clear idea of targets to attack and how that attack should take place.

Within this context, the concept of self-defense as promulgated by the Panthers takes on another meaning. Panthers have claimed that police, as part of a national system of repression, exceed their usual propensity to brutalize blacks when dealing with Panthers. David Hilliard, for instance, was arrested by over fifty agents, who followed him when he left a wedding, forced his car to the side of the road, and carried him off to jail. The charge was threatening the President.

Blacks can never hope to compete with this potential for havoc. Police simply have access to more arms than have black people. But this differential in potential firepower is only another way of saying that black people are poor. As a community, they do not have the resources to command that kind of artillery. A great number of blacks fail to see that there is any necessity to arm. Others, awed by the obvious superiority in firepower available to the police, refuse to think in terms of armed conflict.

But it is not so simple. Few people can reasonably be expected to engage in warfare with police. But anyone, if he has any self-respect, recognizes that there is some form of provocation, some threat to his person, that will elicit a furious response. No one—a legislature, a court, a police department, or an army—can take away or confer the right to self-defense. That is part of the message of the gun. Firearms, shotguns primarily, are ideal tools for defending one's home.

Panthers have insisted that one of the political consequences of being oppressed is a high ghetto crime rate. Some of the criminals are explicitly described as policemen. All of them are identified by their acts, rather than their stations. If someone kicks your door down, he is a pig—not necessarily a policeman, but definitely a pig.

After that comes the politics. Police, they say, function politically, and therefore move to control political expressions that do not meet with the approval of government authority. The history of the civil rights movement alone demonstrates that police are ready to inflict harm on people who defy authority and demonstrate in favor of social change, even when that demonstration does no harm.

Police specifically go after any and all black orientations which they perceive as a threat to them. Historically, every attempt of black people to create institutions for themselves that would corral a modicum of political power has been smashed by the police apparatus, often in combination with the courts. The prime example is Marcus Garvey's movement, but there are others, including the religious commune experiments.

Father Divine, for instance, was described as a religious charlatan, hauled in and out of court for allegedly saying he was God (a charge which he denied, but which, even if true, hardly seems sufficient excuse for criminal prosecution), bedeviled by tax collectors, and generally pictured as an irresponsible exploiter of black people. And yet he shepherded thousands of black people through a depression, provided cheap food for blacks through his restaurants, and cornered (though only temporarily) real estate holdings and business interests that would have made the black community a lot richer, had its members been able to organize around the economic issue of keeping black-controlled wealth in the black community.

The Muslims were attacked point-blank. There is no police authority anywhere in the nation that has hard evidence linking the followers of Elijah Muhammad with any aggressive actions against policemen. Nevertheless, known members, Muslim-owned businesses, and finally mosques were attacked, following battle plans that resembled the one disclosed by Hilliard—because police feared the potential of Muslims. Theirs were political attacks. It follows that the politics of policemen are in sharp opposition to the politics of those blacks who seek to assure that only blacks will make decisions for blacks.

Justice Department teams have been sent to individual cities where, in conjunction with local police officials, they plot out methods of control in time of emergency. The intended object of this control is no secret—black people. National Guard troops conducting maneuvers in riot control in Tennessee actually used a black neighborhood to sharpen up their tactics.

The fear of genocide, so prevalent in Panther rhetoric, accompanies a belief that for all intents and purposes Negroes are controlled by police. Many Negroes who are far removed from Panther ideology are moving toward this belief, recognizing that far more money is being spent nationally to prepare for disorders than to treat some of the conditions which lead to riot. Blacks in general do not trust police, and are not heartened by the knowledge that their local police forces are being provided with improved armaments and can always count on support of the national armed forces.

Distrust of police is not an exclusively black attitude, and the defensive posture of most police departments toward criticism is often in response to observations devoid of immediate racial connotations. One cannot escape the recognition, however, that any improper police action affecting a group of people would in most instances have a disproportionate effect on minority-group members. Moreover, not only have police officials done little to combat the direct expression of bigotry among their officers; they have been traditionally protective of any police officer accused of wrongdoing.

It is also a fact that police departments have never been able to achieve the measure of disciplinary control among their men that the armed services takes for granted. On the question of armament alone, it is difficult to conceive of a soldier marching into battle equipped with a weapon of his own choosing, based on the belief that his GI rifle was inadequate to the task ahead. And yet, in civil disturbances all over the country, there have been reported instances of police officers going to the riot with personal weapons, usually guns more powerful than those stocked and issued by the local police department.

This attitude of individual policemen has long been present in police organization. It has been accompanied by the phenomenon of policemen identifying more with one another, and the abstract concept of law enforcement, than with the people they purport to serve. The result has been a gradual alienation of policemen from the general public.

Corruption, poor judgment, and that sometimes ill-defined item called police brutality have been a part of American police practices at least throughout the present century. Dr. Albert J. Reiss, Jr., a sociologist, published an article dealing with police brutality which began with the following quotation: "For three years, there has been through the courts and the streets a dreary procession of citizens with broken heads and bruised bodies against few of whom was violence needed to effect an arrest. Many of them had done nothing to deserve an arrest. In a majority of such cases, no complaint was made.

If the victim complains, his charge is generally dismissed. The police are practically above the law." This statement was attributed to the Honorable Frank Moss, a former police commissioner of New York City, and was first published in 1903.

Dr. Reiss's article concerned a unique research project in which thirty-six observers accompanied police in their various contacts with citizens in three of our major cities. These investigators witnessed a number of cases in which police used "undue force." Undue force was defined as a situation where an officer struck a citizen "with his hands, fist, feet or body, or where he used a weapon of some kind—such as a nightstick or a pistol."

"In the seven week period, we found 37 cases in which force was used improperly. In all, 44 citizens had been assaulted. In 15 of these cases, no one was arrested. Of these, 8 had offered no verbal or physical resistance whatsoever, while 7 had.

"An arrest was made in 22 of the cases. In 13, force was exercised in the station house when at least four other policemen were present. . . ."

The article further concluded that police brutality operated against victims of all races in equal proportions, and that Negro and white police used brutality in roughly equal proportions, one in ten. "The use of force by police is more readily explained by police culture than it is by the policeman's race." *

At first glance, it seems surprising that policemen, knowing that they were being observed, would utilize force that was clearly excessive. The author of the article offered the plausible suggestion that behavior is not as easily changed as one would assume. The policemen observed were responding to situations in their normal fashion.

* Albert J. Reiss, Jr., "Police Brutality—Answers to Key Questions," *Transaction*, July/August, 1968.

Those defenders of police practices who might accept the statistics would tend to point out that only a minority of police were involved in unacceptable conduct. Such a defense is meaningless. As a rule, officers do not denounce one another for brutal practices and thus help to maintain that level of police conduct which has resulted in general public alienation and a profound mistrust by Negroes. For the first time on a large scale, many policemen are coming into contact with assumed lawbreakers who are of middle-class origins and are otherwise respectable. College demonstrators, the sons and daughters of middle-class people, middle-aged pacifists, non-violent blacks and whites, demonstrating in what they believe to be peaceful fashion, have experienced the sudden, and to them inexplicable reality of police violence. After the experience, they are not the least bit impressed by the information that a minority, say a hundred of the thousand police present, overreacted.

Newsmen have repeatedly found themselves on the receiving end of police-administered beatings; cameramen seem to be particularly vulnerable. In Cleveland, during the disturbances in 1967, two NBC cameramen, Julius Boros and Charles Ray, were beaten badly enough to require hospitalization. Boros insisted that the beatings occurred after police objected to his taking pictures of an arrest.

Oakland's draft-center demonstrations in 1967 were also sources of complaint from newsmen. A California State Assembly committee recorded pages of testimony concerning the outrageous actions of police in controlling participants. Prior to the Assembly hearings, Alexander Bodi, chairman of a Bay Area committee of Sigma Delta Chi, the national fraternity of journalists, complained of police brutality to Chief of Police Charles Gain. The particulars were aired at a meeting where time, place, and the nature of the incidents were clearly laid out. After the lengthy description, Chief Gain responded that if there were any "specific complaints" of unwarranted police activity against newsmen, "I assure you that they will be investigated by our internal affairs department."

Gain, who was invited to the Assembly committee hearings, failed to show. Instead, he sent a representative, Oakland Patrolman William Lovejoy, who told the committee that he was not authorized to say anything, but that Chief Gain would be happy to meet with the committee at any time other than the present, because the chief was busy in Oakland.

Similarly, representatives of other law enforcement agencies declined to discuss the specifics of police actions involving injuries during riots. The most popular reason given for this reluctance to testify was the possibility of having to testify in future lawsuits concerning police actions.

These Oakland demonstrations were particularly significant in the deteriorating history of citizen-police relations. Stop the Draft Week began on Monday, October 7, 1967, with a peaceful and symbolic sit-in by a group of pacifists. Most were persons of known stature in the community, and the arrests which followed their refusal to unblock the doors to the induction center were carried out in a most decorous fashion. The following day, a number of students blocked the doors to the center, and virtual carnage resulted. Demonstrators, onlookers, bystanders, and newsmen were severely attacked by police in a sudden exhibition of officially sanctioned fury that caught everyone, except the participating police, by surprise.

By the end of the week, the site of the induction center was a virtual battleground. Thousands of demonstrators, mainly students, developed spontaneous skirmish tactics that at one point threatened to rout police forces. Sidewalk trees growing in concrete tubs were pulled into intersections to become part of hastily constructed barricades. The tires of several police cars were flattened, and in one instance a police car was overturned. Isolated policemen found themselves surrounded by large groups of students, who, while throwing insults, did not make any further move to attack the officers.

At one point, a police skirmish line was disrupted by students who began to direct traffic at a nearby intersection, sending scores of passing motorists down what had been a blocked-off street.

As a result of that demonstration, seven of the organizers were charged with criminal conspiracy and were acquitted. Before receiving the verdict, the presiding judge talked to newsmen, and described the prosecution's case as "mushy." What was not mushy was the clear evidence that the disruptive acts of demonstrators came after police used excessive and inappropriate force. The group, the Oakland Seven, were successfully defended by Charles Garry, the Panther's leading attorney.

Charges of mass police brutality toward whites have followed almost every large-scale demonstration that has occurred during the past few years. The most thoroughly documented instance of large-scale police violence was the Walker Report, *Rights in Conflict*, covering the disturbances accompanying the 1968 Democratic Party Convention. Dubbed "The Chicago Police Riot," the report set out in voluminous detail numerous instances where police attacked innocent bystanders, sought confrontations with demonstrators, and generally acted like a well-trained mob. "On the part of the police there was enough wild club swinging, enough cries of hatred, enough gratuitous beating, to make the conclusion inescapable that individual policemen and lots of them, committed violent acts far in excess of the requisite force for crowd dispersal or arrest. To read dispassionately the hundreds of statements describing at first hand the events of Sunday and Monday nights is to become convinced of the presence of what can only be called a police riot." *

Blacks reading of the riot were not surprised. Too many of them had experienced arbitrarily dispensed hurt at the hands

* *Rights in Conflict*, a report submitted by Daniel Walker to the National Committee on the Causes and Prevention of Violence.

of police, or were closely related to people who had. Also, they had become acclimated to the sight of policemen wantonly beating demonstrators during the height of the non-violent demonstrations of the early 60's, some of which were led by the martyred Martin Luther King.

The U.S. Riot Commission Report, which covered 164 disorders in 128 cities, 41 of which were classified "major" or "serious" disorders, stated that although specific grievances varied from city to city, at least twelve deeply held grievances can be identified and ranked into three levels of intensity: "*First level of intensity:* 1. Police practices. . . ." * All other complaints, including inadequate housing, unemployment and underemployment, ineffectiveness of the political structure and grievance mechanism, were rated at lesser intensities by Negroes than the all-important item of police practices. An item which perhaps reflects the expectations of Negroes relative to white-dominated institutions is the fact that the discriminatory administration of justice was ranked eighth of the twelve listed items.

The Commission summarized: "What white Americans have never fully understood—but what the Negro can never forget—is that white society is deeply implicated in the ghetto. White institutions created it, white institutions maintain it, and white society condones it." They could have added the fact that, by and large, white patrolmen police it.

Statistics setting out Negro membership in police departments were included in the report. Of twenty-eight departments reporting, the average percentage of Negroes on police forces was 6 percent, hardly representative of the 24 percent Negro population served by these police departments. These figures are further distorted by the pronounced inability of Negroes to gain status within the departments.

* *Report of the National Advisory Commission on Civil Disorders,* N.Y.: Bantam Books, March, 1968.

"One in every 26 Negroes is a sergeant; the white ratio is one in 12.

"One in every 114 Negroes is a lieutenant; the white ratio is one in 26.

"One in every 235 Negroes is a captain or above; the white ratio is one in 53."

The Oakland and San Francisco police departments were included in the statistics. In most categories, both departments were well below the averages presented by the Commission.

	Oakland	San Francisco
Non-Whites as % of Population (1965 est.)	31	14
Non-Whites as % of Officers	4	6
Ratio Non-White Sergeants	1-27	0-102
Ratio White Sergeants	1-7	1-8
Ratio Non-White Lieutenants	0-27	0-102
Ratio White Lieutenants	1-25	1-25
Ratio Non-White Captains	1-27	0-102
Ratio White Captains	1-63	1-110
Ratio Non-White above Captain	0-27	0-102
Ratio White above Captain	1-210	1-165

Two months after the report was released, the San Francisco Police Department swore in its first Negro sergeant. At the time of his promotion, Willie Frazier was a nine-year veteran of the force, a college-trained officer who had received a captain's commendation as a rookie, and who had passed the sergeant's examination a year before he received his appointment.

The black policeman finds himself in an increasingly schizophrenic position on today's police force. He is caught between the demands of a police department insensitive to the perceptions of Negroes, and the pressures which come from the black community. In November, 1967, a Negro officer, Herman George, was shot and killed when on duty in San Francisco's predominantly black Hunters Point section. It is presumed that his murderer was Negro, but there have not been any arrests in connection with the case. A fellow officer, Kelly Waterfield, also Negro, was with George at the time of the murder. Waterfield denied the persistent rumor that George repeatedly brutalized Negroes during a previous tour of duty in the Fillmore District, another predominantly black area of San Francisco.

Waterfield told Rush Greenlee, one of the few black reporters working in San Francisco: "I can't say he was an Uncle Tom or an oppressor. I think he was a very good policeman. I worked with him ten months and I never saw him brutalize anyone. I don't know why he was killed." The fact is that George was killed, and that the event has deeply affected every Negro member of the police force. Other policemen gave harsher opinions of George. Since the killing, however, black officers have become noticeably more militant-sounding as well as increasingly involved in the affairs of San Francisco's black community.

Organizations of black officers have sprouted up all over the country. In Illinois, the Afro-American Patrolmen's League, which claims over four hundred members, was formed in June, 1968. Edward Palmer, executive director and one of the founders, said of the league: "All members of the league have vowed to end police brutality and indignities against Black citizens. . . . To confront changing times, the Black policeman must change. If he is to do his job correctly, he must develop a close relevancy to the man on the street."

Palmer, in an interview with *Muhammad Speaks*, expressed concerns identical to that of the Panthers and other militant or revolutionary black groups: "Black policemen in America must remember that history often repeats itself, and the example of genocide set by Nazi Germany could also repeat itself."

He went on to point out that Jewish policemen were used in Warsaw to herd Jews on trains, en route to extermination centers, and that these Jewish policemen were later placed on the same trains also routed to extermination. "Eichmann insisted he was only doing his job. . . . The Black policeman must have a higher allegiance to humanity. His first obligation must be to his community. . . ."

The AAPL reacted strongly to the killing of Fred Hampton and Mark Clark in an early morning raid on Hampton's apartment. Originally, police claimed that their attempts to gain entry into the apartment were countered by shotgun blasts. It was later demonstrated that all of the shooting was done by policemen. Hampton died in bed, apparently unaware that his apartment had been raided. Clark evidently was standing behind a door when the first volley of shots came through, killing him. Immediately after the raid, the AAPL recommended that whites not enter the seething South Side after dark. Moreover, they volunteered to take over the policing of Chicago's black community.

The policemen involved in the raid were exonerated by the grand jury and were reassigned by Edward V. Hanrahan, Cook County State's Attorney.

There are several black police organizations in the Bay Area. One is the Allied Peace Officer Liaison Association, which includes California highway patrolmen, prison guards, sheriffs' deputies, two attorneys, and policemen from Richmond, Oakland and San Francisco. The group was formed in the aftermath of the riots in Richmond, and one of its attorney members, Henry Ramsey, failed in an attempt to become a member of the Richmond Police Commission. Nine of the members of APOLA are the only black officers on the 149-man Richmond police force.

In January, 1969, these nine officers held a press conference and announced that they had requested a meeting with the city council to discuss their treatment on the force, as well as Richmond police department attitudes toward minority citizens. The officers explained that they had been unsuccessful in their repeated attempts to speak with Police Chief Robert Murphy, to whom they had begun appealing after the July,

1968, disturbances in Richmond, following the killing of a black youth by white policemen. The items the officers wished to discuss included attitudes of white Richmond police toward black citizens, the excessive use of force in the department, with subsequent lack of disciplinary action, and the divisive attitudes among white department members to blacks.

Chief Murphy's response to this petition was that he was personally disappointed by the methods used by black officers in trying to air their concerns. He also pointed out that the officers had violated regulations of the department by holding a press conference. Richmond officers are still trying to effect a review of Richmond police practices relative to the black community.

Friction between black and white officers, particularly in regard to white maltreatment of black people, has been a problem in all Bay Area police forces. In July, 1968, an officer Johnson found it necessary to threaten two white officers who were beating a Negro in the Park police station. Most of the time, black officers witnessing such abuse do not act, but simply experience the dilemma of being part of an organization whose members often brutalize black people. One unnamed officer expressed his feeling of impotence to Greenlee: "You see a black person being abused. You can't side with him and you can't let the incident go unmentioned. What do you do? Whatever you do is wrong." Some black officers have decided what to do. They organize!

In August, 1968, black officers in San Francisco sent a letter to Chief Thomas Cahill asking for permission to form their own organization, Officers for Justice. The officers felt strongly that they needed to emerge as a group that would address itself to the serious internal problems of the Police Department. They also felt the need to identify closely with the black community. The blacks are convinced, they said, "that there is a strong stream of racism in the police department. . . . Heretofore, both black and white officers have refrained from voicing criticism. Our fears of being denounced by the hierarchy of the San Francisco Police association have prevented many officers from speaking out.

"When we disagree with the official Police Department position, we are denounced by the Association's station representatives. This not only reflects racism but indicates a complete lack of concern for the citizenry of this city."

Jake Ehrlich, attorney for the Police Officers' Association, expressed disapproval of the proposed organization. He claimed that the Association spoke for all officers, without regard to color, that the "dissident" petition was not the right thing to do, and that it would lead to a divided department.

Chief Cahill denied the officers the right to organize.

The next step was the Police Commission. A petition which dealt with the Police Officers Association in stronger terms was prepared for an October meeting of the Commission. The black officers stated at the outset that the present voice of policemen in the area, the Police Officers' Association, has an image of being "a septic tank of white killer cops.

"In its wisdom and without conferring with any Black policemen, the POA carries out all of its business. . . . In all of this, not one Black police officer has had one vote or any voice in what the POA had done. . . . Now the POA may not have done any of these things because they are racists or because they approve of 'Gas Huey' buttons, or because they think that the brand of philosophy of Mr. George Wallace is best for our country. . . ." The officers said that they could not be represented by the POA because "We have no way of altering or preventing policies which we find reprehensible to both the Black community and the Black policemen.

"In silence, we have carried the double burden of Black officers and Black men. . . . We have submitted ourselves to white leadership from the beginning to the present. . . . No longer do we feel it necessary for the sake of 'saving face' of the POA, that we maintain the appearance of 'blue brother' togetherness. Those blue brothers that are men enough to stand up and be counted in the fight for equality, we welcome.

And those blue brothers that will stand up and be counted in the maintenance of 'white is right' no matter what, will be attacked."

The petition went on to outline changes the black officers would like to see in the department, primarily in the area of police-community relations, integrating the teaching staff at the Police Academy, upgrading of black officers, and the vexing problem of recruitment.

Across the nation, it has been virtually impossible to recruit black applicants for police jobs. Entire states, such as Michigan, report failure in their attempts to attract Negroes to their police forces. The Officers for Justice felt that "It is Black police officers who can get the recruits," and they might be right. One black San Francisco officer, however, a veteran of thirteen years on the force, reported that he had not had an inquiry from a black youth regarding ways to become a policeman in at least two and a half years. By contrast, this same officer said that in his early days as a policeman he was approached by Negro youth who aspired to the force almost every day.

Illinois State Senator Richard Newhouse, a Negro, felt that the problem of recruiting black policemen was related to the requirement that applicants not have a police record. "For a Black man in the ghetto to grow up without incurring some kind of record is a minor miracle. Therefore, the number of Black men eligible to get on the force is very limited, and those who can proceed up the ladder is highly selective."

Relevant to Senator Newhouse's remarks was a report of an April, 1969, ruling by the New York State Division of Human Rights. It found that grammar questions in a recent examination for New York City police captain were discriminatory and of "limited relevance."

It would appear, however, that the Officers for Justice correctly analyzed the reason for a lack of black police applicants by noting that the feeling raging through the black communities was that "the San Francisco Police Department is a cesspool of racism," and that blacks feel that "the cop is the enemy."

The Officers for Justice were unable to present their petition to the Police Commission because two of the three members had suddenly left town. Prior to the next meeting, Chief Cahill reversed his position and gave Officers for Justice a qualified approval.

The necessity for closer identification with ghetto police problems was also brought home to black officers through the operation of the San Francisco Police Community Relations Bureau. The bureau was started in 1964, largely through the urgings of Terry Francois, a Negro attorney who is now a member of the San Francisco Board of Supervisors. Mr. Francois, one of the few San Francisco blacks who actually thought of the police department in positive terms, was in later years to ask for the resignation of Police Chief Cahill because of the unsupervised mayhem distributed by the Tactical Squad (a group of riot-trained S.F. policemen) as well as the lack of support given the Police Community Relations Bureau.

The bureau was organized originally as a public relations gimmick. Uniformed officers would meet with neighborhood groups in areas marked by poor relations between police and citizens. They would then attempt to convince these citizens that policemen, with rare exceptions, were usually kind, gentle, and often misunderstood people. The reception to this approach was not all heartening to police propagandists. (In Oakland, Chief Gain instituted a system of police information centers. Presumably people who wanted to lodge complaints about police, or who wanted to find out how to secure police services, would present themselves for interview. Within weeks of the establishment of these centers, one was wrecked by a mysterious blast.)

San Francisco fared better than Oakland, primarily because the police went out to the neighborhoods, and also because the policemen assigned to community relations duty returned repeatedly to the same neighborhoods, where they managed to begin to appreciate some of the reasons for the anti-police perceptions so common to the ghetto. At that point a process was begun in which the police on the unit experienced even greater alienation than that of most policemen. The unit made the mistake of attempting to bring basic changes in police practices, thus earning them the enmity of their fellow officers, without materially altering the standoffish, suspicious attitudes of the people with whom they were working.

The inability to become forces for change in the department led a number of the members of the unit to attempt to solve problems not directly caused by police practices. One project of note found the men approaching prospective employers of youths rendered unemployable because of police records. They would explain police practices to these employers, and in a number of instances succeeded in using the prestige of the police department to secure favorable consideration of otherwise marginal applicants.

These limited successes did raise the stock of the unit with a number of minority people, but did not materially help change the negative attitude toward policemen.

The first head of the bureau, Lieutenant Dante Andriotti, has since accepted a position in Washington. When he was leaving the force he had the unique experience of having a testimonial given in his honor by a predominantly black group in San Francisco's Fillmore District. The few temporary changes in police practices which were brought about as a result of PCR activities were almost entirely due to Andriotti. He did manage to have more human-relations material introduced in the training sessions of the Police Academy. He did restrain, in selective instances, the compulsion of police toward the "massive show of force" in response to minor disturbances, and he did pinpoint for the department the more abrasive practices of policemen that could easily be eliminated.

The bureau was reduced in effectiveness with Andriotti's leaving because there was no ranking officer willing to head the unit and also because Andriotti had not been effective in sensitizing other high-ranking police officers to the mood and beliefs of the citizens with whom he worked.

Andriotti was succeeded by a captain, who, because he was a full-time Chief of Inspectors, did not have the time to devote to the further development of the unit. Even without the handicap of another assignment, he probably would not have been too creditable with minority people who knew him as the man who had organized San Francisco's K9 (canine) corps.

Lieutenant William Osterloh was then appointed head of the unit. He was, however, slated to retire and left the department less than a year after his appointment. The post is now held by Rodney Williams, a black patrolman. The announcement of Williams's appointment as bureau chief, the first time any black has commanded anything in the San Francisco Police Department, signaled the resignation from the unit of two white sergeants who, while denying racist sentiments, expressed an unwillingness to take orders from someone with a lower permanent rank. There was some lack of logic in their stance, as they took orders from Chief of Police Cahill, whose permanent rank was also that of patrolman.

One of Andriotti's observations, which received wide circulation after he left, was that the worst officers were assigned to the ghettos in most cities. The better officers, he noted, usually managed to wrangle reassignments to cooler beats. An exception, which he did not bother to mention, were men such as those assigned to neighborhood duty through the Police Community Relations Bureau. Most of these men have remained on duty, working to the limits of their effectiveness during a period when ghetto life is heating up. They have been in conspicuous attendance at most of the disturbances which have occurred in San Francisco, and have managed to keep channels of communication open, even with some of the active civilian participants of the disorders. When relative civil peace returns, these officers find themselves discussing the details of the confrontation with ghetto youth.

Rodney Williams, along with Richard Hongisto, a white member of Officers for Justice, came under fire for their acts during the San Francisco State College disturbances. The two appeared on campus and gave advice to students about methods of avoiding arrest, how to document cases of police brutality, and generally how to survive police-distributed mayhem. The Police Officers' Association was one of the loudest voices raised in condemnation of what they considered disloyalty to the force.

The opposition of the Police Officers' Association to anyone or anything is formidable, as organized police represent one of the more powerful pressure groups in the country. New York's 26,000-member Patrolmen's Benevolent Association, with a known treasury of four million dollars and a contingency fund of unestimated dimensions, forced repeal of a law instituting a civilian police review board for the city. Detroit's Police Officers' Association contributed to the defeat of a similar law. In Boston, the Patrolmen's Association became involved in the Model Cities program because that city's version stressed civilian review of police matters. All provisions of the program relating to police were removed. Philadelphia police won a lawsuit which nullified the police review board that had been established in that city, the first of its type in the nation. In Minneapolis, an ex-policeman was elected mayor on a law-and-order platform.

Police have taken to demonstrating. Picketing New York police have adopted the chant, "Blue Power." But unlike civil rights demonstrators, police often get what they demonstrate for.

The October, 1966, riot in San Francisco came in the aftermath of a policeman fatally shooting a fifteen-year-old black youth in the back. The officer suspected the boy, Matthew Johnson, of stealing an auto, an offense which would have netted Johnson, if convicted, no more than a year in a juvenile detention center. The riot which ensued caused a number of other black youth to be injured by police fire, and a great deal of black-controlled property to be damaged or destroyed.

The officer, coincidentally named Alvin Johnson, was suspended pending investigation, and the announcement resulted in a police demonstration in front of city hall. Angry speeches by POA officials denouncing the coddling of criminals and defining the difficulty of police work without official support were featured. Johnson was immediately restored to duty, and in a subsequent hearing was declared to have been acting properly and in the line of duty.

Police officers in San Francisco have been demonstrating regularly since that event. One of the more recent occasions was sparked by the intervention of Mayor Alioto in a case where three black women had been the victims of unnecessary force at the hands of police.

A white woman, apparently drunk, had run into a parked car owned by a black druggist, Mr. Wayland Fuller. His daughter, Miss Wayzel Fuller, was pushed around and handcuffed by one of the two white policemen investigating the accident after she ignored their order to not photograph the seemingly drunken driver. Another sister, Winifred Fuller, and their mother, Mrs. Hazel Fuller, responded to Wayzel's cries for help. They soon found themselves embroiled in a nightmare of argument, handcuffing and arrest, and the final harassment of being Maced by Tactical Squad members after they had been subdued.

A public uproar ensued following the disclosure that the victims of an accident had been manhandled by police. The situation became even knottier when it was discovered that the Fuller family was being charged with a variety of offenses and that police were being held blameless by their superiors. Serious questions were also being asked about the reason for calling the Tactical Squad to the scene of an automobile accident.

The mayor, when hearing of the incident from several angry delegations, intervened and ordered the charges against the Fullers dropped. He also got involved in the subsequent investigation, which reversed an earlier routine police dismissal of undue-conduct allegations, and resulted in the transfer of one of the policemen involved.

The rally protesting the Mayor's action was a joint production of the Police Officers' Association and Teamsters' Union Local 85, which had over a period of time been attempting to organize policemen into the union. The executive council of the AFL-CIO has given approval for the establishment of a national union of policemen, with a potential nation-wide strength of 300,000. The council did not designate who would have jurisdiction over police, and possible jurisdictional disputes are in the offing. Oakland police are attempting to merge their 650 policemen with Laborers Local 261, a union which, despite a relatively high minority group membership, has not been noted for any affirmative programs to alleviate the employment problems of minority people.

Such an observation can be made of most unions, particularly the Teamsters, which until recently was successful in keeping those union cards that afforded access to high-paying Teamster jobs out of the hands of blacks. Their recent interest in police matters does not seem to have helped increase Teamster appreciation of Negro concerns. Many Negroes in the Bay Area are fearful of the possible coalition of the Teamsters and the police, seeing both as separate, powerful organizations, each of which panders to the sentiments of racists.

Such apprehension is heightened when they hear Jim Rourke, business agent for Local 85, using the rhetoric of law and order—"Police brutality is the famous war cry of those who recognize no authority"—or read of the strange coincidence in which Jim Rourke attended a school board meeting accompanied by a number of very large white men identified as Teamsters, who proceeded to beat up a number of people attending the meeting in support of school integration. Police protection, which normally is over-abundant at school board meetings concerning racial matters, was mysteriously absent.

The two policemen who were present, and who were seen chatting pleasantly with some of the suspected goons, were unable to effect an arrest, and could not identify any of the assailants. Further, they could not successfully summon police assistance, although a police station is nearby.

Supporting the Tac Squad was Ed Heavey, attorney for the Teamsters, and a booster of the POA. Heavey was instrumental in the engineering of a right-wing takeover of the civilian component of the Police Community Relations Bureau. They attempted to use the Bureau to propagandize against any police reform advocated by minority people.

Heavey linked Dr. Washington Garner, the black member of the three-man Police Commission, to the Panthers. Garner had given Charles Garry, attorney for the Panthers and a personal friend, a miniature gold star making him an honorary member of the Police Department. The gesture, which is generally ignored when white officials distribute these honorary badges among their friends, resulted in Heavey and his Police Community Relations organization disrupting several meetings of the Police Commission.

Heavey had previously described a Police Commission decision to investigate complaints brought by Negroes as "being brought down to the level of the Congo." Now he was demanding that Garner be ordered to take back Garry's star. He linked Garry with the Communist Party, called the Panthers "arsonists, murderers, rapists and professional terrorizers," and claimed that only the police recognized Panthers for what they really were, dedicated and trained revolutionaries.

On almost every issue, Panthers and police are diametrically opposed. Police interpret the pressure for social change which they detect as a conspiratorial approach, issuing from the left, for the overthrow of government. Panthers, and others, see police completely aligned with the radical right in a conspiratorial attempt to keep power out of the hands of the blacks and the poor. Panthers are genuinely concerned with the possibility that the demand for law and order will lead to the formal establishment of an American brand of fascism. Their opposition to the practices which constitute the present exercise of police power issues to a large extent from their fear of the formal establishment of a police state.

No organization is self-correcting, and any group which can increase its firepower and at the same time avoid outside control of the use of its armament has a running start on being a power unto itself. Policemen, whatever their individual vices or virtues, have one thing in common: each of them is trained to a discipline which seeks solutions to problems by the assertion of authority backed up by force.

Many policemen complain, and justifiably, that they should not be saddled with the task of solving society's problems. They fail to see, however, that there is a level where police practices are one of society's problems, and that police confound the solution by resisting, often successfully, the attempts that are made to make police departments more subservient to civilian control. Police are only human, we are told, and this makes them subject to human error. The newspapers are filled with these errors.

In Concord, California, a police officer who was part of a posse moving on a suspect thought to have a carload of marijuana shot at three men emerging from a green auto with guns in their hands. They proved to be U.S. Customs agents, whose vehicle had been knocked into a ditch by the successfully escaping suspect.

Two Negro undercover police agents in Washington, D.C., responded to a report of a robbery. They arrived at the scene and jumped out of their cars with guns drawn. Two white officers got out of their cars at the same time, and opened fire. One of the Negro cops was killed and two robbery suspects escaped.

In New York, one off-duty policeman was attempting to take a prisoner into custody when another off-duty policeman made a mistake and killed his fellow officer. This was the second such shooting in New York City within a matter of a few weeks.

However justifiable these errors were, the truth is that the policemen involved were quicker with a ready trigger finger than they were with good judgment.

In San Francisco, Negro Patrolman Troy Dangerfield, a member of the Police Community Relations Bureau, was clubbed by Tactical Squad members before he could identify himself as a policeman. In a previous incident, two officers, Ray Musante and Elbert Boyd, beat a State Narcotics agent so badly that hospitalization was required. The undercover agent, Myron Gilbert, never had an opportunity to identify himself and was clubbed to the ground before an informer with whom Gilbert was working could identify the officer.

Boyd and Musante were exonerated. The explanation given by their superior, Alfred Nelder, who was then Acting Police Chief, was that Gilbert was a "narcotics agent trainee on his first assignment." Presumably, a more experienced officer could have devised a means of self-identification and, therefore, would not have suffered head wounds that required sutures and a badly bruised body. It later developed that Gilbert had been a member of the Oakland police force from 1964 to 1966 and had subsequently worked for the State Department of Alcoholic Beverage Control. Gilbert's immediate superior, Vincent Chasten, in commenting on the incident noted that the police version of the conduct attributed to Gilbert "couldn't be possible. . . . We get some pretty competent undercover men who couldn't possibly do some of the things described."

Officer Boyd was subsequently convicted of beating up several teen-agers when off duty and very much affected by drinking. This conviction resulted in Boyd's dismissal from the force, but did not have the effect of moving the police chief or the Police Commission to take steps that would instill the sort of professionalism in their police officers that would avoid increasing racial alienation. The victims of the attack were Chicanos.

It is easier for police departments to cover up or dismiss mistakes in judgment, or indiscriminate use of force by a police officer, when the victim has no status. But they do not always succeed.

Tens of thousands of dollars have been awarded by Bay Area courts to victims of unjustified beatings or unconscionable shootings by police. Officers have also been dismissed from the force as a result of being found guilty of unnecessarily shooting or otherwise injuring a citizen. But the process of determining the degree of culpability in individual cases is slow, and the effect of treating each incident of police brutality as an isolated instance is to make both policemen and citizens victims of criminal neglect on the part of those who presumably have the power to control policemen.

In a 1970 incident in Los Angeles two unarmed Mexican nationals were killed by policemen looking for a murder suspect. Two policemen from San Leandro, accompanied by Los Angeles policemen, surrounded a house after receiving a tip that the suspect was inside. A Los Angeles detective kicked open the door of a room, tripped and fell to the floor, immediately after shooting at a man he thought was charging him. The detective's partners shot and killed Guillermo Sanchez, thinking that Sanchez had fired a gun. Officers outside of the building, hearing the shots, responded by killing another man who was climbing out of the window of the besieged apartment. A third Mexican was wounded while attempting to leave the apartment, and a ten-month-old baby, sleeping in a neighboring apartment, was missed by four police-fired bullets which came through the wall. Seven policemen were indicted and charged with involuntary manslaughter.

It is true that the incidence of disciplinary action affecting policemen who brutalize citizens is on the increase. But it must be remembered that many of these cases originate in the overreaction of policemen to the perceived threat of civil disorder. Again, the U.S. Commission on Civil Disorders discovered that the highest intensity of complaint to be found in the ghetto related to police practices. In other words, policemen, collectively, contribute to the conditions which cause riots and then overreact to phenomena they create. This sense of fear and threat seems to carry over when police are off duty. It also seems to affect one of their off-duty occupations, the forming of political opinions.

The increasing restiveness of America's Negro population has consistently found policemen, in official and unofficial capacities, claiming that the most vocally protesting black group operated outside of the law and deserved being treated as criminal. Most of the leaders of the now-respectable civil rights groups—NAACP, CORE, SCLC—have spent time in jail for activities that have since been defined as peaceful and constitutionally protected. A number of them, along with their followers, spent part of that jail time nursing injuries inflicted by the protectors of established law and order.

An undeniable truth is simply that police officials have always singled out an organized group of blacks and defined their activities as threatening. The last such group to be on the receiving end of police hostility were the Black Muslims. There was a recent time when their mosques were attacked and their members subject to intense police scrutiny. In Los Angeles, on two separate occasions, masses of police claiming to be acting on reliable information shot their way into a mosque in search of weapons. On both occasions they came out empty-handed and theorized that the Muslims, along with their guns, had escaped via some secret route.

Police have now escalated the war against Negro militancy to the point where some blacks see the need for self-defense. Under these conditions, and without basic reforms which would make police activity responsive to social needs, or at least devoid of paranoid political thinking, everyone—black and white—may discover that the keepers of the peace have become our jailers, and very possibly our executioners.

III

The Cats from the Jungle

ON MAY 1, 1969, Huey P. Newton appeared before a Federal Judge in San Francisco, seeking release from jail pending an appeal of his conviction for voluntary manslaughter of an Oakland policeman in October, 1967.

A rally was in progress in front of the Federal Building which houses the court. "Free Huey" signs were everywhere, nailed to trees, pasted in automobile windows and held by many of the crowd of 6000 or more who filled the plaza and spilled far out into the street separating the Federal Building from the California State office building. For a while a "Free Huey" sign was displayed from the center window of the top floor of the state offices. It disappeared at just about the same time a red flag was run up the flagpole to join the stars and stripes.

There were no uniformed officers on the plaza, but the plainclothesmen were easily spotted. Here and there along the sea of natural hairdos, within the swirl of liberated colors and in the shadow of periodically upraised arms, some holding red books and others clenching fists, stood small clumps of neatly gray-dressed white men, with serious faces and movements that did not match those of the surge of humanity surrounding them. They were ignored, or rather no attention was paid them by the crowd shouting "Free Huey" on cue and screaming "Off the pig" at every possible opportunity.

Attorney Charles Garry yelled, "We've got an uphill fight, friends, but we're going to win. The people are going to win. We need, and we want, Huey Newton out on the street."

"The Black Panther Party," said a Panther captain, "is feeding two thousand young brothers and sisters every morning. If that's subversive, then, dammit, we're subversive. When the Party says 'power to the people,' we ain't jiving a pound. When the people say to Reagan, when the people say to Alioto, when the people say to pig Richard M. Nixon that we want Huey P. Newton free, we're saying, 'You bald-headed pig punks, better get out the way 'cause we're tired and we're saying you better let Huey go.'"

Kids from the breakfast program sang "Free Huey Newton" and "We want pork chops, off the pigs."

Father Neal said he could not relate to the image of a Statue of Liberty that is "a cold marble figure of some dyke woman covered with pigeon droppings sitting in a polluted Bay in the Atlantic Ocean. . . . My Statue of Liberty is a brother on the block, hot, wet and funky, with a smoking rifle in one hand and a flaming torch in the other."

Baby D read the poetry of Bunchy Carter, the Deputy Minister of Information, killed in Los Angeles in January, 1969:

> In Niggertown one day
> four little children kneeled to pray
> in Jesus name.
> Boom!
> Four little children gone
> and your Jesus never came.
>
> Now you say you're tired of all this shit
> You suck-a pawed son of a bitch
> If you was you'd ball your mitt
> DO SOMETHING nigger! If you only spit.

Carleton Goodlett, publisher, doctor, participant in peace conferences all over the globe and recognized "responsible" Negro leader, pointed out, "The issue transcends that of freeing Huey. The issue which we face today centers around the attempts of private citizens in this country to ward off the invasion of fascism in our land. . . . As I visualize the struggle of the heroic black youth in this country, this is what they are saying to me. . . . 'If we are forced in freedom's name to fight for liberty, let us fight and let us die at home.' "

From the crowd, shouts of "Right on." Goodlett continued, " 'Let us conduct, if forced we are, guerilla warfare, in the complex, calm inhuman black steel and concrete canyons of America's vicious cities. If we must die in freedom's name, better to die at home, than to be buried in an unmarked grave in South Vietnam.' "

Cheers greeted the announcement that "A couple of our Chicano brothers took care of business today. They were holding up a place, the cops stumbled on them, so they killed one pig and critically wounded another."

Actually, the shooting had occurred when a group of Chicanos suspected of having stolen goods were questioned by two plainclothesmen. The second officer had been hit by fists rather than bullets. Seven Chicanos were charged with murder and became known as Los Siete de la Raza, the seven of the race. The trial, like that of Huey Newton, found the prosecution claiming that criminal charges were being leveled at the defendants, and the defense insisting that the trial was political.

Charles Garry, Newton's lawyer, became chief counsel for Los Siete. Thus, by some historical coincidence, a rally called to comment on Huey Newton's treatment in the courts became the springboard for a Panther-like organization among Mexican-Americans.

(Los Siete, in addition to raising money for legal defense and publicizing the cause of their accused brothers, started a newspaper, *Basta Ya* [*Enough!*], initiated a breakfast-for-children program, and opened a community information center organized around a restaurant where films are shown, speeches are made and political activity is ever present. They and the Panthers support each other and regularly engage in each other's public activities.)

The Black Panther Party had come a long way from the street-corner meetings it used to hold. It has much further to go before it is in a position to implement the ten-point platform * and program that constitutes the Panther revolutionary mission. The distance it has traveled in the relatively short time of four years, however, has been enough to change both the style of Negro politics and the nature of the response of whites to the pronouncements of black people.

The Black Panther Party comes from a portion of the American social spectrum that has been all but hidden from public view. Bad niggers are what many Panthers are, fresh off the streets, out of gangs, away from the penitentiary, just departed from educational careers stopped short of high school graduation, and suffering from the economic deprivation that is a combination of too little employment and too many welfare workers dispensing more talk than money.

They suffer from a deprivation of manhood—not their own, but that of fathers who left women alone to face the landlord and the bill collectors, and to work to take care of their families. There is contempt for an older generation that did not seek to develop its potential to wrest liberty for black people. "If our fathers had fought the man like we doing," they say, "the struggle would be almost over." They are a ferocious embodiment of the summarizing tenth point of the Panther program: "We want land, bread, housing, education, clothing, justice and peace."

In many respects it is the style rather than the demands of the Panthers that has caused so much consternation. The one

* See Appendix A.

truly revolutionarly plank in their platform is the first: "We want freedom. We want power to determine the destiny of our black community." The other nine, however radical they might seem to some, are items which could be satisfied without significantly changing the power equation that governs present black-white relations.

Their concept of the right to self-defense, armed self-defense, is seen by many as a thinly disguised exhortation to take pot shots at cops. The slogan, "Guns, baby, guns," coupled with the Panther fondness of the phrase, "Off the pig," seemingly supports the observation that the Panthers are tooling up for a war with police. It is hardly that simple.

Panthers are insisting that all blacks recognize that they are in physical peril and that they prepare themselves appropriately. Ironically, Malcolm X's call for armed self-defense, to which the Panthers wholeheartedly subscribe, was heeded by his home state of Nebraska, which passed a law affirming the right of its citizens to own guns to defend themselves or their property. The law seems to have been inspired by disturbances in the ghettos of Omaha.

San Francisco, which requires the registration of firearms, has fewer than 800,000 residents and 400,000 legally registered firearms, or more than one gun for every two people living in the city. There is no method by which the number of unregistered firearms can be accurately estimated, but unquestionably the majority of firearms—registered and otherwise—are in the hands of whites. Again, there is no way to guess how many of these armed whites are capable of finding some reason to attack blacks. But a comparative minority, say 1 percent, would amount to a minimum of five thousand people in San Francisco.

Critics of the idea of blacks arming themselves recognize quite accurately that a visible armed minority is hardly a match for the nation's whites. President Johnson once replied to cries for black power with the observation that 90 percent of America (white) had democratic power. Panthers are only one of several black orientations that recognize that an invisible minority of this admittedly racist society has the capacity and desire to control black assertion by force of arms.

A very logical sequence of experiences, ideas and alternatives led to the formation of the Panther program. The top leaders are all of an age. They were too young to be involved in either World War II or the Korean War, with the accompanying demands for the loyalties and attentions that national conflict brings. Also, they did not grow up soon enough to be heir to the fears of being labeled subversive or communist that is the legacy of many who matured in the 50's and experienced, at least vicariously, the total loss of status, credibility, position and respect afforded the victims of McCarthyism. The time of their birth having spared them the necessity of developing a fear of being labeled for political beliefs; they were free to search both the communist and non-communist world of ideas for what was useful to them, and to form alliances with other groups with which they seemed compatible.

For the most part the Panther leaders were products of a northern experience which included all of the rights fought for in the south. They could easily recognize that if the right to vote, to swim with whites, to travel in other than the back seats of buses, or to eat in public with whites had any true significance to black lives, that black Oakland would be far better off than it was.

Moreover, it became clear that a fantastic amount of black energy, time and money, along with a great number of black deaths and injuries, had been devoted to securing what were at best empty symbols. True, a few Negroes benefited as a result, but they were symbols also. This reasoning was summed up in a position paper presented to the Alameda County Peace and Freedom Party in January, 1968, by Kathleen Cleaver.

"High-placed, hand-picked Negroes were given high-placed, hand-picked jobs as a concession to the pressure of the masses for dramatic social change—but what good does a black Supreme Court Justice do when the entire legal system is racist and dedicated to denying black people justice? . . . Rosa Parks, when she sat down on a segregated Montgomery bus and refused to give her seat up to a white man, launched a movement which sent Martin Luther King to Stockholm to accept a Nobel Peace Prize. Without Rosa Parks there would be no Martin Luther King. But where is Mrs. Parks and how have the conditions of her life changed?"

Dr. King's life, of course, was drastically changed through assassination. The principle remains the same, however. Very little of the honor and respect granted a Martin Luther King has filtered down to the people in whose name he spoke, and for whose cause he was martyred.

The Panthers were a logical development of earlier black revolutionary programs, particularly those of Robert Williams, the Muslims, Malcolm X, and the more activist civil rights organizations such as SNCC.

Robert Williams articulated and demonstrated the principle that blacks must defend themselves against attack from both official and unofficial sources. Williams was the president of the NAACP in Monroe, N.C., a city where Negroes lived in a special section of town approachable only by an unpaved road leading nowhere else. In addition to the frustrations common to poor Negroes everywhere, those living in Monroe had the added disadvantage of being targets for whites who wanted something to do of an evening.

It was a fairly common practice for several carloads of rednecks to drive to niggertown and distribute a few shotgun blasts among the terrified residents. Williams responded by forming the males in the NAACP into a militia-type organization which returned the fire of the next group of marauding whites. He also wrote articles and letters upholding the right of self-defense. As a result he was suspended from the NAACP for six months.

Williams left Monroe in 1961 to avoid a federal fugitive warrant charging him with kidnapping, assault with a deadly weapon, and several other charges. He went to Cuba, mainland China, and Tanzania, and returned to the U.S. in 1969. During the entire time he was gone he wrote an underground newsletter for U.S. consumption. His purchase of a ticket home so shook up the airline that they flew a fully staffed plane from London to New York carrying a single passenger, Williams.

The precise sequence of events leading to Williams's departure are obscured by conflicting testimony. There seems to be agreement, however, that a white couple was detained by Williams' group, and was released unharmed after Williams left town. Soon after, Monroe police, sheriffs' deputies, and ultimately the FBI came. The couple were natives of the area, but claimed to have become confused in the dark and to have ended up in the black section of town. Williams and his supporters say that the couple were either part of a raiding party, or else decoys sent in just to give police an official excuse for opening fire. Whatever the case, blacks fired back at police, in line with the previously announced advocacy of armed self-defense against any and all attackers.

The Muslims contributed to Panther philosophy on a number of levels. Their demand for a physically separate part of the United States, in contrast to earlier back-to-Africa movements, established the notion that blacks had a legitimate and historically based claim for land as a result of having worked (as slaves) without due compensation. This demand that America get off state-sized hunks of real estate and turn them over to blacks is on its face one of the more audacious revolutionary programs advanced by blacks in modern years.

The Muslim demand for land was also rooted in a concept of nationhood, defined by race but also circumscribed by a religion, Islam, through which American blacks could establish close identification with people of color outside the U.S. Thus, it was a nation with overseas allies that sought to establish a political entity in North America, and not second-class citizens with reflexes toward white government that were developed in slavery.

In reality, the Panther approach to the solution of black political problems in America is not dependent on the prior existence of Muslims. A concept of nationhood or extended community, the development of an identity with other similarly deprived peoples regardless of geography, the demand for land, and a determination to self-defense are basic to the formation of a politics of freedom. But the fact remains that Elijah Muhammad and the Muslims were asserting their principles at the same time that the civil rights movement was being put through the excruciating changes of facing whites totally resistant to black self-assertion.

Throughout this entire period, the Muslims were loudly calling attention to an alternative approach to bringing self-determination and Malcolm X was, in the main, the bearer of the message.

The Panthers, in fact every revolutionary black orientation in America, readily acknowledges Malcolm X as the most important influence on their thinking and activities. Almost every issue of the *Black Panther*, the official organ of the Party which began publication in April, 1967, makes reference to the legacy of Malcolm X.

It was Malcolm who moved from street boy, gangster, hustler, pimp, dope peddler, convict, and Muslim convert, to a position of being the most articulate spokesman for black liberation in this modern era. Thus he provided a pattern for emulation, in a cultural context undreamt of by Horatio Alger and his followers, which was specifically relevant to the experience of black youth. It was also Malcolm who could rap, who faced an audience alone, unafraid, and who answered every question with an authority issuing from conviction, commitment and a thorough knowledge of his position.

It was Malcolm who appeared in public flanked by a phalanx of the Fruit of Islam, a mute statement to all on-

lookers that blacks who speak clearly in favor of black liberation are in physical danger. And it was Malcolm who was
assassinated at the point when he was beginning to organize
a movement outside the boundaries accepted by Muslims, a
movement within which, presumably, all blacks regardless of
religious affiliation could find a vehicle for expressing and
achieving their need for independence, freedom and self-
respect.

It was finally Malcolm who reflected the sentiments of
many blacks in the street when he noted that President Ken-
nedy's assassination was a case of "chickens coming home to
roost." His statement resulted in a suspension from the
Mosque, and ultimately in his leaving Elijah Mohammad's
organization in order to found a group of his own, the Organization for African Unity. He remained religiously affi-
liated with Islam, but his politics became more directly tied
up with preparing for an armed struggle and very much
devoid of the sharp racial distinctions made by the Muslims.

Eldridge Cleaver was one of a number of Muslims who left
the Mosque along with Malcolm and who conceived of themselves as members of the OAU. He closes his essay on Malcolm * with the often quoted "We shall have our manhood.
We shall have it or the earth will be leveled by our attempts
to gain it."

Cleaver, while still in jail, conceived of himself as the heir
to Malcolm and set himself the task of rebuilding the OAU.
He subsequently decided that the Panthers were in fact carrying on Malcolm's program and became the Minister of
Information. In this capacity he contributed to the development of Panther political theory.

In April, 1966, when Cleaver was still in jail and the manu-
script of *Soul on Ice* was on its way to a publisher, a meeting
was held in a West Oakland YMCA. A group of fifteen to

* Eldridge Cleaver, *Soul on Ice*, Initial Reactions on the Assassination of
Malcolm X, McGraw Hill, 1968.

twenty blacks, from both San Francisco and Oakland, were attempting to form a group geared toward organizing the black community to fight for self-determination. All claimed loyalty to Malcolm's memory, and each felt that black people were the only ones qualified to determine the future and character of the black community. Two factions developed.

One group insisted that blacks, because of their oppressed condition, were natural revolutionaries. They proposed what was essentially an educational program, in which a sense of community would be developed by making blacks aware of their cultural heritage and the role which Europeans played in destroying that culture. The contemporary problems that blacks faced could then be discussed and dealt with in the light of a history of which they were aware. Such an approach, it was suggested, would automatically lead Negroes to the point where they could determine for themselves when, and if, armed resistance was necessary. To stress revolution to people whose lives would naturally lead them to revolt was considered foolhardy because it would attract unnecessary pressure from white militarists as well as redundant because black people, they felt, did not need lessons in the advisability of shooting when there was no other alternative.

The other faction, which included Huey Newton and Bobby Seale, insisted that the present-day black existence was sufficiently differentiated from white culture so as to obviate the necessity of stressing historical roots. The undefinable but accepted concept of "soul," the commonly shared nuances of language, the essential experience of oppression, unemployment, rejection and insult suffered by blacks at the hands of whites, provided a cultural context which only lacked a tool for collective advancement. That tool, it was asserted, was a gun, which at once earned the sobriquet of "technical equipment." Education, cultural advancement, the development of community through the absorption of history, the adoption of African dress or the learning of Swahili, was considered ridiculous, and also tainted with the white-inspired scholasticism that was the heritage of the house nigger, the slave who was taught to read and write and respond with social grace, for the sole convenience of his master.

The meeting broke up in anger and resulted in two organizations. Those labeled "cultural nationalists," who by coincidence were mainly from San Francisco with its 10 percent black population, formed the Black Panther Party of Northern California. Eventually they established a headquarters and started a newsletter. Their publication, *Black Power*, used a few Swahili words on the masthead and featured a few articles on black history, art, culture and language, but in the main concentrated on contemporary issues, cited the necessity for revolutionary organization, and repeatedly extolled the virtues of an armed black community.

Bobby and Huey, along with the Oakland contingent, returned to Merritt College in Oakland, where they formed the Soul Students Advisory Council, the prototype for the Black Student Unions which were later developed on campuses across the country. They succeeded in the establishment of the first Black Studies classes, when Bobby Seale taught a class in black history. They also formed the Black Panther Party for Self Defense, and went about Oakland recruiting young blacks for what was to become the vanguard party of the Black revolution.

It seemed apparent to outsiders that the differences between the two groups were those of emphasis rather than intent, and that the assertion of individual egos contributed heavily to the argument. An experience common to some of the members of the two Panther parties was past membership in a superficially militant organization headed by Don Warden, an Oakland attorney.

Warden's Afro-American Association was a Negro self-help mini-conglomerate, which in its self-effacing search for an image of black respectability combined the philosophy of Booker T. Washington with the economic separatism of Elijah Muhammad. Warden owed his initial recruiting success to the fact that his anti-civil-rights-movement position could be shared by black youth, who could not accept the voluntary submission to beatings that was required of civil rights activists in the development of the movement.

Warden's approach was shot down in 1968, at the Third International Conference on Black Power in Philadelphia, by a brother from Detroit:

"We've been sold a lotta shit about bringing industry into our own communities. . . . Check it out. See how much land a modern factory takes up. How much vacant land is there in our communities? Man, just to build a tot lot we have to tear down three houses and move thirty families. . . . And the already over-crowded ghetto . . . gets even more crowded. It's land locked by white suburbs, not getting bigger, just getting higher. And babies keep being born and needing more space. . . . Where will the apartment buildings be?—Where we gonna put those damn factories you gonna bring in? . . . I say we got to get our eye back on the ball. Sure, control your own communities—but don't just stop there. . . .

"When your government takes from tax money 40 billion bucks and gives it to some 'private' airplane company to build some goddam SST plane, baby that factory is yours no matter where he builds it—west hell or an all-white suburb—and you better start getting your shit together and figure out some way to get out there and get some that action. . . .

"You're not just citizens of the ghetto. . . . Don't buy this bullshit that just because you might want some clean air and green grass for your kids, that makes you some kind of imitation white man. Dig it, we ain't no more native to the ghetto than the white man is native to America—fact is, if it weren't for him, we'd be back in Africa where we'd have more fresh air, open space and green grass than anyone in the world." *

* Clarence Funnye, "The Untogether People: Separate but Gilded?" *The Village Voice*, September 26, 1968. (In 1970 a black separatist from Detroit seemingly heeded this brother's advice. Milton Henry, vice-president of the Republic of New Africa, an organization that has exchanged gunfire with Detroit police, moved into a $58,000 ranch-type house located in the wealthy all-white community of Bloomfield Township.)

Both Panther Parties, though they had not articulated their positions as persuasively as the unnamed brother from Detroit, were girding themselves to organize their communities and get some of theirs back from the white man. They coexisted, but uneasily.

In January, 1967, the remnants of Bay Area civil rights organizations combined with all of the Negro statewide elected officials to promote a three-day gathering called "Conference '67, Survival of Black People." The theme of the conference reflected the concern being shared by a large spectrum of the black community of the possible future development of an American equivalent of Hitler's genocidal final solution. These fears had been heightened by the summary refusal of Congress to seat Adam Clayton Powell.

Despite the far-reaching implications of the conference title, the sessions were largely old-hat, consisting of militant sounds coming from politicians capable of finding that working toward a black revolution was compatible with efforts to elect Democratic Party candidates, and the cries for social reform emanating from Negro poverty-program officials seeking bigger and better programs. The best-attended session featured Stokely Carmichael and a number of other self-declared revolutionaries, including Ron Karenga and Huey Newton.

Leaders of the Black Panther Party of Northern California were at odds with the planners of the conference, primarily because no provision had been made to guarantee admittance to grass-roots blacks who could not afford the fee. They also felt that the conference should have included some significant mention of Malcolm X, who during his lifetime had repeatedly encouraged Negroes to organize in a fashion that would help to insure their physical survival. They met with Stokely Carmichael before his appearance, to discuss the shape of the movement in the Bay Area and to encourage him to center his speech on the contribution of Malcolm X to the survival of black people.

Carmichael informed them that his speech was already set.

He was delivering a position paper on the subject of alliances, which later appeared as a chapter in *Black Power*. Carmichael said that the conference was not the proper environment in which to begin establishing a respect for the memory of Malcolm X. He supported the idea of a grass-roots-oriented symposium in honor of Malcolm, with mild objections to holding it on February 21, the anniversary of Malcolm's assassination.

"We should celebrate life, not death," he said, "Our black heroes are important to us because of the way they lived their lives, not the fashion in which they met death." He did agree, though, that it was important to get on with the business of healing the breach between black revolutionary groups, and that February 21 was as good a time as any.

Betty Shabazz, Malcolm X's widow, was scheduled to be the featured speaker at the First Annual Malcolm X Grass Roots Memorial, which was held in Hunters Point, in a community-center building that had been San Francisco's first opera house. Disgust with the middle-class-dominated conference's exclusion of Malcolm X caused the two Panther parties to combine forces to provide a bodyguard for Mrs. Shabazz. They appeared at the airport carrying rifles and shotguns and wearing ammunition belts, some of which had pistols attached to them.

"A Frightening Army," headlined the *San Francisco Chronicle*, reporting on what it called an invasion. The Black Panther Party was in the news.

Eldridge Cleaver records this occasion as the first time he met Huey Newton, whom he describes as the "baddest mother fucker ever to set foot in history." Cleaver was working as a *Ramparts* reporter and was in the *Ramparts* office when Betty Shabazz came in with her armed escort.

The pace of Panther activity stepped up considerably after the Shabazz incident. There had already been a feature article on the Panthers in one of the local dailies. Its prime message was that niggers were openly arming themselves to make war on white people. Anyone reading the article would be led to the conclusion that the Panthers were a small band of kooks, hopped up on paranoid fantasies of police brutality, the effects of racism and the enmity white society bore toward black people. There was absolutely no attempt to describe the Panther program, develop the rationale which led to it, or discuss the proposition that continued denial of equality to Negroes must at some point in time lead to organized aggressive activities within the community.

It is useless to describe the mass media approach to the Panthers as racist. The term is accurate, but not descriptive. The media, along with a majority of whites, assume that the minority status of Negroes will, in and of itself, temper the expressions of hostility emanating from the ghetto. In its simplest terms the argument is that Negroes know that they are greatly outnumbered, and will therefore restrict the expression of their unhappiness relative to the black condition to tactics calculated to avoid the unleashing of majority hostility toward blacks. It follows from this assumption that the Panthers must be aberrant blacks, unable to appreciate the arithmetical racial facts of life.

Another assumption is that Negroes, when articulating their discontent along with proposals for change, are directing their message to those who can make changes, white people. Also taken for granted is that whites and Negroes, because they are both products of an American culture, get exactly the same message from a newspaper article or television report. Not only do they not get the same message, but the bland, business-as-usual put-down of particular blacks puts Negroes on notice about a possible positive element coming out of their community. Positive at least in the sense that whites are sufficiently bothered to use time and newsprint to take official notice of black activity.

One aspect of the black community ignored by whites is that it is comparatively small and possesses the urban equivalent of the jungle telegraph: When the newspapers were reporting the airport incident and even before, when the *San Francisco Examiner* "exposed" the Panthers, Oakland blacks were aware of the Panther patrols, small groups of young blacks, visibly armed, who observed police making arrests and on occasion were arrested themselves. Articles about the Panthers, then, let Negroes know that Panther activity was beginning to get to the man. And, while many might not approve of the specific acts, almost all could identify on that most common level of enjoying a spectacle where the man catches hell.

Minor confrontations with police continued, but a near-crisis occurred when a Richmond youth was killed by an officer of the Contra Costa Sheriff's Department.

Denzil Dowell, according to official sources, was shot and killed when running away from a sheriff after refusing to identify himself and submit to arrest. His relatives say that he was shot by an officer who knew Denzil well, and who on previous occasions had threatened him with death. Panthers went out to Richmond to conduct their own investigation, and satisfied themselves that Denzil was incapable of running as described because of a previous hip injury, that the body had been moved from the original point of death, and that valuable evidence was being suppressed.

A series of street-corner meetings were held, all featuring a group of armed Panthers deployed in skirmish lines set up to repel any attack by police. Bobby Seale reports that at one street-corner meeting, local residents supplemented the armed patrol with guns of their own.

"This time it wasn't only the Black Panthers who came, but other people came there, with their rifles, with their guns, and with their pieces. I noticed some older brothers come out and they were shaking hands with a lot of us, and they had their pieces under their shirts. They just carried them concealed. And some sisters. One sister came out and jumped out her car with an M-1. We saw the black community people getting uptight and ready." *

The Panthers, on their way to organizing a Richmond chapter, not only held meetings, but also visited a local school to express their disapproval of teachers hitting black pupils. They instructed Richmond residents on the implications of the Panther political program, including the care and use of firearms, and paid an armed visit to the Contra Costa sheriff's office to complain about his men's actions. Sheriff's deputies would not allow the Panthers inside the building when wearing arms. There was at least one standoff, where Panthers and police leveled loaded guns towards one another, but there were no arrests and no incidents. There was also no satisfaction to be gained from speaking to the sheriff. None had been anticipated.

Blacks from Richmond accompanied the Panthers to the sheriff's office, and it was they whom the Panthers wanted to impress. How the sheriff would respond was unimportant. It was only blacks that counted. They were expected to observe and discover the style necessary to confront white authority. After that, they could join the Panthers, support their activity, or else strike out on their own, armed with an increased political sophistication.

The Richmond adventure started a new phase in the forming of opinion regarding the attempts of Panthers to organize blacks. Within the ghetto, there was ambivalence aplenty. It was one thing for a group of young blacks to be belligerent toward white society and white police in general, and another for them to be rigidly disapproving of assumedly nonrevolutionary black activity.

Many Negroes read the term vanguard to mean that Panthers thought they held a privileged position that allowed them to run over blacks as well as whites. There was, of

* Selections from the Biography of Huey P. Newton, Bobby Seale, *Ramparts Magazine*, November 17, 1968.

course, the constant fear that the Panthers were overplaying an emphasis on guns, with the result that some young blacks, who would have been thugs in any event, rationalized their holdup attempts with politically oriented phrases. Suddenly they were liberating, or fighting the oppressor on his own ground, or driving the racist capitalist away from exploiting the black community. To complaining blacks the actions still looked like burglary, a downtown mugging, or the holdup of a white grocery store in a black neighborhood.

The main objection, however, was that many of the Panthers seemed to be more zealous in their condemnations of black people than in the ways they moved against whites. Panthers were seen as separating themselves from the black community's daily activities toward reform, the easier to belittle blacks whose earnest and honest attempts toward betterment were frustrated by the acts of whites in power.

It is difficult to evaluate the truth of these charges. A number of the Negroes most vehement in condemnation of the Panthers are very obviously threatened with the thought that they might have to defend Panther activities. By and large, these are Negroes who have some communication with whites in power, and who prefer to maintain these liaisons without the pressure of a new dissident orientation.

There are also the complications related to class position. Many middle-class Negroes are acutely distressed at any display of the Negroness they have worked so hard to eliminate in themselves. It will probably take a long time to appraise accurately the degree to which the self-hatred that has been inculcated among Negroes has handicapped them in progressing toward real freedom, a component of which is genuine self-respect.

The Panthers did get themselves involved in community affairs in Richmond. To be precise, it was in North Richmond, an unincorporated enclave of over 6000 deprived blacks, located between the county dump and the city's heavy industrial area. Usual city services such as street sweeping, sewer maintenance, garbage collection are at a minimum. Every winter the annual heavy rainfall turns sections of North Richmond into a shantytown, ghettoized version of Venice, Italy. Insurance rates are high, if and when insurance is available at all. Police protection is low, and protection against police, nil.

The killing of Denzil Dowell in April, 1967, was only the last of a number of incidents involving the Contra Costa Sheriff's Department, and only one of the issues raised by the Panthers in an unsuccessful attempt to move North Richmond blacks to incorporate themselves into a city.

"Bad roads, dilapidated housing, rampant unemployment, inferior education, brutal cops—cop cars with a dog behind the steering wheel and a dog behind the screen—bad sewers, bad lighting, no drainage system, no say-so over the decisions that control our lives—this is a portrait of the horrible inhuman conditions that the white power structure forces black people in the North Richmond area to live under." * This was the Panthers' description of the election issues.

Incorporation, whatever the drawbacks to a poor community, would have placed North Richmond citizens in a position to have their own police department, and if desired, their own schools.

A little more than a year after Denzil Dowell was killed, Charles Mims, a fifteen-year-old black car-theft suspect, was shot and critically injured. Three days of looting and burning of businesses followed. Afterwards, as has happened in other cities, the cry for law and order was louder than the pleas that the root causes of the disturbances be discovered and corrected.

One of the loudest voices for the establishment of law and order is that of Assemblyman Don Mulford, whose Assembly district includes the troubled U.C. campus in Berkeley. Mulford, apparently disturbed by the popularization of guns in neighboring Oakland, introduced a bill that would make it illegal to carry loaded firearms within a city limit. It was seen

* *The Black Panther*, June 20, 1967.

as an anti-Panther bill by many, including Huey Newton; and the Panthers decided to send a delegation to Sacramento to express their position. Newton himself did not attend; instead, Bobby Seale went and read a statement:

"The Black Panther Party for Self Defense calls upon the American people in general and the Black people in particular to take careful note of the racist California Legislature which is now considering legislation aimed at keeping the Black People disarmed and powerless at the very same time that racist police agencies throughout the country are intensifying the terror, brutality, murder, and repression of Black People." *

The statement was read at some point in the midst of total confusion beginning with Governor Reagan running at the sight of the Panthers, and ending with the arrest of twenty-three Panthers. Over the years, the State Legislature at Sacramento had witnessed sit-ins, sleep-ins, pray-ins and other protest activities on behalf of black people. They were all eclipsed on May 2, 1967, when the Panthers held a gun-in. Every single Panther—with the exception of Eldridge Cleaver, prevented by his parole conditions from the carrying of firearms—came, armed to the teeth, to call on the legislators.

Upon entering the capitol grounds, the group fanned out into a formation that resembled an attacking skirmish line. They rounded one corner of the building, only to run into a group of young people who were visiting with the Governor. Reagan wordlessly cut the audience short and trotted to comparative safety indoors. The Panthers hardly noticed him; they were intent on finding their way into a capitol building none of them had visited before. They soon found the route, with the help of newspapermen.

Cameramen who had been covering the Reagan story, and others who were in the pressroom, photographed, interviewed and guided the Panthers on their way to the Assembly chambers. Calm deliberation went out the windows with the

* See Appendix B for complete statement.

entrance of the Panthers, preceded by what must have been the entire Sacramento press corps. They had intended to go to the visitors' gallery, but had inadvertently come onto the floor, from which the public is barred during sessions. The visitation was probably the purest example of cultural clash ever recorded.

On the one hand there were California state assemblymen, most of whom had never heard of the Panthers, but who had been convinced up to that moment that a combination of legislative immunity and the capitol cops served to keep guns off the Assembly floor. And then there were the Panthers. The majority of them had never been out of the Bay Area—indeed, Oakland. As for official buildings, the only ones most had previous contact with were schools, police stations, jails and courts.

So there they stood, surrounded by the unaccustomed opulence of the Assembly, and facing the obviously frightened visages of men listed as top wheels in the power structure. They had nothing to say to each other; the gulf of noncommunication was too great. On one side were men who passed laws governing the lives of people they did not know, and on the other the people who did not have the vaguest idea of how to get a point across to a legislator. Both groups did the only thing possible: They ignored each other.

An assemblyman, not identified, began to shout that the cameramen and reporters had no business on the Assembly floor. Meanwhile, Panthers were busy condemning police. "Bobby Hutton was cussing the pig out who had snatched his gun out of his hand, who had snuck up behind him and snatched his gun out of his hand . . . 'What the hell you got my gun for? Am I under arrest or something? If I'm not under arrest, you give me my gun back. You ain't said I was under arrest.' " *

Several guns were taken from the Panthers, who in actuality

* Selections from the Biography of Huey P. Newton, *op. cit.*

had not come to Sacramento to do any shooting. Next, the entire group, both the armed and unarmed, were pushed, herded, escorted, and otherwise encouraged into a 'down' elevator, where they eventually found their way back to their cars. The Panthers were arrested before they left Sacramento on charges which included the carrying of concealed weapons, conspiracy to disturb the decorum of the legislature and a number of other misdemeanor charges. The final outcome was that six of the Panthers pleaded guilty to a misdemeanor charge of disrupting a legislative session.

There is a distinct possibility that the six-month jail sentence which Bobby Seale served for disrupting the legislature indirectly resulted in Huey Newton's imprisonment for manslaughter.

Huey and Bobby were a team. Most of the time the two were inseparable, a fact which contributed to their working well together. But Huey tended to become upset more quickly than Bobby in response to an assumed insult or attack. Seale, although he did not totally avoid arrest prior to becoming notorious as a Panther, was more successful than Huey in avoiding direct confrontations with police when it was not desirable.

When Huey Newton was stopped by Oakland police in October, 1967, Bobby was still serving time on the Sacramento case. Had he not been in jail there is an excellent chance that he would have been with Newton, and that events would have turned out differently. Of course, that is all speculation. It is doubtful that the Panthers could have survived for long without being involved in an exchange of gunfire with police, and it is very possible that Huey would have been one of the Panthers so engaged.

Huey was very active in the patrolling aspects of the Panther program. This was an adaptation of police surveillance techniques that several ghetto communities used to reduce arbitrary police violence in the course of arrests or questioning.

Groups of citizens, usually wearing large identification badges, would patrol ghetto streets, particularly those with a high incidence of arrest. Whenever they came upon an arrest in progress, the citizens would stand far enough away to avoid being charged with interfering with an arrest, but sufficiently close to observe everything going on. In this way, they would be witnesses to the arrest and also, because of the identification badges they wore, give notice to the officer that he was being observed.

Panther patrols were similarly conducted, but the official means of notification were the very obvious weapons carried by Panthers. There have been no reported incidents arising out of this practice.

Considering the tenseness that has characterized relations between police and Panthers, it is amazing that more difficulty has not been experienced. One of the factors which might have contributed to this uneasy peace was the Mulford Act, which made it illegal for a citizen to carry a loaded gun within city limits. The passage of the law made it impossible for Panthers to patrol legally, as they had prior to September, 1967.

Following Sacramento, the pace of Panther activities increased, as did their scope. One of the first items of business was securing exclusive use of the Black Panther name.

Joint activities between the Black Panther Party for Self Defense and the Black Panther Party of Northern California had not worked out, some of it due to antagonisms between Eldridge Cleaver and black radicals who had been active in community affairs long before Cleaver came to the Bay Area. Even if the antagonisms did not exist, however, it was becoming impossible for two organizations, both identifying themselves as Black Panthers, to function in the same community without causing a great deal of confusion. The task was accomplished, after argument, more friction, and reportedly the firing of a gun by one of the more trigger-happy Panthers.

No damage was done, except to injured feelings and the floor of a San Francisco apartment.

The outcome has probably been beneficial from the Panther point of view. They succeeded in getting exclusive use of the name, but they also alienated a number of blacks whose revolutionary orientation is similar, if not identical, to that of the Panthers. Many of these brothers have remained outside of the Party, and form what might be thought of as a loyal opposition. Because the community is relatively small, criticisms of Panther Party structure, activities and programs get back to Panthers in short order. Some of these criticisms are acted upon, and generally have helped to make the Panthers more responsive to community control than they might have been had they succeeded in corralling all black radicals in the area.

The Panthers then set out to strengthen themselves both politically and programatically.

Merritt College, where Bobby and Huey had been students, had already taken positive steps in response to the surge of revolutionary nationalism coming from many of its black students. Black Studies courses were introduced. The college took official notice of the economic problems of its predominately black student body and organized the bookstore and cafeteria so that prices would be lowered, and so that a portion of the profits would be used to benefit students.

Changes were not without conflict, but by June, 1968, the black revolutionary orientation was sufficiently strong at Merritt to prompt the election of a Panther, Fred Smith, to the student-body presidency. Smith resigned several months later. Included in his resignation statement was the observation that college officials were particularly uptight at the thought of a Panther as president and did not afford his administration the cooperation normally expected.

Merritt is a two-year college. Across the Bay is San Francisco State College, a four-year institution where Panthers made more of a mark. One Panther, Minister of Education George Murray, caused a furor without even trying.

Murray was a graduate student in English, whose background included an affinity for the ministry. In fact, he had been a lay preacher prior to joining the Black Panther Party. Murray was one of several students who helped form the Black Students Union.

It took little time for BSU to absorb the Negro Students Association, a rather mild-mannered organization with little real influence on campus. BSU then began to make demands in the name of black students, and succeeded in bringing about basic changes in campus practices. They persuaded the college to establish a Department of Black Studies, and initiated a special admissions program that partially compensated for the relatively small percentage of minority students attending the college by allowing a limited number of students to enroll at San Francisco State who showed academic potential, but did not meet the normal entrance requirements.

Their thrust toward equalizing education through special admissions was sufficiently powerful to cause admission practices throughout the state college system to be modified. BSU also influenced the student government to stop the practice of subsidizing athletic events, and instead to spend money on developing community-based programs. San Francisco State then became involved in a variety of tutorial and college commitment programs, supported by student government funds.

Murray was one of a small group of students who had been identified as the attackers of several members of the staff of the *Golden Gater*, the campus daily. Reportedly, the attack was occasioned by annoyance over a consistently racially biased approach of the paper, which became intolerable when it published uncomplimentary remarks about Muhammad Ali, and specifically, negative comments regarding his change of name from Cassius Clay. The incident occurred in November, 1967, and Murray was sentenced to a six-months' suspended sentence and a year's probation. At the time of the sentencing, in March, 1968, he was working for the college as a part-time instructor of English. He was rehired to teach in the English program set up for the special-admission students who would be entering in the fall.

In August, 1968, Murray, in company with Landon Williams, a psychology student at San Francisco State, and David Hilliard, the National Chief of Staff of the Black Panther Party, were summarily deported from Mexico City, an act which prevented them from going to Havana to attend a conference. In a press conference discussing the incident, Murray spoke of his admiration for the Castro regime, his admiration of Mao Tse-tung, and his conviction that he had been kidnapped by the CIA in Mexico City and sent to New York, where he had to find plane fare to get back to Oakland. Murray subsequently succeeded in traveling to Cuba, this time via Prague, apparently with Captain Joudan Ford, the head Panther of the New York chapter.

In September, 1968, the *San Francisco Examiner* "exposed" Murray as a revolutionary, and reported that he had been appointed as an instructor at San Francisco State College. They did not include the fact that Murray had satisfied the appropriate hiring committees of his professional competence, and that his views were well known to his colleagues on campus. Murray the Panther, therefore, was an issue before the semester began.

The *Examiner* article was followed by a press conference held by Nick Verreos, then a candidate for the State Assembly. He pledged to see that the educational system would not be perverted toward narrow revolutionary ends. He characterized Murray as a propagandist for Communist causes. Verreos was not elected, but Murray did begin to teach. This was not to the liking of the State College trustees, who immediately passed a resolution asking that Murray be dismissed. College President Robert Smith declined to act on this request, pointing out that "George Murray was hired according to established procedures and we have neither professional nor legal grounds to change his status." Next, Chancellor Dumke ordered Smith to fire Murray, and Murray was suspended effective November 1. November 6 was the beginning of the BSU strike, and George Murray was the subject of one of their demands.

The demands, however, had been drawn up before the Murray suspension, and actually reflected the knowledge that Murray had a very tenuous hold on his position. In reality, the BSU demands concerning Murray were based on the principles contained in their own ten-point platform and program, a version of the Panther program adapted for student use.*

Murray was arrested January 6, 1969, following a complaint signed by Dr. Hayakawa for unauthorized use of a bullhorn. Murray was the only one of scores of speakers who used the banned bullhorn to be arrested for that reason. On January 24 Murray was again arrested, this time because a highway patrolman, who found it necessary to search Murray's car after stopping him for a traffic violation, discovered two pistols in the automobile. Murray insisted that the guns had been planted. Bobby Seale testified in his behalf, saying that Murray, as a member of the Panthers, had been specifically ordered not to have firearms in his possession.

The result was a series of jail sentences for Murray. His probation was revoked, and the resulting jail term was longer than he would have served following his first conviction. In July, 1969, while still in jail, Murray announced that he had experienced a new call to the ministry and that he was resigning from the Panthers. At this writing he is teaching English in an all-black school that was established as an alternative to public education.

The Murray case illustrates the obvious lack of grace with which Panthers are handled by officials. In doing so, it exposes severe contradictions in the social fabric. Murray has never denied being a Panther, and in fact was proud of his position. No charges were ever made that Murray used his

* See Appendix C—BSU 10 Point Program.

position as an instructor to politicize or propagandize his students. The charges against him related to two speeches, one made at San Francisco State, another at Fresno State College, and both made out of the classroom and in his capacity as the Black Panther Minister of Education.

Murray did not say anything in his speeches at the colleges which he would not have said when speaking in the ghetto. And an attempt to have him indicted for inciting to riot fizzled, because investigators, armed with witnesses and transcripts of his speeches, claimed that he had not engaged in speech that was criminal.

The conclusion is that Murray was fired for bringing his Black Panther message to white students. Also, the implication is that black students who are being integrated on white campuses cannot hear, on campus, what is constitutionally protected in the ghetto. In other words, colleges, at least the California State Colleges, may very well be doing what the Panthers claim—concentrating on the care, feeding and training of house niggers.

Another program initiated by the Panthers is Breakfast for Children, an activity which created controversy before it was three months old. Breakfast for Children was an enterprise which seemed to contradict the criticism that Panthers contented themselves with playing black revolution while staying aloof from the everyday problems of black people. Panthers, on the other hand, were insisting that they only sought to meet the needs of black people. "We are the people's ox. All we ask is that they ride us." In Breakfast for Children, Panthers found a popular ox ride, but they also found people were trying to hamstring the ox.

The program began in mid-December, 1968, at St. Augustine's Church.

What began as a pilot project involving a few dozen kids soon grew to accommodate over 200 children from eight to twelve years old, every school morning. Projects sprung up in San Francisco, Berkeley, Sacramento, Vallejo, Richmond, Marin City, Los Angeles and, in fact, in each of the over forty-five cities where there is a Panther chapter. There are no restrictions, even of race. Any child who appears in time for breakfast gets fed.

The program has run into some resistance. Within communities with a Panther chapter, questions have been raised about possible attempts to indoctrinate the children.

Panthers have attempted in every way they know to get their message across to anyone that is receptive. Considering their conviction that black people are in danger of being placed in concentration camps, or subject to genocide, they would be betraying their own beliefs by not pushing a little political orientation along with the grits, bacon, eggs, sausage, toast and hot chocolate they dispense in the morning. The message isn't particularly heavy, simply that the Panthers are doing their revolutionary duty in feeding them, and that Panthers can always be counted upon in emergencies and in time of trouble.

In truth, a large part of the propaganda job has been accomplished just by setting up the program. Parents of children who are fed better at Breakfast for Children than at home of necessity feel somewhat kindly disposed toward the people who provide food, no strings attached. In addition, the Breakfast for Children program attracts volunteers who would otherwise not be in contact with the Black Panther Party. A certain amount of loyalty to the Panthers, along with an occasional member, can confidently be predicted as a result of Breakfast for Children.

Two other sets of charges have arisen in connection with the breakfast program. The first is that the Panthers, in soliciting donations from merchants, have been zealous to the point of extortion. Panther Captain Robert Bay, who was in charge of the first program established in Oakland, was arrested when he attempted to solicit the aid of businessmen. He was charged with five counts of robbery and attempted assault. After Bay spent a month in jail, pending trial, the charges were dropped.

In another instance, the manager of a Safeway store near St. Augustine's refused to contribute. Panthers proceeded to mount a picket line seeking a boycott of the store. Business fell off, and the management of the store insisted that the Panthers were attempting extortion. After a time the store began to contribute.

Another charge arose in connection with the distribution of a Black Panther coloring book. The book was reportedly discovered through the program conducted at Sacred Heart Church in San Francisco. It depicted policemen as pigs, and was filled with pictures to color showing black children stabbing, shooting and otherwise assaulting policemen. National prominence was given the booklet when San Francisco Police Inspector Ben Lashkoff testified before the Senate Permanent Investigations Subcommittee, whose chairman is John L. McClellan (Dem. Ark.).

Both Bobby Seale and David Hilliard denied that the book was an official publication of the Party. Seale explained that the book was "first published in 1968 by a young Party member from the Sacramento chapter. He was not politically mature and was not aware of the class position of the Panthers." Seale said that the Panthers stopped production of the book after twenty-five copies were printed. He further identified a James Teemer as author of the book, and said that while he was still a member of the Panthers, he was not allowed to do propaganda work. Seale went on to say that Larry Clayton Powell, who had testified before the Subcommittee charging Panthers with a variety of crimes including conspiracy to commit armed robbery, had reproduced a thousand unauthorized copies of the booklet.

A copy of the coloring book reached Vice-President Spiro T. Agnew, who sent it to Chairman McClellan, recommending that a law should be passed banning the distribution of "inflammatory propaganda" by revolutionary groups in the United States.

Despite the complaints about the program, Panthers continue to feed more and more children every school day. In doing so, they reveal a deep and basic flaw in the social structure. However much people complain about the damage to children that might come out of Breakfast for Children, none of the complainants are willing to mount a breakfast program of similar dimensions, meaning that for the moment when hungry kids get fed hot breakfasts in our cities it will be the Panthers who feed them.

The Panthers have struck out in a number of political directions. In June, 1967, Huey Newton issued Executive Mandate Number 2, which drafted Stokely Carmichael into the Black Panther Party for Self Defense, invested him with the rank of Field Marshall, and delegated the responsibility to

> establish revolutionary law, order and justice in the territory lying between the Continental Divide East to the Atlantic Ocean; North of the Mason-Dixon Line to the Canadian border; South of the Mason-Dixon Line to the Gulf of Mexico.

The Panthers had divided the territory, retained the western third for themselves, and assigned blackdom's heaviest brother, Stokely Carmichael, to take revolutionary care of the rest.

Actually, the move to draft Stokely was the first act in a drama that was to involve all of SNCC in the affairs of the Panthers.

The Panthers were angling for some sort of relations with SNCC, which was greatly respected on the West Coast. SNCC's newsletter, written by H. Rap Brown, began to be a regular feature of the *Black Panther*, and the paper's coverage broadened to include news of the movement in the south.

As an organization, SNCC was on the decline. Its articulation of black power, coupled with the associated rejection of whites in the central council of the organization, made it unpopular with donors who give money to liberal causes. In addition, numerous arrests of SNCC leaders caused a drain on an already overextended budget, and made it difficult to sustain a program. But the name SNCC was still magic, particularly because of the heavy names attached to it. H. Rap Brown, Cleveland Sellers, James Forman and, of course, Stokely, were household names to everyone interested in black-liberation politics. Panthers recognized that, at the very least, an association with SNCC would add glamour and credibility to the West Coast group.

October 28, 1967, Huey Newton received a telegram in his room at Highland Hospital, an Alameda County Hospital with accommodations for prisoners in need of medical attention.

> VIOLENT COP ATTACK AGAINST YOU IS PART OF WHITE AMERICAN PLAN TO DESTROY ALL REVOLUTIONARY BLACK MEN BROTHERS AND SISTERS IN SNCC SUPPORT YOU ALL THE WAY WE PRAISE AND WELCOME YOUR FINE EXAMPLE OF ARMED SELF DEFENSE YOUR ACTION IS INSPIRATION FOR BLACK MEN EVERYWHERE SNCC STANDS UNITED WITH YOU AND READY TO HELP IN ANY WAY POSSIBLE YOURS IN LIBERATION
>
> BROTHERS AND SISTERS IN SNCC

With one policeman dead, another wounded, and Huey in a hospital suffering from multiple gun wounds, it was an appropriate time for black organizations, particularly those which lay claim to revolutionary fervor, to support the Panthers. At the same time, however, the Black Panther Party was making moves to align with white radicals, a goal that seemed somewhat inconsistent with the aims of black power, and the clearly expressed sentiments of Eldridge Cleaver, Minister of Information.

In July, 1967, Cleaver attacked white "mother country radicals," particularly the Communist Party and Socialist

Workers Party. He pointed out that the Communist Party supports Russia against the People's Republic of China, and was, therefore, a traitor to the best interests of non-white peoples throughout the world. He could have gone further. The Communist Party USA, at a convention held that July, found in its own wisdom that the white working classes were not ready for revolutionary activity. Communists then advised black revolutionaries that they should wait until the time was right, and then the Party, along with the masses of people, will support blacks in their fight for liberation.

"From now on," said Cleaver, "the Socialist Workers Party and the Communist Party should not be allowed to function in the black community at all. . . . The literature on Malcolm X which the bloodsucking Socialist Workers Party has grown fat on should not be allowed in the black community. Their newspapers and so forth should be banned from black communities. The black flunkies who are members of these groups should also be barred from the black community.*

This seemed to be a sound decision. Although communist theoreticians have been able to deal with racism as a phenomenon which had implications over and beyond that of class, they have been incapable of acting upon these implications. An attempt was made in the 40's, culminating in a special issue of *Masses and Mainstream* dealing specifically with America's color question. The Party then came to the conclusion that Negroes, because of the special conditions under which their lives were lived, should be considered a nation, and that the Negro struggle must be interpreted as a move toward national liberation. This would imply that the Communist Party was ready to meet with blacks on their own terms, and to support the independent black political decisions coming from the community.

Instead, the Party decided to integrate. That is, it would

---

* *Black Paper,* presented by Eldridge Cleaver to the Peace and Freedom Party Founding Convention, March 16, 1968.

purge itself of "white chauvinism" by giving Negroes an equal share in the governance of the Party. In practice, this led to a cumbersome system of co-chairmanships in which the most doctrinaire and loyal Negro communists would co-chair a unit along with an even more doctrinaire, and generally more experienced white communist. In a number of cases the chosen Negro was felt to be incompetent, or at least not ready for the position. But the Party prevailed. Those whites who complained about a particular Negro choice were obviously chauvinists, and blacks who were unhappy about either choice were labeled black bourgeois revisionists. In all instances, as chronicled by Harold Cruse in *The Crisis of the Negro Intellectual*, the Communist Party would not countenance the development of an independent black communist position based on the experiences of its black membership.

The Socialist Workers Party made its own contribution to impeding the development of an independent black radical politics, primarily by being enemies of the Communist Party. In a very real sense, American blacks have been victimized within white radical circles because of a basic argument between communists. The SWP has never forgiven the CP for countenancing the murder of Trotsky, a non-racially-oriented event that split the Party into two conflicting factions. The split was further aggravated during World War II, when some Trotskyites went to jail rather than fight on the side of a country that had made a treaty with Hitler, while Stalinists raised no protest in their behalf.

After the war ended, part of America's political adjustment included the purging of all communists, and suspected communists, from positions of power or authority. Negroes, though second-class citizens within the Communist Party orbit, had managed to achieve some real gains because of the reduced racism within the Party. Very real strength existed in unions such as the Mine, Mill and Smelter Workers, United Electricians, the Marine Cooks and Stewards, and the National Maritime Union. Without question, the relative position of

Negroes vis-à-vis organized labor would have been considerably stronger today had those unions been allowed to continue
functioning. They were not. And the SWP, apparently operating on the premise "that the enemy of my enemy is my
friend," took an active role in denouncing known communist
labor leaders. Few Negroes were directly involved in the
purge, but many were affected.

In sum, the Panther position seemed unassailable and emi-
nently correct. They had contemporary grievances: "Those
black revolutionaries who understand the value of a coalition
between white radicals and black revolutionaries have had the
ground cut out from beneath their feet by the nefarious activities of these white radicals. . . . They are nothing but hitch-
hikers on the black revolution. . . . The Socialist Workers Party
went so far as to try to kill off the Black Panther Newspaper
by refusing to allow the paper to be sent out of its various
branches around the country. The Communist Party is nothing but a white NAACP." *

The Panthers then proceeded to set up alliances with other
white radicals, setting up what might be described as a mutual
hitchhiking relationship.

Huey's arrest created an immediate need for money and
publicity, not to mention skills necessary to raise funds and
get the Panther message across. The black community didn't
have any and the liberals wouldn't get up off of any, leaving
only the white radicals. Also, there was the question of nationwide contacts. Although the Panthers were beginning to
branch out into other cities, individual chapters were primarily
involved with solving the problems of organization and could
not immediately be counted upon to divert local funds and
talent to a long-range effort.

At that point, the Peace and Freedom movement, a loose
coalition of white radicals representing every spectrum of left-
ist thought, appeared on the scene. Peace and Freedom de-

* Ibid.

clared themselves in favor of immediate U.S. withdrawal from Vietnam, against racism, and for a political alternative to the Democratic and Republican parties.

The Panthers had been through the white radical hassles in the financial confusion surrounding the original forming of the Black Panther Defense Committee. They discovered that the most vocal anticapitalist tended to believe that giving or raising money placed him in a policy-making position. Peace and Freedom, then, became a hope, insofar as it was a new organization, without a concrete platform, containing some white radical members trusted by the Panthers. It was also obviously headed toward third-party status, an event which in the future could provide the Panthers with the opportunity to present their program as part of a political campaign.

The first move toward cooperation with radical whites occurred in October, 1967, when the Stop the Draft Week committee immediately supported Huey Newton, without benefit of a talk from a Panther. By April, 1968 their slogans had grown to include "Free Huey" and "Cops out of the Ghetto." Known leaders of the group found themselves as subject to sudden arrest as Panthers. Panthers in turn supported the leaders who were indicted for conspiracy.

Panthers insist that in making coalitions with whites they have followed the rules as laid down by Stokely Carmichael—first, that the coalition be for a limited and clearly defined purpose; second, that the coalition last only so long as it is mutually beneficial; and third, that it be a union of equals, thus guaranteeing that one member of the coalition does not dominate the other.

These conditions were apparently met in the coalition with the Peace and Freedom Party. A founding convention was held in Richmond, March 16, 1968. Actually, the Panthers and Peace and Freedom had been working together since October, 1967, on matters directly related to Huey Newton's defense. But the formalization of a political party also required that the relationship between the Panthers and Peace and Freedom be clearly laid out.

"The Black Panther Party looks upon the black members of the Peace and Freedom Party as misguided political freaks who are trying to maintain their dual status in an incorrect manner; they have one foot in the mother country and the other foot in the colony, and their political manhood gets strangled on the borders separating the two nations." *

Cleaver proposed, and the convention accepted, a situation in which the Panthers would not be members of the Peace and Freedom Party. They would, however, use their "papier-mache right to vote to help strengthen the Peace and Freedom Party." Peace and Freedom would in turn accept as their candidates Huey P. Newton for Congress and Bobby Seale and Kathleen Cleaver for State Assembly, and also support a six-point program proposed by the Panthers. In addition to running the Panther candidates, the program required Peace and Freedom to support the calling of a national black plebiscite, and the backing of a Panther request for UN observers to come into the ghetto and oversee the actions of police.

Peace and Freedom was to join with the Black Panthers and participate in the Stop the Draft Week demonstrations in April, and also support the demand that police who patrol black neighborhoods live in them.

The Peace and Freedom Party also had to deal with Cleaver's "misguided political freaks," who had formed a black-brown caucus with other minority-group delegates. They demanded equal voting strength on all matters pertaining to minority citizens, along with a number of other racially oriented proposals.

The issue was resolved by creating a permanent organization of minority people which was independent of the Party for purposes of considering racial matters. The black-brown caucus did not seem to be so misguided as to oppose the Pan-

* Ibid.

ther proposals, and harmony of a sort reigned. Panthers did not get elected, but they did manage to get a lot of nation-wide rapping done between March and November.

By aligning with white radicals, even on a limited basis, the Panthers caused quite a few revolutionary blacks to dismiss the Party as being run by white people. Some did not go that far, but were very seriously questioning whether the Panthers could keep their organizational integrity while working closely with whites. They were particularly bothered by the Panther entrance into electoral politics. The coalition was viewed as a sign of weakness, and also as an indication that the Panthers were placing themselves in a position to betray revolutionary principles other than the one they had already forsaken, with-drawal from the political life of the mother country. Questions were also being raised within SNCC.

An alliance was announced February 17, 1968, at a massive birthday party held for Huey Newton at the Oakland Audi-torium, an easy rifle-shot distance from the Alameda County Courthouse where Huey was imprisoned on the tenth floor. Stokely Carmichael was the featured speaker, but there was an added surprise. H. Rap Brown, Stokely's successor as SNCC chairman, and James Forman, then heading up SNCC's New York office, also came and spoke.

The rally was enthusiastically attended and substantially en-riched the Panther coffers. Much of this money was drained away in bail bonds, however, as a week after the rally sixteen Panthers were arrested on a number of charges, all of which were subsequently dismissed.

Despite the apparent show of togetherness at the rally, there were differences in style and emphasis between the Panthers and the brothers from SNCC which seemed to relate to the question of coalition with white radicals.

Stokely, Rap and Forman laid down a line that seemed harder and heavier than most of the Panthers' statements.

Rap Brown: "I've got a program that can employ every

black person in this country overnight. Nobody in Vietnam is unemployed."

Carmichael: "We are talking about survival. We need a generation of warriors who are going to restore our dignity. If they execute Huey, the final execution rests in our hands. We must discuss revolutionary tactics—how to do the maximum damage to them and the minimum to us."

Forman (setting out the retribution he expected if he were killed): ". . . ten war factories, fifteen power plants, thirty police stations, one southern governor, two mayors and fifty cops. For Stokely Carmichael or Rap Brown the price will be tripled. For Huey Newton, the sky is the limit."

The brothers from SNCC talked black revolution and third-world retribution. They put down honkies in passing, not with specific attacks, but with a disdain sufficiently universal to include the whites in the audience. At one point, Stokely seemed to question the Panther Peace and Freedom alliance:

"So when you talk about alliances you recognize you form alliances with people who are trying to rebuild their culture, trying to rebuild their history, trying to rebuild their dignity, people who are fighting for their humanity. Poor white people are not fighting for their humanity, they're fighting for more money. There are a lot of poor white people in this country, you ain't seen none of them rebel yet, have you? Why is it that black people are rebelling? Do you think it's because it's just poor jobs? Don't believe that junk the honky is running down. It's not poor jobs—it's a question of a people finding their culture, their nature and fighting for their humanity."

Panthers were articulate, as usual, but they did not seem to come up with a revolutionary fervor comparable to that enunciated by the SNCC delegation. Undoubtedly, some of the difference could be explained in terms of experience. Forman, Brown and Carmichael had been speaking to audiences about black liberation a lot longer than any of the Panthers. But subject matter had something to do with it. The announcement by Eldridge of the candidates the Panthers were putting up for office could not compare with Forman's demand for the lives of southern elected officials.

Bobby Seale denying he's a racist (". . . That's the Ku Klux Klan's game. I hate oppression and the system. We are organizing to stop racism") could not, in his defensive posture, compete with Stokely: "We do not care about honkies; but if in building that concept of peoplehood, the honkies get in our way, they got to go. . . . We are not concerned with their way of life, we are concerned with our people."

Nothing more was heard of the alliance with SNCC for several months. The Panthers were too busy to make announcements, however. Even Huey Newton became eclipsed when, on April 4, Martin Luther King was assassinated, and two days later, eight Panthers including Eldridge Cleaver were arrested after a shooting incident with Oakland police that wounded Cleaver and another Panther, Warren Wells, and killed Bobby Hutton. Support for the Panthers automatically increased within the ghetto, just on the basis of the damage that had been done to the house where Hutton and Cleaver had been hiding.

The modest four-room bungalow was perforated. Some of the holes were almost an inch in diameter. There was evidence that some of the bullets had gone completely through the house, and the fire which had started in the basement harboring Cleaver and Hutton had been so intense that the exterior wall of a house more than six feet away was badly fire-scarred.

White support of the Panthers increased also. The Medical Committee for Human Rights, a group of Bay Area physicians and health workers, announced a broad program of support for the Panthers. In addition to pledging emergency medical help when needed, the doctors offered to provide attorneys and help with legal services, patrol the ghetto to discourage police "from singling out Panthers and other blacks," and to create a speakers' bureau to take the Panther story to whites. Dr. Philip Shapiro, a psychiatrist and chairman of the group, announced the speakers' bureau by saying, "Frankly, I am white and a professional man. Perhaps the white community will listen to me."

Seventy-five University of California law students sent a letter of condemnation to Oakland Police Chief Charles Gain, accusing the Oakland Police Department of "a deliberate program of oppression and brutality in the black community of Oakland." Even prospective white preachers got into the act when forty-seven divinity students, most from the Church Divinity School of the Pacific, wrote a letter in support of the Panthers.

Harry Edwards, organizer of the black boycott of the 1968 Olympics, announced that he had decided to become a member of the Black Panther Party. He announced his affiliation at a press conference in which he urged all Negroes who had achieved social standing to join, and thus serve notice on the society that "You can no longer ignore the Black Panthers." Seventeen white Bay Area college professors also attacked the "systematical harassment" of Panthers, and urged the U.S. Civil Rights Commission to investigate the Oakland Police Department.

Panthers were not exactly ignored. Over fifteen hundred people attended Bobby Hutton's funeral, and about five thousand were present at a memorial service held in a park across the street from the County Courthouse. Also in attendance was an immense contingent of policemen—most of them stuffed on every floor of the courthouse building. Four Panthers were arrested at gunpoint following the memorial service, and charged with the holdup of a shoe store. They were released on bail and charges were subsequently dropped.

Bobby Seale, the only ranking Panther on the streets at that time, made a return trip to Sacramento on May 2, the anniversary of the original gun-in, a few hours before he was found guilty of violating an 1867 law banning guns in or about a jail.

Finally, in July, SNCC announced an informal working alliance with the Panthers. James Forman said that he had accepted the post of Minister of Foreign Affairs, H. Rap Brown was Minister of Justice, and Stokely Carmichael was Prime Minister. SNCC was careful to point out that there was no organizational merger involved, an emphasis which seemed calculated to establish a warm working relationship at arm's length. Reportedly the SNCC staff was wary of the Panthers. They did not accept the Panther ten-point program, and also rejected the idea of conducting a black people's plebiscite. The plebiscite was a program thought up by Eldridge Cleaver, and SNCC might have rejected it on that basis. Cleaver had not exactly endeared himself to SNCC when he described them as being primarily composed of "blippies," black hippies.

The alliance went swiftly downhill. After weeks of rumors, SNCC announced in August that Carmichael had been expelled from the organization. Also included in the statement was a rejection of any association with the Panthers, although SNCC reaffirmed its position that Huey Newton should be freed. SNCC had already notified the Panthers that their alliance had been terminated, reportedly on grounds that the alliance had been made by individuals within SNCC, rather than the organization as a whole. The SNCC press release also made reference to a power struggle, involving Carmichael, which almost resulted "in physical harm to SNCC personnel."

Rumor has it that the power struggle was actually a violent argument in which Panthers went for, or threatened to go for, their guns. Cleaver was quoted as commenting on the incident with "The feeling at that time was that a few of them should have paid for their treachery with their lives." Cleaver, however, is known for his uncompromising and sometimes extreme language, and the quote is too oblique to be considered a confirmation of the rumor.

Rap Brown and James Forman also resigned from the Panthers, leaving Stokely Carmichael as the only reminder of the SNCC-Panther agreements. He came to the Bay area in August, 1968, and was present at the beginning sessions of Huey Newton's trial. He helped the Panthers organize, and made numerous appearances at all-black meetings in the area. Carmichael was also a driving force behind the formation of the Black United Front, an umbrella organization embracing all black people, whose function it would be to concentrate on the question of the future survival of the black community as a physical entity.

Carmichael's position in fostering such an organization had been articulated on numerous occasions. He insisted that revolutionaries had to develop an "undying love" for black people. "Every Negro is a potential black man," he felt, and it was necessary to organize them and bring them home. "The bourgeoisie is very, very minute inside our community. We have to bring them home. . . . We have to bring them home because they have technical skills which must be put to the benefit of their people. . . . One of the ways of bringing our people home is by using patience, love, brotherhood and unity—not force. . . . We try and we try and we try. If they become a threat, we off them. . . ."

The Panthers had never preached undying love, and though they applauded Stokely when he announced his position, they were moving in another direction. Members of the black bourgeoisie were usually described as bootlickers, toms, lackeys, house niggers and other terms which did not imply a patient attitude. Most negative comments made by blacks about the Panthers are particularly condemnatory about what appears to be an insufferable intolerance toward Negroes who are not moving in Panther-approved fashion. There have been accusations that the Panthers have physically attacked Negroes with whom they disagree; but thus far the allegations have not been proven.

One problem is that few people can actually identify Panthers, outside of the most prominent leaders and a comparatively small group of young men who are very visible at Panther functions. There are a fair number of youths who affect the Panther uniform, and who may in fact be Panthers in training. Theirs is a nebulous status, and the Party takes no responsibility for acts committed by them when they are outside of the Party's control.

Whole chapters have been purged, some of them because they were allegedly organized by police agents.

Relations between Carmichael and the Panthers became increasingly acrimonious. Stokely seems to feel that the Party is too rigid in its posture, tends toward totalitarian rule and is deficient in the development of a politics which would include the concept of Pan-Africanism. He seriously questioned the ability of the Panthers to control their alliances with whites, and implied that the organization might not be controlled by blacks.

On the other hand, Panthers accused Carmichael of being the worst kind of cultural nationalist, a racist, a seeker of individual glory and an inept rhetorician. They also point out that Bobby Seale is facing a murder charge in Connecticut as a result of testimony provided by a friend of Carmichael's.

Apparently Carmichael personally intervened on behalf of George Sams, who had been expelled from the New Haven Panther Chapter, and effected his reinstatement. Sams ended up confessing to the murder of Alex Rackley, who police claim was murdered because he was thought to be a police informant. Sams said that he killed Rackley following orders from Bobby Seale. After Sams's confession, Carmichael lost whatever dwindling credibility he might have had with the Panthers.

Carmichael could not resolve his differences with the Panthers, even after having long discussions with Eldridge Cleaver in Algeria in July, 1969, at the Pan-African Cultural Festival. During the conference he removed himself from the Panthers ideologically, by rejecting Marxist-Leninism.

"I believe that people who talk about 'Marxist-Leninism' so hard, in such a hard line, are the people who are groping for an answer. They seize on 'Marxist-Leninism' as if it were some sort of a religion. Marx becomes, in essence, Jesus Christ. Now anything you cannot answer you take over and bow to Marx. That, in my view, is absolutely absurd." *

Panthers leveled charges about Carmichael's activities that were more serious than that of being ideologically irreverent. They began to feel that he was more cooperative with the federal government than he let on. Stokely, accompanied by his wife, Miriam Makeba, returned to the United States in March, 1970, after fourteen months in Africa. He was immediately subpoenaed by the Senate Subcommittee on Internal Security and appeared before an unannounced meeting of the subcommittee (notices did not even appear in the *Congressional Record*, which routinely lists all committee and subcommittee meetings). The only member present was Senator Strom Thurmond, who refused to answer reporters' questions about Carmichael's testimony. Stokely, himself, said that he invoked the Fifth Amendment.

On August 26, 1970, Huey P. Newton held a press conference to repudiate the allegation that the Panthers had "a delegation of Panther members led by Stokely Carmichael, in Jordan . . . We further charge that Stokely Carmichael is operating as an agent of the CIA."

If that were not enough, Newton proceeded to further widen the ideological chasm that existed between the Party and Carmichael.

"As you very well know the Black Panther Party does not subscribe to 'Black Power' as such. Not the 'Black Power' that has been defined by Stokely Carmichael and Nixon. They seem to agree upon the stipulated definition of 'Black Power,' which is no more than Black capitalism, which is reactionary and certainly not a philosophy that would meet the interest of the people."

If SNCC and Carmichael have had hassles over the Panthers, so have the Peace and Freedom Party, the Committee for New Politics, and SDS. In fact SDS, once strongly sup-

* *The Black Scholar*, November, 1969, p. 38.

portive of the Panthers, split into pro- and anti-Panther factions at their convention in 1969, the meeting which marked the birth of the Weathermen.

There are a great number of reasons why some white supporters of the Panthers have become critical of their actions. A number of white organizations are unwilling to accept the Panther demand that their program be supported in its entirety, and that white allies refrain from taking any position on black people which in any way deviates from that of the Panthers.

Another problem inhibiting uncritical support of the Panthers by white radicals is the Party's alleged anti-Semitism, charges based primarily in the Panthers' total opposition to the war policies of Israel.

Some of those who recognize the Panther's anti-Zionist stance as a natural and expected extension of their anticolonial politics have trouble handling the militant anti-American attitudes of the Panthers. It is one thing to be in virulent opposition to the war in Southeast Asia and another to cheer loudly at the notion of an American military defeat.

Huey Newton, upon his release on appeal of his manslaughter conviction, announced that "In the spirit of solidarity with the people of the world and the Third World or the developing world in particular, the Black Panther Party would like to extend the friendship and spirit of revolutionary solidarity. We will give a declaration to the Paris peace talks where we will commit an undisclosed number of troops to the National Liberation Front in order to show solidarity— in order to help the Vietnamese people fight the cowardly American aggressors."

There are those who call themselves revolutionary who cannot accommodate the thought of fighting on the other side in any conflict involving America.

There is some criticism expressed by women liberationists at what they perceive to be male chauvinism among Panthers. They see female Panthers playing traditional female roles within the ranks of the revolution. The typing, cooking, phone-answering, and message-relaying is done almost exclusively by women. Those women attached to the Panthers stay out of the women's liberation movement, perform tasks assigned to them, and are more into liberated revolution than the bulk of Women's Liberation supporters.

Without question, the women in the Panthers have kept the Party together through much of its existence. Panther males go in and out of prison at fantastic rates. As a result, a level of female leadership has emerged that guarantees a perpetuation of the revolutionary ardor of the Panthers.

There are substantial differences in the liberation being sought by black women. Predominantly white middle-class ladies are complaining about being assigned housemaking roles, while many black women are seeking liberation from the necessity of being breadwinners, rather than homemakers. In terms of revolutionary activity, the Panthers have developed a phenomenally dedicated and capable group of sister revolutionists.

The Panthers maintain that the vanguard, being way out front in the liberation movement, develops a perspective which will ultimately be proved correct.

Polarization of the society is welcomed by the Panthers. They seek alliances, but only on their terms. What they actually are looking for is the commitment of the black community. Eldridge Cleaver put it right on the line: ". . . if we have to use the only power that we have, the only power that can never be taken from anybody when everything else is taken, and that's the power to destroy, the power to disrupt, the power to throw a nigger in the machine."

Panthers are doing just that, and in the process they are commiting blacks to some aspect of their program. The cost in leadership is frightening:

Bobby Hutton, 17, first Panther recruit and once Treasurer of the Party, killed April 6, 1968. Police called it justifiable homicide.

Fred Hampton, 21, NAACP activist in Maywood, Illinois. Joined the Panthers in 1968 and died in his bed, a victim of a one-sided shootout called justifiable homicide.

Mark Clark, 22, killed along with Fred Hampton. Justifiable homicide.

Alprentice Carter, "Bunchy." "Bunchy like a lot of greens," he described himself. Bunchy, poet, Muslim, ex-convict who served time with Eldridge and left jail to become Eldridge's lieutenant. Bunchy, who Kathleen Cleaver says went around murder-mouthing: "You motherfucker, I'll kill you. I'll kill your dog, I'll kill your cat. I'll kill your goldfish, I'll kill your alligator. I'll kill your parakeet!" And then he'd smile just enough to let the knowledge that he was putting someone on seep through and relax tensed muscles.

Bunchy, who went back to L.A. at Eldridge's request, rounded up an uncontrollable group of young thugs and disciplined them through lavish use of that profane love available only to a poet or to a man totally dedicated to his people. He'd line his delinquents up in the Panther office, repeat the rules so that everyone would know, and then distribute sticks to his chosen lieutenants. "If anybody fucks up in here, beat him with those sticks."

His life a poem, light, air, humor, compassion, did not deserve death. It came at UCLA in January 1969, at the hands of two assassins from US, the Swahili-oriented, politically polygamous black national group that managed to keep their revolutionary rhetoric from interfering with their good connections with Sam Yorty, the Mayor of L.A.

This is a partial roll, a few of the events that mold the character and convictions of anyone who would assume leadership in the Panthers. In their search for the symbols of humanity, political freedom, predictable justice in the courts, a patch of beauty surrounding their persons, they have picked up the gun.

Huey Newton came out of jail August 5, 1970. Bobby Seale was then in Connecticut facing a charge of murder. He has been in jail since August, 1969. Eldridge Cleaver is living in Algeria, where he went after Havana, and from where he attends conferences in Moscow, Pyongyang, and other portions of the Communist-dominated world. Kathleen Cleaver bore a son, Antonio Maceo, named after a black Cuban revolutionary, while in exile in Algeria. She went to North Korea for the birth of her second child.

Several grand juries and congressional investigation committees are continuously inquiring into the Panthers. Police play the role of big white hunter searching for big game, causing the Panthers to dig more firmly into their lair, the black community.

The Panthers, despite the upheaval of their political existence, seem to be growing and gathering support. They are national in scope and international in concept. They maintain that the role of a vanguard party is to stay visible until the oppressor drives it underground. Right now they are still very much above ground, as are the conditions which helped to create them in the first place. The struggle is intensifying and it looks like both the cats and the jungle will be with us for some time.

IV

The Big Black Cats

ON SUNDAY, March 22, 1970, the springswept Bay Area atmosphere exuded a balmy sensuality that compelled great numbers of residents to go somewhere, just for the luxury of exposing their nerve endings to the sometimes miracle that is California weather. At Stanford, the day before, about one hundred people had attended an afternoon reception to welcome Jean Genêt and several Panthers and support their efforts to raise funds to defend Bobby Seale, who was about to face trial in Connecticut. About seven hundred people showed up the same evening, to listen to Genêt voice his concerns. Both gatherings ended abruptly when the Panthers and Genêt stalked out of the room.

"A bunch of white racists," was Hilliard's economical description of the people he left behind at Stanford, raising hackles among the white activists to whom he directed his observations. These whites, some of whom had worked in support of Panther-related activities such as the defense fund, or the Breakfast for Children program, felt, though they would not say, that Hilliard might be displaying what has to be known as black racism—racism in reverse. Hilliard was extended the benefit of the doubt. He was described as bellig-

107

erent, acting as if his shoulder supported a large chip, argumentative, totally unreasoning and, through his iracund behavior was blamed with causing white support to turn away from Panther concerns.

Many of these whites were active in the peace or antiwar movements, and shared negative views about Hilliard's performance on Moratorium Day:

> Hilliard: So then, we would like to ask the American people do they want peace in Vietnam. Well, do you?
> Audience: YES ! ! !
> Hilliard: Do you want peace in the Black communities?
> Audience: YES ! ! !
> Hilliard: Well you goddamned sure can't get it with no guitars, you sure can't get it demonstrating . . .

And at the end of his speech, immediately after the remark which earned him a Federal indictment:

> Hilliard: We ain't here for no goddamned peace, because we know that we can't have no peace because this country was built on war. And if you want peace you got to fight for it.
> Audience: NO, NO, NO, PEACE, NO ! ! !

Hilliard's "All power to the people" was drowned out in the chorus. Prominent over the heads of many of the crowd of over 30,000 was the waving of the two-fingered V that has been converted by present-day antimilitarists from a symbol seeking victory in war to a gesture indicating a desire for peace.

White members of the audience got the message. Hilliard was contemptuous of their movement. He demanded more of them than simple opposition to the war, and he did not believe that it was theirs to give.

That was the situation on Sunday afternoon, when Genêt, with Hilliard, D.C., Masai, and Emory—the four members of the Panther National Central Committee still in the country and on the street—angrily left a cocktail party given in their honor.

Behind them was confusion. Tom Hayden was speechless. Stew Alpert's girl friend was screaming, "I didn't see any black people on the street when Bobby Seale was sentenced." Mike McClure was intoning, "It's always the children who get hurt," while his wife was attending to the practical business of comforting her child.

The rest of the ninety or so guests milled about, exchanging information, collectively establishing what the fuss was all about, and cementing their private opinions about Hilliard, and through association, the rest of the Panthers. Many of them had been too busy pouring down the free cocktails and sandwiches to pay attention to what was going on in the living room.

Some of the cause of the confusion dates back to August, 1968, when Bobby Seale, substituting for Eldridge Cleaver, flew to Chicago, delivered two speeches to the predominantly white youth gathered there in response to the organizing efforts of leaders like Hayden, Hoffman, Rubin, and Dellinger. These speeches landed Bobby Seale in Judge Hoffman's court, charged with crossing state lines to organize a riot and conspiracy to do the same.

Hilliard—in fact the Panthers generally—were very unhappy about this indictment, as it was a direct result of the Panther association with white radicals. The indictment was confirmation for a number of black people of their belief that a black-white radical alliance could only bring trouble to the Panthers.

One example of this feeling was the Black Guards, an all-black security force headed by a Muslim, Sultan Nasser Ahmad Shabazz. Shabazz was once an active member of the San Francisco Mosque who decided to move on his own and get closer to black political activity than organized Muslims are allowed to go. For a time, Shabazz worked with the poverty program in San Francisco's Western Addition. He was separated from EOC when its white administrators became uptight about what they described as Shabazz's corruption. An accompanying charge that he was building a personal empire within the poverty-program organization.

Shabazz formed the Black Guards several months after leaving the poverty program. Members of the group wear a uniform which includes combat boots, tucked-in black trousers, a black shirt, and an ankh-decorated combat helmet, also black. They are often seen accompanied by formidable-looking German shepherd dogs, guarding a business, a home, or a place where a meeting involving blacks is taking place. Shabazz objected to the Red Book as insufficiently black and supplied his men with the Black Book, the sayings of Nkrumah.

In August 1969, Shabazz called a press conference just to condemn the Panthers in their alliances with white groups. "Eldridge Cleaver did a good job of selling the Black Panther Party to the Communists and Socialists. . . . The Black Panthers are becoming more red each day. . . . When the Black Panthers say 'power to the people,' they also mean power to whites. . . ."

From Shabazz's point of view, one shared by other blacks, the entire point of black revolution is to seize power from whites, not share it.

Shabazz referred to his personal history of being an eleven-year member of the Communist Party, "working for what I thought was the good of the black people. . . . I was being used." He referred to a past prison term of four years in Louisiana in which the communists did nothing to defend him. "Communists and Socialists have infiltrated every group," he said, "and after these groups have served their purposes, they're left to rot in jail, with no help from the Communist Party to get them out."

Shabazz was not involving himself in the narrow doctrinal distinctions which neatly separate white leftists into various brands of socialist or communist. His condemnation echoed a genuine fear that blacks, just by involving themselves with so-called white revolutionaries, would reap political disadvantage.

Shabazz's stance did not in itself shake Panther leadership. They were, however, by virtue of their alliance with left wing whites, subject to extreme criticism from a number of black groups. When Bobby Seale was indicted behind Yippie activity in Chicago there were a lot of black mouths sounding I-told-you-so's.

Soon after the Chicago Eight were indicted, a meeting was held at Charles Garry's home. Stew Alpert, a writer for the underground press, Kathleen Cleaver, Tom Hayden, Dave Hilliard, Bobby Seale and Garry were present. The meeting was somewhat tense, primarily because the Panthers recognized Bobby's indictment was a side product of the push to get white radicals. It didn't take too long for the decisions to be made concerning the upcoming trial. Bobby Seale refused to be represented by anyone but Garry.

Garry in turn insisted that he would not have Bobby involved in a common defense unless he was recognized as the chief defense counsel. There wasn't much argument. Phone calls between California, Chicago and New York verified the arrangement, and the defense questions were settled. Garry was dealing from a position of strength. He had Bobby Seale. He had also just won his case with the Oakland Seven, the group which stood trial for conspiracy following their organizing of the 1967 Stop the Draft Week, an exercise which exploded into violent confrontation between demonstrators and police.

The meeting was cordial enough but there was none of the camaraderie which was common to earlier white radical-Panther get-togethers. A year before, Kathleen Cleaver, George Murray and other Panthers, accompanied by a group of whites including Tom Hayden and Stew Alpert, took their guns to the Chabot Gun Club, a private shooting range in the Oakland hills catering to off-duty policemen and right-wing whites. Alpert describes them as, "freaked-in lunatics of the anal power trip . . . an assortment of Minute-Man arrogance, Bircher paranoid scared virgin housewives, and skinny sexless men in search of a hardon."

The usual customers at the range, plinking away at bull's-eyes located above an imaginary heart of Huey Newton, took off, deafened by the harsh sound of the heavy semi-automatic weaponery lugged up to the hills by the Panther-hippie-Yippie forces. An hour before the usual closing time the owners of the range decided to shut down.

A year later, the Chicago indictment had driven a wedge between the Panthers and their long-haired allies. There was no open breach, but rather a reticence on the part of the Panthers to assume automatically that they and the Yippies were headed in the same revolutionary direction.

Hilliard, before leaving the meeting at Garry's, had pointedly questioned Alpert's and Hayden's understanding of Marxist-Leninist principles. Hilliard, more than any of the other Panthers, gauged actual revolutionary fervor and commitment by what he perceived to be the degree that a so-called revolutionary reflected the tenets of Marxism-Leninism.

The strained relations that began to display themselves at the meeting at Garry's were very much apparent at the March 22 cocktail party. Kathleen and Bobby were obviously not there, but Garry was, as well as Stew Alpert, Tom Hayden and David Hilliard.

Alpert made his contribution to the annoyance of the Panthers right away. His role as a writer had been resented from the beginning, not so much for what Alpert wrote as for the position he assumed in writing. Alpert was an inside man for the white movement. He wrote of the Panthers in intimate terms. There was a *Berkeley Barb* article, for instance, that began, "I was the last reporter to interview Huey P. Newton before the Man put him under wraps at Vacaville. We spent three rewarding hours together . . ." —no mention was made of the fact that Garry and several other reporters were present at that interview. "Much of what Huey told me is too hot to reveal right now . . ."

Alpert walked into the cocktail party and headed for Don Cox, the Panther National Field Marshall known as D.C., who was seated at one end of a couch which held three of the four Panther leaders present, as well as two other blacks who were apparently sitting in. He notified D.C. of his intention to run for Sheriff of Alameda County in order to "effectively politicize the community." Alpert said that he was uniquely qualified to run because he had gained first-hand information about jail conditions while doing time at the suburban county jail.

"How much time did you do?" asked D.C., who was under indictment for a charge that could earn him five years in jail. (He was subsequently charged with murder, and dropped out of sight.)

"Sixty-five days," answered Alpert.

Considering the amount of jail time each of the Panthers on the couch (except Emory) had served or were facing, Alpert's time in the county lock-up seemed trivial.

At the other end of the couch sat David Hilliard, who seemed to be gazing past Tom Hayden, who had chosen to sit down an arm's length away from him. Reportedly, Hayden's ideas influenced the conduct of the Chicago trial. He had rejected the Rubin-Hoffman approach that would have turned the trial into a total display of guerrilla theater. Hayden had hope that the court would deal favorably with their case, a fantasy not shared by the other defendants.

Hayden's stance, his perception of what was necessary to defend the conspiracy charge, did not jibe at all with that of the Panthers. They saw Bobby Seale as fighting a lonely battle, involved in a trial almost without relevance to issues which concerned black revolutionaries. They were aware of the fact that the wives, girl friends, and relatives of the white defendants were present in court every day of the trial, while Artie Seale, Bobby's wife, and her relatives were ushered out of the court the day they first arrived. To add to Panther rancor, the white defendants were free on bail, to enjoy something that resembled normal social, familial and political relations, while Bobby was in jail, usually in isolation. The recognition that even those whites close to the black liberation movement could fail to understand the black imperative, and the recognition that whites, even those in revolt, are routinely treated with more consideration than blacks set the emotional climate.

Immediately after Genêt recognized Hayden and asked him to speak, Hilliard jumped up.

"Yeah, goddamnit, get up and explain just why you're out on the street and Bobby is in jail."

Hayden was jolted. "I don't know what that was all about," he began, apparently referring to the known fact that Bobby was then in jail because of a murder charge in Connecticut.

Hayden, in taking Hilliard's accusation literally, was avoiding the central issue. The question actually was why Hayden was not in jail. Bobby had been indicted, tried, placed in chains, and was subsequently sentenced to four years in jail for contempt of court as the result of a casual speechmaking excursion into a scene of hippie-involved political mayhem. Hilliard's words implied that if Hayden and his fellow defendants were really the revolutionaries they claimed to be, they would have closed ranks and stood on their conspiratorial constitutional rights when Bobby Seale was denied the right to represent himself, and if necessary force the court to chain them all. It didn't happen.

Hayden's remarks did still more to alienate the Panthers. He chose not to confront Hilliard's distress and only commented on Bobby's plight in general terms. Bobby, he said, proved that the courts were corrupt. "We must seek our judgment in the streets," he said, to what appeared to be expressions of approval from the crowd.

There is a kind of unreason in this racist society that prevents whites from actively dealing with directly expressed anger. The society insists that communication, in order to be meaningful, productive, or informative, must avoid all but the delicate nuances of emotion. Passion must be avoided when discussing serious subjects.

Somehow, the entire definition of violence to white America begins with the raising of a voice in what they consider to be an important discussion. Intense emotion might be sympathized with and the reason for the display understood, but an emotional outburst is considered only an indication that there are underlying discontents which require close attention whenever it is possible to return to calm, reasoned dialogue.

What whites fail to understand is that there is a level of communication, an exchange of real information that occurs in the very midst of an emotional tirade. Their automatic withdrawal from any attempt at emotional discourse tends to intensify the situation in precisely the way that a refusal to respond to reasonable questions might be upsetting to them. "You don't have to get excited," or "we can't reach any understanding if you insist on being emotional," is a denial of essential fact. Whites refuse to allow visible emotion any communicatory legitimacy.

Good manners first, communication next, seems to be their cultural bag. A black trapped in this inflexible approach to dialogue experiences the frustration of being treated like a child who is throwing a temper tantrum, or a somewhat addled dimwit who cannot perceive the necessity of speaking so that others can understand. This was Hilliard's position. His urgency was sidetracked by the lack of emotional resonance on the part of the white audience.

When Hayden finished speaking, Hilliard again started snapping angry questions at him. Stew Alpert, in an obvious attempt to conciliate the developing ugly situation, started to move toward them, all the while making soothing sounds.

"Fuck you, Alpert, you jive-ass revolutionary. We can do without you and your shitty writing."

Alpert stopped.

At that point another would-be conciliator stepped between Hilliard and Hayden. With the movement of whites toward the trouble center, the Panthers jumped up and moved closer to Hilliard. The four-man wall of black menace never got into action. The fellow who moved between Hilliard and Hayden was evidently unaware that a would-be peace-maker does not inject himself between people, particularly with his hands upraised. Rather, he comes behind the person he knows best (which in that case would have been Hayden), reaches around, and pulls him away from the spot, all the while expressing his disinterest in seeing a fight.

The act of inserting himself in the middle only served to provide Hilliard with two adversaries rather than one. In one rapid motion, Hilliard pushed the newcomer away, picked up a glass wine decanter and threw it at the back-pedaling intruder. The decanter found its mark and bounced harmlessly away, only to fall on the head of the thirteen-year-old girl who had been seated on the floor very close to the action.

The Panthers then swept out of the room, leaving behind them a mass of confusion, and the beginnings of a hard line toward Hilliard evident in the seemingly innocent question, "Isn't it a shame that Hilliard had to throw that bottle at an innocent girl?" He didn't throw it at her, but the damage was done. Hilliard's actions were perceived by many of the remaining guests as the kind of behavior expected of a madman.

The charismatic leader as revolutionary is almost a cliché. But all revolutionary leaders are not charismatic, and Hilliard is one of them. He is an effective leader, however, even though he does not possess the impelling ability to command loyalty as do Huey, Bobby, and Eldridge.

Panthers follow Hilliard because they know that there is business to take care of. Hilliard is not likable. He lacks Huey's magnificence of imagination, Bobby Seale's ability to shift rapidly between high comedy and basic political belief while describing society as he sees it, and Eldridge's total irreverence.

Hilliard comes at the world with more than the conviction of being right. It, they, you, whatever, is wrong, and that's all to it. He is military to the core, and there is no Panther in the entire square footage that is America that has been drilled by a harder-cadenced soul than David Hilliard. The word came out directly from Huey that Panthers had to relate to the black community, specifically that large portion of the ghetto which relates more to church than to profanity. Some church-going folk, particularly those who are righteously disgusted with the nature of their lives, can be reached only through language short on four-letter anglo-saxonisms. Hilliard responds, sort of. He is impelling, but gentle in language, when talking to a black, non-Panther audience. The rest of the time he is a terror.

Hilliard sharply condemned everyone vaguely connected with the blockage of his first attempt to get to Cuba in 1968. He scornfully described the group that arrested him, Landon Williams and George Murray in Mexico City, as "at least one Nicaraguan, two Mexicans, and some European CIA agents."

Most of Hilliard's tenure as a Panther has seen him acting in one capacity or the other, taking up the leadership slack caused by court actions or jail sentences imposed on other Panther leaders. Hilliard was the *de facto* head of the Panthers on a number of occasions, all the while being hassled by every level of police authority from the municipal to the international. In the face of all this, Hilliard's anger has been classic. He completely eschews the scholarly truculence that passes for anger exhibited occasionally by an older generation of blacks such as A. Phillip Randolph, Whitney Young, or Roy Wilkins. He puts it where it's at, and doesn't waste too many words doing it.

In April, 1969, Tommy Jones, an ex-Panther, claimed that Ron Black, his cousin, was murdered by the Panthers. Bobby Seale answered the charge with "The Party has no information about the shoot-out."

From Dave Hilliard came "Fuck their charges."

A month later, Larry Powell and his wife Jean reported to the McClellan Committee that the Panthers derived much of their income from crime. According to the Powells, Ronald

Black had been murdered by sixteen- and seventeen-year old boys on assignment from the Panthers. They further testified that Panthers literally raped fourteen-year-old girls, that they maintained a maximum-security room below their Berkeley headquarters where Party discipline, in the form of severe beatings, was handed out, and that fifty to a hundred thousand dollars a month came into Panther headquarters and was not accounted for by the Party leaders.

The Powells claimed that Stokely Carmichael, Donald Cox and William Hall went to Mobile in August 1968, to teach young blacks how to manufacture and use firebombs.

They said that their good standing with the Party lasted only as long as they planned and executed successful holdups, and turned one-third of the take into headquarters. But, they said, immediate expulsion from the Party followed their arrest for sticking up a nightclub even though they did so on orders from the Panthers. Powell said that he had risen to the rank of captain, ran the National headquarters office for a time, recruited his wife into the Party, and then was abandoned in jail after his arrest. The Party, they averred, did not spend any of its wealth on behalf of Panthers who were arrested as a result of Party assignments.

Hilliard was a particular target of this couple. According to the Powells, Bobby Seale began to deteriorate soon after Huey Newton was jailed. Bobby, they claimed, consistently looked at the world through scotch-affected nerve endings. All that Bobby could do, they claimed, was to talk, and even then his speeches were written by David Hilliard.

Seale and Hilliard responded immediately, each in his own peculiar style. Hilliard's response to Powell's testimony was, "He's a liar! The people know that, period!" Bobby explained that the Black Panther Party had purged itself of police agents, provocateurs and adventurers, in order to maintain the Party's revolutionary integrity. The Powells, they said, were both crooks and provocateurs, and they were purged along with the other undesirables.

The Powells' testimony is slightly suspect. They had been co-defendants along with Wendell Wade for a holdup in an East Oakland tavern. Wade had earlier been involved in the April 6 shootout. Wade received a sentence of five years to life in state prison for his part in the robbery. Larry Powell, charged with five counts of robbery and one count of assault with a deadly weapon, was sentenced to three years' probation, with just eight months in the county jail. To add to this brand of judicial leniency, Powell was not sent to jail, but was released on the basis of time served while awaiting trial. He had served only three months.

Powell's charge of Bobby Seale's alleged scotch-influenced dependency on David Hilliard seems libelous. As long as Bobby was out of jail he was the chief spokesman for the Black Panther Party. What he had to say, and the manner of his delivery, did not add up to a Hilliard-written speech. When he reached Judge Hoffman's court, Bobby was totally on his own. A reading of that transcript clearly indicates Bobby Seale in full command of his faculties, profoundly articulating his sense of being an aggrieved person before the bar of justice, while demonstrating his extraordinary ability to think on his feet. The description of the relationship between Hilliard and Seale that was given by the Powells is on its face somewhat other than entirely true.

Bobby was the workhorse of the party, and his capacity for achievement was diminished only by the assaults made on his freedom, his person and finally his right to life.

An amazing portrait of Bobby was presented on KQED, San Francisco's educational TV outlet, via a television interview filmed in the San Francisco jail between Seale and Francisco Newman, a black reporter. The interview ranged over a variety of subjects, Bobby's early life, his attitudes toward American society, experiences in and out of the party, favorite poems, people and even recipes and descriptions of his confrontations with bailiffs and jails. He spoke of the hole, where he was confined after taking a beating from San Francisco county sheriff's deputies.

"... It's no hole. It's a door, a big thick steel door ... and it's a cold floor, you have to sleep on the cold floor, you don't have no bed. It's a seven-foot-long, five-foot-wide box."

And in response to a question of how he kept his spirits up in the hole: "This is the way you beat the cat. You see, when you're a revolutionary you don't let them break your spirit that way. The real thing is to understand the psychology of the cop. They are the ones who really couldn't stand it to be in there. That's why they create that kind of thing."

"Who were you," asked Newman, "before you were Bobby Seale, Chairman of the Black Panther Party?"

"Another brother in the community, man. I went in the service. I got kicked out of military service because I got into an argument with a white colonel who thought he was God—who tried to mess over me and my drums. I was a drummer. My father taught me to be a carpenter. I'm a journeyman aircraft sheet-metal mechanic. Let's see, what other trades have I got? I'm a general machine operator. I know all kinds of magnaflux and nondestructive testing methods. . . . I was a comedian, a nightclub comedian. . . . But you can't tell jokes about the revolution, the revolution's real. . . . I don't tell jokes much anymore . . . I use my skills for serving the people now."

He did not include in his listing of skills that of author. His book, which was the outgrowth of a series of articles in *Ramparts*, had been released a few months before the interview.*

The Panthers specifically denied that their income approaches $50,000 a month. Moreover, they asserted that most of their funds went into bailing Panthers out of jail or otherwise paying for legal assistance. It is matter of record that the Powells were kicked out of the Party at the same time

* Bobby Seale, *Seize the Time*, Random House, 1970.

that a general purge was announced. Whole chapters were shut down, Panthers in Sacramento, Oakland, Philadelphia, Chicago and Los Angeles were condemned in the Panther Paper, and a statement describing the purge and the reasons for it was published months before the Powells took the stand.

There is the possibility that the nationwide crackdown on the Panthers occurred because the purge was successful, leaving police departments without any clue as to what the Panthers were involved with. After all, there are still questions about Willie Brent, who was purged along with the Powells.

It is an undeniable fact that after April 6, 1968, Hilliard inherited more responsibility for guiding the Panther Party. Eldridge was not released from jail until June 12, and during this period both Kathleen Cleaver and Bobby Seale were involved in establishing political liaison with white radicals, particularly the Peace and Freedom Party, and most of all, in making paid appearances in order to add to the Party coffers.

Hilliard had the frustrating experience of having charges of attempted murder, growing out of the April shoot-out, dismissed because of insufficient evidence by a Superior Court Judge who was then reversed by the State Court of Appeals. September 15, 1969, was the date set for that trial. Meanwhile, Hilliard had to dispose of several other pending cases. He was acquitted on a charge of attempting to free several blacks, arrested for loitering, from a police car. Police claimed that Hilliard got out of a car in which he had been sitting with Bobby Seale and another man, walked over to the patrol car, and tried to open the back door where the prisoners had been sitting.

Seale, who at the time of the trial was in San Francisco county jail awaiting extradition to Connecticut, was Hilliard's prime witness. Seale insisted that Hilliard approached the police car only to obtain information and that the cops panicked. Where police had estimated that a crowd of 150 had formed, presumably developing the nucleus for a riot, Seale and Hilliard insisted that the number on the corner was closer to thirty-five. Both Panther officials described police as waving rifles in their direction. This allegation was denied by one police witness, Officer Joseph L. Bean. He did admit that he had cocked his weapon in preparedness. Preparedness for what was never specified.

In December, Hilliard was again on trial, this time in connection with a gun charge that was levied in February, 1968, when Bobby Seale and his wife were arrested for conspiracy to commit murder. The prosecution made it a political trial. Articles from the *Black Panther* paper were quoted out of context to prove that Hilliard, because of his political beliefs, was duty-bound to carry a gun and ideologically prepared to use it against police at any time. Hilliard flatly denied that he was carrying a gun at the time of arrest. He was found guilty of unlawful possession of a loaded gun, in one of those split decisions that defy analysis, for the jury hung on whether or not the weapon was concealed. While it was entirely possible that Hilliard was in the car with the gun in his hand, or openly displayed in a holster, it is unlikely. Moreover, that was not what police testimony alleged.

The gun charge was Hilliard's first conviction for any crime. Despite this fact, the judge gave him the maximum sentence, six months jail and $500 fine. A new date was set to consider the concealed-weapons charge. Garry's motion for another trial was denied, and the decision was appealed.

The charge which really can hurt Hilliard is that of threatening the President. Conviction carries a maximum sentence of five years and a $1,000 fine. Attorney Garry bristled at the charge and pointed out that Hilliard had only been using rhetoric and that there was no clear and present danger to the President. The judge didn't agree, and set bail at $30,000. After that, an Alameda County judge had to block the attempt of an insurance company to withdraw the $25,000 bail which keeps Hilliard on the streets until his shoot-out trial is decided.

In a sense, the argument that Hilliard's remarks about killing Nixon is rhetoric can be dismissed. Of course it is rhetoric, but the truth is that the Panthers, and any other revolutionary orientation in the country, could move to kill anyone if they were convinced that the action would advance them politically. If a Panther, a black man, or even someone a little swarthy offed the President, all blacks in this country would be imperiled. Forget the elaborate precautions made in the name of protecting the President, and assume that some dark man got through them. Who knows how many white private citizens would then take it upon themselves to avenge their President?

Hilliard knows that killing the President is not political. It would eliminate only one man and not change the system. To move on the President, then, would have the potential for bringing a reign of terror to the black community for an act that in no way would reduce the commitment of the nation to a racist capitalistic economy.

Hilliard, therefore, was using rhetoric. He had no choice. His charge that his remarks were taken out of context makes sense. But a wider frame is needed. The phrase on which the government chose to prosecute was taken without reference to the context of Hilliard's speeches. Hilliard comes down heavy naturally, and he's been talking that way a long time. At the May 1 rally, Hilliard lashed out at Mayor Alioto, because of the police raid on Panther headquarters just three days before.

". . . If Alioto fucks with the Black Panther Party, not only will we deal with the Molly McGuires manifested in that fool Cahill (Chief of Police), but we'll deal with the Mafia. We say fuck the Mafia, fuck anybody that's trying to trample upon the rights of the people. Because we know that the power is manifested in the people. We say that it wouldn't make us one bit of difference if those motherfuckers moved on Bobby and myself this afternoon, because we know that the people will follow through with this shit. Fuck Alioto in his stupid ass. I think we were right."

In November 1969, Garry, Hilliard, and Bobby's mother participated in a press conference deploring the chaining of

Bobby Seale in Chicago. In response to an interviewer's question asserting that Bobby Seale "has been somewhat of a nuisance in court by shouting and refusing to listen to the Judge," David exploded:

"Motherfuck the judge . . . the man is a fascist . . . Bobby's rights have been violated. . . . Fuck that judge, fuck America. What Bobby's doing is all that he can do. The judge is a criminal. Bobby is a victim of pig persecution because he's a black man."

Hilliard knows how to use the language, and chooses the words he uses to fit the audience or the medium. When he appeared on *Face the Nation* on December 28, 1969, he defended his statements eloquently and without profanity. But when he stood in front of 30,000 peaceniks at the November 15 Moratorium he was shaking his fist in the face of the nation with magnificent style.

Eldridge, in past speeches, had done more to threaten the President. He had challenged Presidents Nixon and Johnson and Governor Reagan to a duel, and gave them a choice of weapons. Duelling is against the law, and the country has, with the memory of Alexander Hamilton's sudden exit, a decisive indication that higher government officials might not survive duels too well.

There is one logical explanation for this idiotic charge. Some language-uptight character in the justice department became completely unhinged at hearing Hilliard call Richard Milhous Nixon, thirty-sixth President of the United States, a motherfucker. There was no real fear that Hilliard, or some other black, would attempt assassination. Nixon has made it a matter of administration policy that black folks not get too close to him. But to call the President motherfucker, not once but three times, to have a nigger do that, to witness a disloyal, gun-carrying, avowed, communist nigger, revolutionary freely apply to the President the monstrous kingpin of all obscenities, and to do it three times before so many witnesses, was more than that loyal agent could take.

Perhaps part of what revolutionary politics is all about is

calling names. Most of what has come down on the Panthers has been directly because of speech, nothing more. Hilliard, who is pretty mad-making to some of the black folk that surround him, has naturally got to uptight whites, particularly those in authority who cannot recognize a man who is a past master at the art of insult, who enjoys doing it, and who is totally willing to fight if his remarks inspire more than a verbal counterattack.

People who want to identify with individual Panthers, rather than with the total effort, are in a position to raise questions about a choice of words, or otherwise suggest that particular expressions coming from one Panther, say Hilliard, represent something other than the sentiments of the leaders they would rather support. Actually, Hilliard seems to be at one with Panther political expressions. The shock with which his remarks are received betrays insensitivity to a very obvious fact. Hilliard's uncompromisingly harsh and profane public character serves as the perfect vehicle for displaying the unequivocal hard line which underlies the Panther political program.

This fact might be more obvious were it not for the need of Panther commentators to assume that Party leadership rests solely with one man. The Panthers have always had a collective leadership, a fact which is obscured by the tendency of the media to zero in on one individual. This habit led everyone to assume that Hilliard was in complete command of the Panthers, and that Ray "Masai" Hewitt, the Minister of Education, would be the person to assume leadership when Hilliard was finally placed behind bars. This assumption betrays more the inclination of the news media to concentrate its attention on a Panther to whom it has paid scant attention, than it does the reality of Panther leadership.

If there is any credence to the idea that the Panthers are run from the top by one man, Huey Newton is that man. Huey is the main man, the mythical black hero who formed the Party and whose image served to keep it together through difficult times.

He is the original vanguard, the person who set an example that has resulted in the fact that Panther leaders are subject to a short life outside of prison, a quick death at the receiving end of massively directed gunfire, or a rapid exit from the country. It was Huey who developed a few black-beret-topped naturals, jaunty walks and allegiance to the gun and the Red Book into a dominant threat to domestic tranquillity. Huey has to be credited with inspiring the most gargantuan aggregate of massed power, wealth, and prerogative in the world, the United States of America, to commit itself hysterically to the massive overkill effort necessary to control a small army of ill-armed blacks marching under the banner of the Panther.

Huey the man, and Huey the myth, are completely intertwined at this point. The combination of his writings and his actions, however, serves to indicate who he is and the influence he has over the Panther operation. Hilliard, when he appeared on *Meet the Press*, responded to a question from Bernard Nossiter of the *Washington Post*:

> Mr. Nossiter: Mr. Hilliard, you speak of criminal activities of police. But don't the Panthers stock and collect guns themselves? Isn't this an invitation to the police to take action?
>
> Hilliard: First of all, the Panthers do not stock guns. We are very aware of the gun laws. We advocate each individual having a shotgun in their homes, as spelled out under the Constitution of the United States. It is not our purpose to assemble large caches of weapons. If we have weapons, we would distribute the weapons in the community for self-defense, but we do not have armories. And, even if we did, we would expect the same treatment under the law that is given to members of the Ku Klux Klan . . .

Hilliard's remarks were a replay of a basic policy laid down by Huey Newton. Huey points out in his short essay, "In Defense of Self Defense": "If the party is not going to make the people aware of the tools of liberation (guns) and the strategic method that is to be used, there will be no means by which the people will be mobilized properly."

Eldridge Cleaver said that Huey and Bobby had seriously started to plan a bank robbery, only to discover that they were actually talking liberation politics. They did not turn their backs on crime, but rather found it irrelevant to their purposes. The two began to find money for guns after Huey discovered one place to buy Red Books for thirty cents and another where he could sell them for a dollar.

The first guns purchased with the proceeds went to the Panther nucleus that was forming. After the Party was underway, Huey made certain that the Panthers were a conduit of guns into the hands of black people. This concept of the vanguard, gleaned in large part through a combination of Mao and Malcolm, is Huey's constant strength. He is preparing for a war of liberation by bringing to the black community the recognition that it might be necessary to fight that war.

Newton actually has at least two images. There is the one that became more and more mythical when Huey was in jail, of the well-armed black who inspires by example, and who exhorts his followers to emulate his example as a vanguard revolutionary leader. This is the Huey of lawbook and riot gun who Eldridge describes as the baddest motherfucker to set foot in history. There is also Huey the public figure. Here his ferocity is replaced by a display of implacable conviction and his demeanor remains ever open to inquiry.

Huey has probably been interviewed more than anyone who has passed through the American prison system. Invariably, reporters who come into contact with him project in their stories the picture of a calm, reasoned man sustained by a belief in the necessity of black liberation. Unquestionably, Huey is a total political person, a condition which does not allow for any fragmentation of character. He is as tranquil in his resistance as newspapermen portray him, but he is much more.

One of the reasons that an image of Newton's more revolutionary aspects, those that resemble more the direction that Hilliard takes, does not come across is that he responds, in interviews, to the structured needs of the establishment press. The rules of the prison at San Luis Obispo are such that only pressmen associated with daily papers were given permission to interview the Minister of Defense. This regulation had the effect of eliminating that order of newsgathering peculiar to the black press.

Most Negro newspapers are weekly, meaning that black people were denied the right to read a Huey Newton interview conducted by representatives of a periodical geared to their interests. This subtle and almost totally selective censorship reduced Huey's ability to directly influence black political thinking during his imprisonment.

Prison officials could not stop the flow of directives to the Party, and also they could not filter out all of Huey's hardline sentiments. The fact that Huey issued a directive from his cell ordering Panthers to cool the city of Oakland following the assassination of Martin Luther King has been told and retold. In March, 1968, he ordered the Panthers to resist with force of arms any assault upon their homes including those mounted by police. Then, in January, 1969, he ordered an unmerciful purge of the party.

Huey, as disciplined revolutionary, maintained the kind of commitment that serves to keep him an example of vanguard mentality. He absolutely refused to work for about three cents an hour, the rate that prison officials pay inmates, well below the minimum wage as prescribed by law.

Once, in an interview with a reporter from a San Francisco paper, Newton showed some unaccustomed anger. "Those freak-show degenerates," he exclaimed, succinctly summing up his view of prison officials. "They think they can rehabilitate me. How do you relate to a person who is so absurd?"

His remark was similar to Eldridge Cleaver's comments: "Rehabilitation in the State of California is less than a bad

joke. I don't even know how to relate to that word, 'rehabilitation.' It presupposes that at one time one was 'habilitated'
and that somehow he got off the right track and was sent to
this garage, or repair shop, to be dealt with and then released. . . . I just want to tell you this. I've had more trouble
out of Parole officers and the Department of Corrections
simply because I've been relating to the Movement than I
had when I was committing robberies, rapes and other things
that I didn't get caught for."

The most compelling fact about Huey is that he tightened
the reins of leadership after he went to jail. He had worked
with Bobby a little more than a year, Eldridge for less than
nine months, Hilliard for slightly less time than Seale, D.C.
for about six months, and in that time established a model of
collective leadership.

"When the oppressor makes a vicious attack against freedom fighters because of the way that such freedom fighters
choose to go about their liberation, then we know we are
moving in the direction of our liberation," says Huey; and his
entire political strategy issues from a position of finding out
what people-oriented program to institute, and then pushing
for it with the vigor that invites and attracts repression.

It is through this repression, he argues, that the masses begin
to see the true nature of the society, and seek to further educate themselves in the details of how blacks seek national
liberation. "The vanguard party is never underground in the
beginning of its existence, because this would limit its effectiveness and educational processes. How can you teach people
if the people do not know and respect you? The party must
exist above ground as long as the dog power structure will
allow, and hopefully, when the party is forced to go underground, the message of the party will already have been put
across to the people. The vanguard party's activities on the
surface will necessarily be short lived." *

* Huey P. Newton, *The Correct Handling of a Revolution.*

Thus far, the party has not been driven underground, or more accurately, there is a visible above-ground Panther operation. There haven't been additions made in the Panther paper to the listing of members of the Central Committee since July, 1969, when Ray "Masai" Hewitt's name supplanted George Murray's as Minister of Education.

Masai is an old friend of Eldridge Cleaver and came into the Panthers as a member of the Los Angeles chapter. He was at one time the Deputy Minister of Information. He is articulate, literate, forceful, well-informed about matters that affect black people, and skilled in the use of that combination of rhetoric and erudition that has become routine with Panthers.

He was a member of the Los Angeles chapter in 1968, when three of the chapter's members were shot by police. The spokesman for the chapter at that time was Earl Anthony, who held the post of Deputy Minister of Defense. The indignation which Anthony then heaved on police has since been directed at the Panthers. His book concentrated on the rifts between Party members, the political infighting between Panthers and other groups, and his eventual disillusionment. When last reported, Anthony was touring Africa in search of another book.

Masai, early in his career, began to travel on Party business. He helped found several Panther chapters, did troubleshooting, and was one of the Panthers who made the international circuit. He was one of those accompanying Bobby Seale in his tour to Scandinavia. In November 1968, Masai was one of the Panthers who disappeared for a short time, only to turn up in Montreal at an international conference called the Hemispheric Conference to End the War in Vietnam.

A rumor that Eldridge might appear at the conference resulted in the wholesale deploying of government agencies north of the border. Some twenty-five Panthers, many from the Bay Area, showed up at the conference and took part in the proceedings. Seale, Hilliard and Masai popped into view the last day of the four-day conference, spoke, and then faded out of sight, only to show up the following day in the Bay Area.

Masai did get together with Eldridge the following July, when Eldridge surfaced in Algiers, just prior to the opening of the first Pan African Cultural Convention. From that point on Masai began to be known. He took over the Ministry of Education post when George Murray decided to leave the Panthers and return to the ministry. In this position, Masai is very critical of Black Student Unions, allowing that although the Black Panther Party had been instrumental in developing BSU's, it had been unable to infuse them with the proper political perspective.

BSU's, he charges, are not living up to their early promise of helping to forge the black college experience into something more relevant to the educational needs of the black community. He says that the organizations are too abstract in their theoretical approach and too removed from the ghetto from which they sprang. He particularly condemns the tendency of BSU's to seek the spectacular when pressing demands. Strikes, building seizures, and the obvious display of firearms gain notoriety and publicity at the expense of the more solid goal of achieving educational politics and racial effectiveness.

Here, Masai seems to echo the advice of Stokely Carmichael, although he, along with the entire Panther apparatus, finds Carmichael complete anathema. At the May 22 cocktail party, Masai spoke out harshly against Stokely. His comments caused one of the black women present to object. She felt very strongly that Masai was airing black business in an inappropriate forum.

Masai disagreed, but he seemed to shorten his remarks about the former Prime Minister. He probably did not do so in response to the criticism. More likely, Masai became aware that most of the whites present were not in a position to appreciate the political distinctions made within the black revolutionary community.

This lack of insight into black politics probably explains why whites seeking parallels within the Panthers to the prerogatives of their own community, conclude that Masai would automatically inherit the mantle of supreme leadership supposedly held by Hilliard. The casual acceptance of the proposition that the Panthers are run from the top down makes observers blind to how a tightly held sense of politics and goals shapes cooperative leadership and renders absolute rule by one man anachronistic and antirevolutionary.

The position of Field Marshall has been listed for the longest time as "underground." But one of the Field Marshalls, D.C., was very much overground. D.C. (Don Cox) joined the Party about April 1967 and is credited with setting up the office procedures of the Panthers. With his large afro hair style, that tends to emphasize the lean readiness of his body, D.C. looks like a greying lion. Even when standing still, his hands clasped behind him and his shoulders slightly bent, D.C. seems to be stalking something or someone. His gaze, steadily focused on infinity, was possibly developed during the days when he walked the ghetto streets of Oakland and San Francisco equipped with a camera and a fantastically discriminating eye.

At that time, D.C. was an enthusiastic admirer of photographer Gordon Robert Parks. Two years later, Parks, on special assignment for *Life*, photographed D.C. along with several other Panthers who were working in the San Francisco Chapter.

If someone tried to search for the source of disillusion or enlightenment that led D.C. to the Panthers, other than the black experience itself, they might find it in his civil rights background. D.C. was one of those CORE activists who accepted the principles of nonviolent civil disobedience and sat-in, prayed-in, picketed and generally participated in that protest activity which has all but gone out of style within the black community. There was a point when his efforts seemed to have paid off.

A vigil at Sacramento, held by CORE members in 1964, who brought sleeping bags and slept in the rotunda of the capitol, resulted in the passage of a fair-housing law. In 1964 and 1965 Don was involved in the series of protests directed against the Bank of America, San Francisco hotels, rental agencies and the automobile industry. Each of these protests was finally resolved by signed agreements, which on paper increased the hiring of black people in greater numbers and in capacities theretofore denied them.

The housing law proved to be ineffective, the agreements made with employer groups turned out to be unenforceable, and the response of the courts to what were misdemeanor charges developed into demonstrations of the arbitrary course that justice can take. Defendants who had sat side by side and were accused of the same offenses were jailed or set free, fined or given probation, strictly according to the vagaries of chance which brought them before one judge rather than another.

Further, those who were put in jail found themselves subject to sentences that were harsher than any similar decisions meted out by southern courts.

D.C., at the time he joined the Party, was the production manager of a San Francisco advertising firm and mail-order house. In this capacity, he supervised every step in the processing of advertising matter beginning with the art work, through the layout and printing, and finally to the stuffing of envelopes and their mailing. His disillusionment with the society was partially a function of integration. Repeatedly, Don would express disgust at the lack of real values in the advertising world. He had arrived, and found himself nowhere.

So, he joined the Panthers when the Party's address was a post office box in Emeryville. Soon after, an office was opened in Oakland, and it was D.C. who established the rules by which the office would be run. He rationalized procedures so that messages could be received and transmitted, set up regular job stations, and generally made the Panthers more businesslike.

There was another side to D.C.'s activities, one which brought him instant notoriety. The *Oakland Tribune* reported that he had made several trips to Reno in order to purchase guns. Knowland's newspaper "exposed" the fact that D.C., who was not violating any laws, had purchased several hand-guns from a Reno gunshop. D.C. freely admits to this activity, but because of the unsought publicity he soon ended his gun-purchasing trips. He was afraid that California authorities would find some obscure law that might land him in jail. Long after he stopped making the Reno trips, D.C. was hung up on a gun charge.

D.C. had been convicted of a felony in 1957. He insists that he was railroaded. A result of that conviction was his being made legally unable to own or possess a firearm. In September 1969, San Francisco policemen raided Panther headquarters, following their attempts to arrest two Panthers accused of illegal use of sound-truck equipment. The office was tear-gassed, desks were upset and general mayhem was distributed. In the process, D.C. was arrested and charged with brandish-ing a weapon in a threatening fashion. Purportedly, he had pointed a shotgun at one of the invading policemen.

Months later, a federal indictment was issued. At the time, D.C. was in New York. The subpoena, issued in San Fran-cisco, resulted in the surprise swooping down of several federal agents, who promptly arrested him and transported him back to San Francisco where bail was posted. His passport was lifted, and his ability to travel restricted between the Bay Area and New York, respectively his place of residence and the location of many of his family members whom he visits whenever possible.

Before federal authorities moved on him, D.C. had done a great deal of traveling for the Panthers. He was one of several troubleshooters who visited Panther chapters in order to assure that a minimal level of standardized procedure existed. He was a member of the Panther delegation that was hung up in Paris for two days en route to Algeria to visit Eldridge Cleaver.

He was also the subject of a federal grand jury inquiry that oddly enough was instituted at the very time that Huey Newton was being tried on charges of killing an Oakland policeman. It was announced that the Grand Jury wanted to establish whether or not D.C., along with Landon Williams (who was jailed in Denver and charged with complicity in the murder of Alex Rackley), had visited Panther chapters in order to instruct blacks on the fine art of manufacturing and using explosive devices.

D.C. was not one of those subpoenaed to appear. If he had been, he probably would have refused to testify on fifth-amendment grounds, the same stance taken by the Panthers who did appear. The charge has not developed into a criminal complaint. But, it is highly probable that a number of Americans, including the members of the grand jury, will continue to believe that specific members of the Panthers, including D.C., are running around the country, dusky reincarnations of the bearded, bomb-toting anarchist.

D.C. is a likely suspect. A column appears sporadically in the *Black Panther* paper called "Organizing Self Defense Groups." In these columns, the Field Marshall lectures on types of armament and their use.

"From seeing too much Wyatt Earp and Mat Dillon too many people think that if they have a hand gun, either pistol or revolver, that they are ready for anything. All that is necessary to give you a different perspective is to examine the armament of the pigs that occupy our Black communities anywhere in Babylon."

What follows is a description of three types of weapons, the shotgun, the rifle and the handgun, accompanied by terse, ambiguous suggestions. For instance, "Most national guard units, at least here in California, are equipped with the M-14. Check your local National Guard availability."

Much of D.C.'s time has seen him involved with the non-

Molotov type of cocktail. He was the featured speaker at a cocktail party given by Mr. and Mrs. Leonard Bernstein, which reportedly raised between ten and twelve thousand dollars for the legal expenses of the New York Twenty-One. Both he and Masai were present at a less profitable, but equally improbable, society bash thrown by the Sidney Lumets, of filmmaking fame.

"This isn't exactly your regular charity ball set," Mrs. Lumet is reported to have said, apparently in explanation of the fact that only a few hundred dollars had been raised. D.C. has a resigned attitude toward these fund-raising parties. He is more at home among blacks, and prefers to deal with the community rather than its financial benefactors. He does his duty, however, attends when necessary, and is not the least bit unhappy when a party ends early as the result of ideological or other kinds of conflict.

D.C. has now gone underground. He disappeared after a murder charge, similar in some details to that lodged against Bobby Seale, was entered in Baltimore. Huey Newton confirmed rumors that D.C. was in Algeria when he announced at a press conference, ". . . we do have an international section in Algeria headed by the Minister of Information, Eldridge Cleaver, and our Field Marshall, Donald Cox."

Algiers is a likely place for any black revolutionary to go when leaving America. Algeria does not have an extradition treaty with the U.S. Also, Algeria, in achieving independence after waging an anticolonial war of liberation (the subject of the film, *The Battle of Algiers*), serves as a model for black revolutionaries. Algiers was also the adopted home of Frantz Fanon, one of the prophets and architects of worldwide anticolonial revolution.

It is no accident that Fanon is one of the prophets of black revolution and that the Algerian experience provides clues for North American blacks seeking liberation. *The Battle of Algiers* is a must for Panthers—the perfect revolutionary film.

Algiers, it should be noted, was a colony which France did

not want to give up. The French attempted to render the Algerian claim to independence invalid, informing the restive population of a portion of a continent removed from Europe that they were a part of France. The French, smug in the legal fiction that they had created, declared that Algiers was little more than an extension of Paris, meaning that Algerians had no more right to revolt than the residents of the 12th Arrondissement, who were historically bound to France by antiquity, and also by the fact that the Bastille was located there.

Even Camus, a rabid antiracist, a lover of freedom and that existentialist thinker who made the concept of the absurd available to American revolutionaries engaged in guerrilla theater, could not hack Algerian independence. He was Algerian, the descendant of French colonizers who moved to Algeria, fell in love with it, and denied its natives the right to share ownership in the land of their birth. Camus said, despite his absolute fidelity to freedom on the European political scene, that Algerians were Frenchmen, and that's that. This is a brand of insensitivity to one's own moral precepts that has parallels in white America's approach to black demands for dignity, and which is labeled by blacks as racism.

Fanon provided American blacks with an accurate description of the colonial mentality that would deny essential suffrage through the device of providing the oppressed people with symbols of full citizenship. At the same time, he provided a description of the European-influenced colonized individual who, in denying his identity with his people, became mentally diseased.

"Black men want to prove to white men at all costs, the richness of their thought, the equal value of their intellect," * he stated. And later:

"The black man who arrives in France changes because to him the country represents the Tabernacle: He changes not

---

* Frantz Fanon, *Black Skin; White Masks*, N.Y.: Grove Press, 1967, p. 12.

only because it is from France that he received his knowledge of Montesquieu, Rousseau, and Voltaire, but also because France gave him his physicians, his department heads, his innumerable little functionaries. . . . He leaves from the pier, and the amputation of his being diminishes as the silhouette of his ship grows clearer. In the eyes of those who have come to see him off, he can read the evidence of his own mutation, the power. . . . 'Good-by bandanna, good-by straw hat . . .' " *

The words are reminiscent of the white-man-inspired Sporting-Life article of faith, "There's a boat leaving soon for New York," "Good-by Catfish Row—Hello, Harlem."

It was Fanon who made it clear to those who dreamt of black liberation that the colonizing mentality was universal, carrying with it an eroding effect on black consciousness totally independent of whether the ruling whites dominated by numbers as in America or by the combination of military and economic power which defines the relationship of Europeans to black Africa. It is whiteness which becomes the yardstick, the same whiteness which offers the hope for happiness only to those Negroes who can come to terms with the inevitability of the insufficiency of black people. This is the logic that has controlled the lives, fortunes, fantasies, ambitions, hostilities, politics, economics and sex lives of blacks, too many of whom have responded to this cultural and psychic genocide by willingly developing an inadequacy of manhood.

The Battle of Algiers had the dual benefit of being Fanon-linked and explicit in the ways of organizing for guerilla warfare. Whenever the film was shown in the Bay Area, phalanxes of Panthers attended. They found satisfaction in the flick. The natives won. They defeated a government that was more powerful, and in doing so, transcended the nonsense of class and assumed patriotism, both of which are claims on individuals which intensifies and consolidates their colonial status.

* *Ibid.*, p. 23.

Most of the young revolutionaries who saw the film concentrated on the terroristic activities, the cell organizations, the singleminded dedication of the Algerian freedom fighters. For some, the essential knowledge transmitted occurred at the very end. The Algerian revolution became a fact at the point that the masses, unarmed but vocal, both shielded its freedom fighters and took to the streets in protest.

The movie did not include the details of how the populace became educated to their role in that revolution. Some of their awareness was obvious. They were exposed daily to the oppressive necessity of the French army, which through searches, raids, and obvious discriminations directed toward non-whites, demonstrated that some departments of the French government were more equal than others.

There had to be more communication, however, communication that was not indicated in the film. There was a need for political information detailing the roles available to Algerians interested in actively supporting the move toward independence by joining with or acting on behalf of the active revolutionaries. This, in turn, had to be part of an overall propaganda effort geared toward explaining to the bulk of Algerians, most of whom did not pick up guns, that the political goal of the revolution was an independence with which they could identify. Tactics and politics, means and ends, had to be transmitted to the masses.

Emory Douglas, Minister of Culture for the Panthers, has taken on much of the responsibility for educating black Americans to the tactics of liberation. He was prominent in the visit to Sacramento, and along with Eldridge, Bobby and Huey developed the format for the Panther newspaper. Emory is responsible for the concept of policemen as pigs. He is also one of the few original Panthers still on the street.

The only word which describes Emory, in person, is reticent. He is shy, almost apologetic. His demeanor makes him seem much smaller than his six feet. He answers almost every comment about himself with a tentative smile and a demeanor which makes it seem as though he is stepping back in order to get out of that limelight which is the attention of another person. Emory is inspired to talk only when he can be persuaded to discuss art—but not his art, revolutionary art in general. At that point his stature becomes apparent, his animation is fluid, free and expressive of the artistic renderings he has not yet committed to paper. His presence becomes impressive, almost dominating, and the floods of words coming out of his mouth tumble freely over one another in such profusion as to give the listener the impression that he is stuttering.

Emory is also commanding when there is the possibility of a fight. If one of his comrades in revolution seems threatened, he visibly grows to gigantic and menacing proportions.

Emory's views on the purposes of revolutionary art have had a decided influence on the politics of the Party. Although he accepts suggestions from others about possible pictures, he tends to come to the drawing board with ideas of his own. When it comes to revolution, art both precedes and interprets politics. He has traveled as much as any of the Panther national leadership, and possibly more. He is privy to the innermost workings of the Black Panther Party and constantly contributes his perceptions to the formulation of policy. Emory knows the ways of the ghetto streets, the intimacies of firearms and the imminence of death or imprisonment for daring to denounce the land of his birth. He is also an artist.

BSU's have adopted his painting of a loin-clothed black man with a gun in one hand and a book in the other as the symbol of their educational aspirations. A Panther greeting card features an Emory drawing of a bandannaed and faceless black woman holding both a baby and a rifle. Accompanying the drawing is a quotation described as a revolutionary Cuban proverb: "If I should return, I shall kiss you. If I should fall on the way, I shall ask you to do as I have in the name of the revolution." Many black homes have copies of the bright red, brown and black painting of a black mother and her naked boy child who is playing with a child-sized gun.

In one of Emory's earliest articles in the *Black Panther* paper he stated:

"Besides fighting the enemy, the Black Panther Party is doing propaganda among the masses of black people.

"The form of propaganda I'm about to refer to is called art, such as painting, sketching, etc. The Black Panther Party calls it revolutionary art—this kind of art enlightens the Party to continue its vigorous attack against the enemy, as well as educate the masses of black people—we do this by showing them through pictures—'The correct handling of the Revolution.' . . .

"We try to create an atmosphere for the vast majority of black people—who aren't readers but activists—through their observation of our work, they feel they have the right to destroy the enemy. . . .

"This is revolutionary art—pigs lying in alleyways of the colony dead with their eyes gouged out—autopsy showing cause of death: 'They fail to see that majority rules.' Pictures we draw show them choking to death from their inhuman ways—these are the kinds of pictures revolutionary artists draw—

". . . We must draw pictures of Southern cracker Wallace with cancer of the mouth that he got from his dead witch's uterus—

"Pictures that show black people kicking down prison gates—sniping bombers shooting down helicopters police mayors governors senator assemblymen congressmen firemen newsmen businessmen Americans—

" 'We shall conquer without a doubt.' Revolutionary Artist—Emory" *

Other examples of revolutionary art are beginning to show. For the most part, the artists have not come into their own and are imitating Emory. The comic book deplored by Vice-President Agnew and held up by the McClellan Committee as

* *The Black Panther*, May 18, 1968.

an example of Panther perfidy is an outgrowth of Emory's efforts. As far as one can determine, these artworks are constitutionally protected. They are obviously inflammatory, but not so specific as to inspire prosecution. The message is explicit—kill policemen, organize for guerrilla warfare, the only good nigger is an armed nigger and black liberation means armed struggle.

Emory, with his revolutionary art, is clearly demonstrating that the Panthers should be considered as something other than urban reformers. As an artist, he has more effective freedom of expression than Eldridge as a writer, or Hilliard as an orator. Emory, as artist, is more of a vanguard than Panthers as politicians. To look at his works is to arrive at the gates of the political dilemma which opens wide on that asylum where America's fears are sometimes tranquilized, increasingly given shock therapy and more often than not left unresolved to ultimately break out and command attention.

At issue are questions of advocacy, clear and present danger, and ultimately that organized violence which can be perceived as conspiracy. Is Detroit's Reverend Cleage advocating violence when he sermonizes that slum dwellings should be burnt down in order to exterminate the rats and the roaches? Was musician Les McCann disloyal when, at a Swiss jazz concert, he referred to "the goddam nation"?

Did Malcolm threaten the domestic tranquility when he insisted that blacks should attain their liberation, "by any means necessary"? And is Elijah Muhammad guilty of advocating cosmic genocide when he teaches that the blue-eyed devil will be exterminated?

Three of the eight Panthers indicted as a result of the shoot-out where Bobby Hutton was killed were turned over to the police by black people. In a genuine revolutionary situation the few blacks who might be inclined to notify police could almost guarantee that some form of reprisal, ranging from ostracism to assassination, would rapidly follow the act of disclosure. Emory in his art, and the Panthers in their gen-

eral pronouncements to the black community, advocate, under
the rubric of black solidarity, that black people should accept
and protect all blacks who commit "crimes" against the white-
ruled government or its agents.

Panther intentions are clear, and Emory graphically depicts
them. The legal alternatives facing the nation involves choosing
the method by which these revolutionaries can be controlled.
To continue to persecute Panthers because of their intent,
rather than their acts, is to bruise the constitution seriously
and concomitantly to unite the black community. On the other
hand, to successfully embark on a project of isolating the
masses from their revolutionary vanguard requires the genuine
production of equitable opportunities for blacks to regain and
retain their humanity. In other words, the society can have
racism and revolution, or reconciliation and reform. To com-
pound this dilemma, there is no set of laws or approach to
order that will serve as a guideline. Revolutions cannot be
prevented; they can only be made irrelevant or unnecessary.

If there is a political rosetta stone capable of translating the
passion of the Panthers into a philosophically sound program,
understandable by many, Cleaver is that instrument. Eldridge
is the common link to all Panthers. He embraced the theory,
practice, vanguardism, humor, irreverence, and the necessity
for black survival in one package, his life. It is Cleaver who
sets the other black cats in perspective and brings the Panther
necessity down front where it can be seen.

Cleaver was thirty-one when he joined the Panthers, and
had spent almost seventeen of those thirty-one years locked
away. He was paroled December 12, 1966, to San Francisco;
and not quite two years later—November 24, 1968—he went
into exile. Two months of this time, between April 6 and June
12, 1968, Cleaver was in jail, charged with complicity in an
alleged ambush that amounted to a violation of probation. In
other words, it took exactly twenty months of freedom for
Eldridge to rip off a piece of revolutionary history for himself, and to get out with something resembling his skin.

Huey was sent to jail nine months after Eldridge joined the Panthers, and at that time Bobby Seale was three months into a six-months jail term for his part in the Panther Sacramento adventure.

Right up to the moment he left the country, Cleaver was a mainstay of the Party, a leader, an order giver, an organizer, with talent, drive and inexhaustible energy, and an orator who combined wit, blasphemy and revolutionary messages in an unpredictable mélange that always made a lot of sense and constantly delighted his audiences.

As the Minister of Information, Eldridge assumed responsibility for contributing to the development of the Party's political theories and informing the community about both the theory and practice of black revolution. The character of the party, and that which is Eldridge, are indistinguishable from each other—they are stamped in each other's image.

Chances are that if Cleaver had not left the country to avoid serving more penitentiary time he would have figured out some way to relate to an international scene. Cleaver's intellectual loyalty is global, his overwhelming appetite for revolution embraces the entire world and his prime contribution to contemporary thought will eventually be in the field of international relations. It was that way from the beginning.

When Eldridge was in Soledad writing *Soul on Ice*, he wrote a short and unpublished article called "Birth of the White Backlash" that placed America's approach to its racism, wars of national liberation, the Cuba missile crisis, Soviet-American relations, nuclear warfare, and the inability of the non-white and oppressed to form common cause in clear relation to one another.

His thesis was that Russia, in removing its missiles from Cuba, gave America the heart to oppose revolutionary struggle everywhere in the world. Cleaver's contribution to domestic revolutionary theory is entirely embraced by the ideas in this article. In October, 1969, he attempted to push Russia into an act calculated to restore the balance of terror that existed before Cuba, and also, in the process, to assume the right of the Black Panther Party to engage in world politics.

Cleaver delivered a speech at Pyongyang, North Korea, at an international conference of journalists. His remarks were made in behalf of the American people, he explained, "because the Black Panther represents the United States and its best interests." He then scolded Russia for limiting its arsenal to Europe and not doing enough with its atomic might to stop the killing of Asians and Africans, and also for not giving Korea and Vietnam sufficient products of its technology to bring liberation to those countries. He assumed his right to speak "as a member of the world Communist movement which had made many sacrifices for the Soviet Union," and urged the Russians to provide nuclear weapons for the fight against the United States in Vietnam.

That is Eldridge's scope—world revolutionary—he strides along, a golden button in his left ear, telling off every entity which he perceives as counterrevolutionary, from the creator on down. Eldridge has monumental gall and a spirit that makes it look like heroism.

He once spoke at San Francisco State College, and suggested that if Adam had adopted Huey P. Newton's ten-point program and platform, history's first eviction might never have taken place. He made this observation with a studied wistfulness that projected the impression that he wouldn't mind challenging God right now, if it would get the revolution moving in the right direction.

In another speech he said, "We say this, that the people have a right to the best because this is all that we know that we have in this life. Those who believe that they can suffer now and get theirs after death, when you go before the throne of the Lord, tell him that Eldridge was sincere, but he just didn't know. . . . Maybe those that made it across wouldn't want to mention such things to the Lord, so I'm going to tell him myself when I get there. Because, if he tries to put me in hell and put some fire on my ass, I'm going to look around, and find some beautiful people there and say, let's organize a Black Panther Party and a Peace and Freedom Party, dig? . . . And if God himself would wield such misery for people whom I love, I would say let's deal with him, dig? Let's deal with him, and if we can deal with him on that level, if we can understand that, then certainly we can deal with these buffoon pigs who are running around here. . . ."

Eldridge offered to slap President Johnson and challenged Governor Reagan to a duel in an introduction to a chapter of Bobby Seale's book that appeared in *Ramparts.* He began, "I have never liked Ronald Reagan. Even back in the days of his bad movies—bullshit flicks that never turned me on to any glow."

He then proceeded to identify Reagan as Mickey Mouse and Superintendent of Public Education Max Rafferty—who was then involved in an unsuccessful campaign for U.S. Senator—as Donald Duck. He castigated Reagan for attempting to deny him the right to lecture at the University of California.

"Big deal. Who in the fuck do you think you are, telling me that I can't talk . . . all and each of you [including Rafferty, Assembly Speaker Unruh and a John Birch member of the California legislature] can kiss my black nigger ass, because I recognize you for what you are, racist demagogues. . . ."

He finished his remarks to Reagan saying: "I think you are a cowardly, craven-hearted wretch. You are not a man. You are a punk. Since you have insulted me by calling me a racist, I would like to have the opportunity to balance the books. All I ask is a sporting chance. Therefore, Mickey Mouse, I challenge you to a duel, to the death, and you can choose the weapons. And if you can't relate to that, right on. Walk, chicken, with your ass picked clean."

On September 11, the University of California at Berkeley announced that a new course called Social Analysis 139X would feature ten weekly lectures by Cleaver, and caused the entire California right-wing establishment to froth at the mouth. Rafferty and the Governor led the infuriated pack. Neither of them was mollified to hear that the University would not be using state funds to pay Cleaver, and both insisted that the University's Board of Regents immediately overturn the decision.

The State Senate voted 33 to 2 to censure UC officials for permitting Cleaver to lecture. The Assembly overwhelmingly passed a resolution censuring UC, and the Regents met and fought over Cleaver's appearance. Senator Schmitz, the Bircher, introduced a measure that would have withheld the next year's budget from UC Berkeley, unless Cleaver was fired within two weeks. The measure was amended when it was pointed out that the 1968 legislature could not bind the 1969 legislature to withhold funds.

Faculty sponsors of the course insisted that Cleaver would teach regardless of what the Board of Regents decided to do. The problem was that Cleaver was hired as a guest lecturer and not a faculty person. Any ruling made by the Regents that would bar him from speaking might operate to prevent any person from lecturing at the University who did not have credentials to teach. The Regents compromised, established a policy that all guest speakers would be limited to one appearance, and also passed the most stringent rules in forty years regulating faculty. The Regents also censured the UC faculty who thought up the course.

Governor Reagan was unhappy that Cleaver was OK'd for even one lecture. Eldridge, in the meantime, commented that the Governor was uptight about the course, because he had heard that Cleaver intended to discuss some of the former actor's movies. "One of the lectures will deal with negative influences of Grade B movies on the American mentality, using Mickey Mouse Reagan's career as a text," he said.

The ruling angered the students and faculty, who immediately organized mass meetings to protest the Regents' actions, while vowing that Cleaver would deliver all ten lectures.

Bobby Seale addressed one of the rallies and encouraged the students to stand up for free speech. Meanwhile, Cleaver further angered the powers that be by appearing on a panel at the University of California at Irvine. Arrangements had been made the previous June, including the payment of a $400 fee. Eldridge, referring to his well-placed opposition as "buffoons," vowed that he would deliver twenty lectures, saying that he has only one thing to say to Ronald Reagan: "Fuck you."

While all of this was going on, the Trustees of the State College system were zeroing in on George Murray, Huey Newton was found guilty and sentenced to jail, and Cleaver himself was ordered back to jail, but given a sixty-day stay. Cleaver appeared at Stanford, repeated his suggestion concerning the Governor's sex life, again challenged Reagan to a duel, while calling him a coward, and was apparently prepared to deliver his first scheduled lecture the following day.

Rafferty, in a near apoplectic fury, told all state school officials that their jobs would be at stake if they sent students to hear Cleaver. He was later to issue an edict banning the use of books by Leroi Jones and Eldridge Cleaver as auxiliary texts by school districts, an order which he did not have legal authority to issue. He was reversed by the courts.

The Governor responded to Eldridge's challenge to a duel, and chose his weapon—"words—words of more than four letters each." Cleaver won that duel.

He proceeded to lecture as scheduled, although 139X was not being offered for credit. Eldridge's weekly lectures were interrupted in the latter part of October because a student boycott of all classes was called. Cleaver agreed to honor the strike, and participated in a teach-in rather than lecture. Reagan continued to rail against Cleaver saying that, "no tiny faction of malcontents are going to be allowed to tear down our institutions of learning." Cleaver continued to teach. He did not appear for his lecture November 25. Instead, Cleaver chose to absent himself from the country rather than obey a court order that would have returned him to jail November 26, the day before Thanksgiving.

Eldridge had more than overwhelming nerve and intellect going for him. He had Kathleen. Her father, a diplomat, adheres to a more traditional political orientation, and was never reported to shout hallelujah when she married Eldridge. She refuses to be classified according to her background, looks, sex or whatever other yardsticks one might employ. Kathleen, who has seen a lot of the world and knew a couple of its languages by the time puberty was a recent memory, went from coed to a year of lying around listening to records, mostly in New York, to SNCC and meeting Eldridge.

On April 7, 1967, Kathleen saw Eldridge off to California, decided she wanted to be closer to him and got herself to California. On the eve of this anniversary, in 1968, Eldridge was shot, wounded, jailed and presumably put away for a long time to come. In the two months he was in jail, Kathleen came into her own as Communications Secretary of the Party. She dealt with the problems of keeping the Panther organization together and became involved in a political campaign that used the running of Huey, Bobby and herself for various legislatures, and Eldridge for President, as a platform from which to push the Panther Program. With Eldridge's release she became really heavy.

Kathleen managed to run a home (her husband liked to eat her cooking when he could), to be political (she had something to do with a black uprising at all-girl Mills College in Oakland), to write position papers for the Panthers, and to get pregnant. When Eldridge disappeared it was Kathleen who had to face and be followed by every brand of intelligence agent that had been invented. She just went on moving with a kind of light-headed intensity that, because of its arbitrary dips and turns, confused her watchers.

The Cleavers shared a life style based on a sense of personal freedom that was so intense as to liberate them from every societally programmed hangup that did not relate in positive terms to the ultimate liberation of humanity. When they took off to Algeria, the Black Panther Party lost immediate contact with two of the most important people it had attracted.

Both raced across the country, speaking, organizing, sometimes even relaxing, and always dispensing arguments, reasons and logic in support of universal liberation based in the black necessity for an end to racist oppression. All the while, they looked down the barrels of guns.

The Black Panther Party, that collective of profane poet prophets, with leadership of differing but complementary revolutionary styles, owes much of its character, drive and validity to Eldridge Cleaver.

Disharmony, the inability to get together for more productive purposes, is also an implication of Cleaver's history in the movement, and represents in microcosm the unhappiness that some segments of the community have with the Panthers.

There is, first, the question of politics. Blacks have always been indifferent to all brands of communism. In most instances there is no hostility involved; communism just hasn't turned on black folk. On a practical basis, blacks, probably most people, can be moved by programs designed to fit their needs, but not by ideological arguments.

The Panther Ten Point Program in many ways can be criticized because it is not as revolutionary as the Panthers would have it be. Harold Cruse suggests that Black revolution is handicapped by the fact that individuals and movements that have used the revolutionary tactics of confrontation have not actually had a revolutionary ideology around which people rally. Black revolutionists discovered the need for black self-determination before blacks determined that they had a need for a collective self, apart from this nation.

"The radical wing of the Negro movement in America sorely needs a social theory based on the living ingredients of Afro-American history. Without such a theory all talk of Black Power is meaningless. . . . He [the black] is so bedazzled by the personalities of his chosen leadership symbols that he cannot peer behind the façade and examine what were the political, economic, class, and cultural trends that influenced the actions of those chosen leaders." *

Panther social theory is subject to that criticism. The rejection of "cultural nationalism," coupled with the failure to develop a well worked out theoretical approach to black ideology and black seizure of economic gain, leaves the Panthers to struggle without a program which has extensions well beyond the obvious charisma of the present leadership. Much has been said about 400 years of slavery, but almost nothing has been done by the Panthers to make the lessons learnt during that history available to blacks seeking freedom. A unified theory of Black American history is sorely needed, and without it the Panther political effort will always be rooted in the immediate perceptions of the present, while utilizing ungainly adaptations of revolutionary rhetoric developed by Asians.

There have been black-based approaches to the economic problems, beginning with the Freedmans Bureau, and ending for the moment with the movement of the Muslims to buy large tracts of farmland in the South. Cleaver criticized Elijah Muhammad's approach to land. He noted that Muhammad was careful not to identify any specific geographical location when he called, "We must have some land of our own, or else!"

Eldridge said, ". . . there is something inadequate, something lacking in that particular slogan because in practice it impeded rather than enhanced movement. In the first place, it is merely a protest slogan; there is nothing revolutionary about it, because it is asking the oppressor to make a gift to black people. The oppressor is not about to give niggers a damn thing."

Cleaver's words were written before the Muslims actually began buying land. There is no argument about the appropriateness of revolutionary ideology in the recognition of the

---

* Harold Cruse, *The Crisis of the Negro Intellectual*, N.Y.: William Morrow and Company, 1967, pp. 557, 560.

need for land, but in reality, the Muslim quest for land, and the attendant difficulties they have experienced, is contributing toward the development of a revolutionary land-based consciousness among blacks.

In Alabama, Muslims bought over 1000 prime acres of farmland from a white automobile dealer who was a member in good standing of a local bigoted group. The move exposed one method of getting a bigot to serve blackness—appeal to his greed. The white man who sold them the land looked at his cracker ideology, counted the money that was offered him, and found his ideology wanting. His fellow crackers, including his own brother, then proceeded to burn out his business and run him out of the neighborhood.

Next, the Muslims moved in. They hired local people, including some whites, at rates higher than those generally paid. Almost immediately they were attacked. First, their cattle were poisoned. Next, the KKK bought farmland surrounding the Muslim spread and proceeded to patrol the fences with guns, and to trespass obviously, in a clear attempt to get the Muslims to react aggressively so that the race war could begin.

Instead, under the glare of nationwide TV, the Muslims announced that they would move away. A victory for the Klan? Hardly. The Muslims demonstrated to everyone, particularly crackers, that even the most hardened bigot can be softened up with money. Thus, local whites began eyeing each other, warily trying to estimate how much black money it would take to corrupt a neighbor's will to whiteness. More important, the Muslims brought home to thousands of rural blacks the real nature of their condition—that whites will band together to deny them any measure of self-improvement. Thus, Muslims are actually revolutionizing black southerners by indirectly appealing to what Eldridge described as a "deep land hunger in the heart of Afro-America," and showing them the extremes that whites will take in order to keep that hunger unsatisfied. Moreover, they did not move, and instead enlarged some of their land holdings.

The argument is not that the Muslims have a revolutionary ideology superior to that of the Panthers, but rather that they have placed themselves in a revolutionary position by applying a developed ideological approach to economics in a way that forces blacks to understand their political situation. Panthers have only succeeded in bringing about a recognition of the political significance of guns through demonstrating the oppressive role of police. Their programs, including breakfast for children and the free medical clinics they have established, are not quite so politically viable.

To be certain, they fill a need. But these programs do not go to the heart of black discontent, and in the absence of a program which can educate black people as to how free breakfasts and free medical attention fit into a total scheme for black liberation, the Panthers are involving themselves in nothing more than mild reform.

There is a large gap between a breakfast program and the development of black revolutionary ardor. Government authorities, even private enterprise, can, at a moment's notice, cancel all of the political implications of the Panther's social programs by simply putting in a few of their own. True, the Panthers can move on and develop other model programs, say educational ventures, a comprehensive system of free legal aid, or a Panther-inspired approach to the widespread rehabilitation of prisoners. These programs also can be co-opted, primarily because reformist programs, however much accompanied by political rhetoric, remain reforms, and as such are totally vulnerable to a takeover by a society well versed in the techniques of substituting small and symbolic gains for real social progress.

The Muslim land program, on the other hand, will hardly be taken over by government or private interests. The creation of real black wealth, a power base of land, is something alien to present concepts of government prerogative. Cleaver is right: the oppressor is not about to give niggers a damn thing, meaning that the struggle for land, with or without revolutionary rhetoric, will always be basic to the development of black revolutionary ideology.

Panthers have not been as active as they might be in bringing real power to the people. More precisely, they have not, as Panthers, involved themselves in programs designed by blacks to meet their needs. There is, for instance, an urban land question that repeatedly comes up in relation to urban redevelopment, freeway planning, and the condemnation of black-occupied land so that white-dominated institutions (hospitals, colleges, office buildings) can expand.

Education is also an issue. Point 5 of the Panther Party Platform and Program demands "education for our people that exposes the true nature of this decadent American society. We want education that teaches us our true history and our role in the present day society." The creation of BSU's was essentially the only move made by the Panthers in the educational field. And now they are unhappy about the direction which these organizations have taken. Small wonder. If there is to be a black revolutionary approach to education it must of necessity be developed where black people are.

White college campuses, the homes of BSU's, are not the place. These black students are effectively not a real part of the black community. They are isolated by the class implications of college attendance, as well as the ideological fact that the black community has not been educated to the value of the institution that is college for the betterment of their own lives.

A Panther effort to develop a black educational approach by revolutionizing black colleges, or joining with blacks in Oakland and trying to take over the Oakland public school system, makes more revolutionary sense. By joining with neighborhood groups who oppose urban development schemes, and bringing a revolutionary perspective to them, the Panthers would be on firmer ground. Redevelopment is of prime importance because black communities are constantly being shifted, broken up, or partially dismembered, without the consent of the residents.

An orientation that preaches firm resistance to the wholesale removal of blacks from urban centers which are developed by government fiat, and which joins with indigenous centers of that resistance, automatically helps blacks proceed to a revolutionary understanding. What it amounts to is that the vanguard has not yet devised an approach that has, as a priority, the merging of revolutionary organization with black-based programs of immediate concern.

This Panther isolation from programs meeting the needs of black people, as developed by nonideological blacks, extends even to their pet peeve, police departments. In San Francisco, the police community relations committees were taken over by right-wingers. In Richmond, the efforts of a black attorney to be elected to the Police Commission failed. Panthers, who have involved themselves in the symbolics of national elections, could have moved in total support of this attorney, with the objective of seizing the immediate power to affect police practices in Richmond.

There are other examples, but to list them would not add any more understanding about the ways in which Panthers have failed to mesh their programs with those of those blacks who in the course of struggling for a limited objective have developed a readiness for ordered and logical radicalization.

Because these essential links were not made, Panthers to a large extent became a spectator sport for black people. The big black revolutionary cats were applauded, denounced, sympathized with and evaluated from a distance. Their spectacular images caught the imagination of youth, but their inability to translate the Ten Point Program into a programmatic approach to the problems of black survival, as defined by blacks in the neighborhoods, made them appear as something that was not quite of the black community.

Their adoption of Marxist-Leninist political cant, along with the taking over of the Red Book, and their unspecific call for socialism, requires more development before it is actually applicable to the everyday black political situation. The Marxist approach to social stratification and class must be modified locally before it can be applied with any validity to black people. Recognizing that black people are in danger of genocide, and that blacks are politically and economically powerless, the concept of class struggle—particularly that portion that condemns the bourgeoisie—needs drastic modification in order to satisfactorily describe social class within the black community.

The black middle class differs drastically from its white counterpart. It has no power, even when it has status. Under these conditions, the Panther condemnation of most black middle-class people (as opposed to specific persons whose activities can be described as injurious to black liberation) becomes divisive rather than illuminating.

Cleaver himself ran into a tremendous amount of resistance to his leadership within the black community. He was blamed by a number of black revolutionaries for exacerbating the abrasive relations between groups. Eldridge showed up on the scene fresh from prison, made a few connections, and then proceeded to judge the revolutionary aptness of the approaches of people who had been around the area for some time. He may have been correct. The fact is, however, that organized revolutionary thought among blacks had not yet developed to the point where serious ideological differences should have led to bad feelings.

He successfully weathered the split that resulted from his forceful separating of what he considered revolutionary wheat from the chaff of cultural nationalism, at least as far as the Panthers were concerned. But he was then placed in the position of not having any contact with those blacks he had declared nonrevolutionaries, despite the fact that many of the Panthers did maintain their ties with the rejected blacks, and were, therefore, more sensitive than Cleaver to the developing subtleties of approach in non-Panther black revolutionary circles. Cleaver may very well have been reflecting his hurt at being separated from some black revolutionary intellectual circles in the Bay Area when, two years after the basic split between his version of the Panthers and other orientations, he unleashed, in *Ramparts*, a scathing denunciatory rehash of his personal disagreements with some of the individuals involved.

The intolerance for blacks who were not stamped out of the same revolutionary mold as the Panthers was shared by the entire Party leadership. However valid their approach, or their descriptions of non-Panther blacks, the truth is that the Panthers operated with the disadvantage of not having any substantial sympathetic base within the ranks of established black leadership, including those who were recognized as radical or even revolutionary.

There is, to be sure, substantial community support of the Panthers at this point in time. But it is not based on the proven correctness of Panther theoretical constructions, or on the mellowing of Panther condemnation of blacks outside their ranks. Even the Panther programs in the community did not create a tremendous amount of actual support. It was policemen and courts that did the trick. The wanton killing of Panthers, the obvious declaration of war by the massed forces of government, forced an approach to black solidarity which could not be developed by Panthers themselves.

The NAACP Legal Defense Fund announced its intentions of contributing to the defense of the New York Twenty-One. Black congressmen and black policemen in Chicago took radical positions in support of the Panthers following the killing of Fred Hampton and Mark Clark. Clergymen in Los Angeles mobilized behind the police attacks on Panther headquarters. In San Francisco, a group of black politicians negotiated with the Police Department to develop a scheme whereby they would operate as buffers between the police and the Panthers.

Even Nasser Shabazz, whom Cleaver had described as "a sneaky looking fellow," reversed his denunciation of the Panthers. The beginnings of some understanding between the two groups occurred in August, 1969, when the Panthers and the Black Guards engaged in a community meeting where their views of each other were aired. Shabazz left, still convinced that the Panthers were supported by Communist money and were much too cozy with whites. The Panthers also did not revise their opinions of the Black Guards, noting that the organization, while calling itself revolutionary, actually hired itself out to white businessmen as guards for the property whites owned in the ghetto. Shabazz nevertheless dropped his complaints and called for the black community to "come to the rescue" of the Panthers, after it became obvious that police were out to kill as many Panthers as they could.

Publisher Carleton Goodlet, who has been the target of attacks by the Panthers, and has tossed a number of insults in their direction, summed up the problem of black unity under a revolutionary banner in a speech delivered at a Huey Newton birthday rally February 15, 1970:

"The Black Panther Party is in serious trouble in USA-1970. All the paramilitary and military forces of racist America have been assigned the task of stamping out the Panthers. The infectious virus of Black Pantherism cannot be contained. If the entire membership of the Party were to be destroyed, tens of thousands more would rise up because they too would have been infected by the concept of Black Pantherism.

"Nevertheless, the fact remains: after three and a half years of struggle the Black Panther Party has succeeded in aligning against it all the forces of reaction. How well the Panthers have organized their oppressors is shown by the estimated twenty-eight fallen Party members and the quarter of a million dollars required in bail fees.

"On many occasions I have criticized your Party's rhetoric which often could be characterized as the trumpeting of an elephant while in reality your comparative strength in Fortress America is similar to the muscles of a mouse.

". . . We remind the Panthers that if jawboning and badmouthing would have liberated black people, we would have been liberated decades ago. . . ."

Goodlet was particularly critical of the Panther adoption of Marxism. "Two hundred and fifty years of slavery and one hundred and seven years of crypto-freedom, out of the black experience, contain enough suffering, pathos, agony and sacrifice for liberty to have developed a rhetoric which would have communicated with and united black America, rather than by its very nature as a Marxist ideology separated us. . . . Three and a half years of going it alone, setting yourself apart from ninety-nine-plus percent of American blacks, has led to your present precarious position. No revolution can succeed without the indivisible support of a total people."

His main point contained the dilemma which now faces Panther leadership as it seeks to further develop its programs and policies.

"Do you have in your limited ranks the skills, the capacity, the experience, the exposure to this technological society, sufficient to establish the Black Panthers alone as the leaders who will program and win the black revolution? One of our big arguments against 'The Man' has always been that we are not allowed to participate at the decision-making level. If we are now involved in a life and death struggle, it might be conceivable that no one segment of the black community has the right to make these serious decisions alone and without consultation. . . . Black America does not yield to the Black Panther ideology one bit when it comes to our demand for freedom, human dignity and self-determination. In freedom's struggle the question has always been to set the agenda and agree upon the timetable. Above all, the most important task in a revolution is for its important functionaries to remain alive and maintain mobility in the struggle. . . . The Black Panther Party must become a viable part of a broad coalition which amasses American Black physical, psychological and human resources in a united phalanx against oppression from the political, military and industrial complex—the true enemy. . . ."

There it is, the reality and challenge of Black Panther Party leadership. An amazing number of top leaders have been killed or are in jail. No movement can afford to pay those dues. These losses occurred within a political context that did not have a mechanism of replacing these leading figures with black converts of proven leadership from other organizations.

In the main, Panthers have developed their own leadership apart from the rest of black organizational efforts. This leadership, in turn, has brilliantly represented the Panthers, eloquently presented reasons for blacks to develop a revolutionary consciousness, and logically described the nature of the oppressive force that is well-policed America. They have not been so successful at analyzing the roots of hostility toward oppression that exists within the black community, and harnessing this hostility in an effective manner. This failure is directly due to the fact that Panthers could not develop a role for non-Panther blacks that could satisfactorily create bonds between themselves and the rest of the community.

There was some mutuality involved in this failure. Middle-class blacks, even those who might secretly sympathize with the Panthers, did not want to be publicly linked to those crazy niggers with guns. They were also ideologically unprepared to accept the term revolution as anything more radical than the revolution described by, and limited to, the increasing abandonment of docile black styles. The middle-class black revolutionary was willing to talk of black liberation, eager to identify himself with black assertiveness, but hardly prepared to conceive of himself as advocating the overthrow of the government, with or without violence.

The Panthers, on the other hand, had adopted Malcolm X's division of the race into "field niggers" and "house niggers." To be a house nigger was, if anything, worse than being a Tom. A Tom at least had a function, a role to play, a purpose. He could be perceived as acting in a political fashion in order to achieve certain goals.

The fact that these goals did not jibe with the wishes of black people, and were in many instances in opposition to those wishes, was to be expected. The house nigger, on the other hand, was a breed. His every act, in and out of politics, constituted a repudiation of his field-nigger heritage. Where the Tom was condemned for his acts, the house nigger was held in contempt for his very life style, his middle-classishness, his automatic reflection of white-inspired values.

The middle-class black could do no right, until and unless he allowed himself to be programmed by the Panthers. Few men, whether or not they deserve to be described as house niggers, could take this devastating assault on their psyches. As a result, they sidestepped even token representation in the revolution that was swirling around them. They went further in their nonactivity than avoiding the Panthers. These men effectively avoided any activity that smacked of political militance. They sought to avoid being falsely labeled as leaning toward the Panthers in style, and also did not wish to subject their militant mode to further Panther derision.

Much of the black middle class were ready to be recruited, however, as long as they could be gunless revolutionaries who were not forced to focus too closely on the fact that revolutionary activity invariably is directed toward the seizure of power. The Black United Front and the United Front Against Fascism attracted numbers of middle-class blacks who subsequently drifted away from these organizations precisely because there were no revolutionaries around to provide day-to-day middle-class revolutionary programming.

The debacle at Stanford, and at the May 22 cocktail party, might never have occurred had middle-class blacks been utilized. The Panthers had no business fund-raising. They were marked men, with little hope of remaining out of jail, whose consciousness was filled with the knowledge that their bail-bonded freedom might end with death. The intense emotional expressions of blacks have always been uncomfortable, if not abrasive, to whites—except of course, when that emotion is structured in song, literature or some other form of entertainment. Hilliard's grief was real, and too overwhelming

to be shared, absorbed and understood by people who viewed
the Panthers as news items, or at best as heroic victims of the
failure of America to come to grips with its imperfections.

Tom Hayden's presence only provided a specific target.
Had he not been there, there is every reason to believe that the
sound of laughter and conversation which drowned out Jean
Genêt's speech, or the sight of well-fed and allegedly well-
informed whites who persist in dealing with the events described by Panthers as abstract problems of bringing social
equity to America, or the delivering of comments by middle-
aged professionals sagely finding parallels in the communist
persecutions of the 40's or the McCarthy demagoguery of the
50's would have caused Hilliard to explode.

The Panthers need a buffer. Black middle-class would-be
revolutionaries, who, house nigger or no, have acquired social
skills less ruffling to the battered social consciousness of whites,
who perceive themselves as rebuffed supporters of black
political development, could have handled the situation while
still getting Hilliard's point across.

A more pressing need than a social buffer, however, is the
type of skills which middle-class blacks can bring to bear in
support of Panthers. The Party has been constantly under
attack because of its dependency on whites in critical areas.
There must be more potential for black legal support, black-
directed publicity efforts, and black development and articulation of revolutionary ideology than has been garnered by the
Panthers. As remarkably able as this leadership has been, the
Party has managed to generate more enthusiasm for its goals
and purposes among middle-class whites than middle-class
Negroes.

This form of integration lacks the capacity to convert
knowledge of the martyrdom of Panthers through death or
imprisonment into a contemporary form of history that has
meaning to blacks, and which gives purpose to their efforts.
When Bobby Seale entered that court in Chicago he should
have been surrounded by a phalanx of the best talent the

black community had to offer. They should have been there simply because the messianic mission that Panthers have accepted should have affected a broad spectrum of black legal expertise and inspired them to defend Bobby every step of the way. When black lawyers finally accept the challenge of defending the Panthers politically, they will begin a process that will either bring a judicial system free of institutional racism into being, or else determine for all time that justice for a black man is unavailable in America's courts.

Panther leaders, beginning with Huey, have repeatedly denied that they, or the Party, is racist or separatist. In one of his jailhouse interviews, Huey remarked that the Panthers were among the last integrationists. The difference between the Panther stance and that of integrationists who preceded them is the idea that blacks, as free men, should decide where, when, how and with whom this integration is to take place. The idea of a black plebiscite, in which blacks would determine their political future, does not do violence to the idea of integration. By developing the political muscle of the black community, however, the Panthers can help to make certain that integration does not become a substitute for absorption, amalgamation and ultimately cultural genocide.

Indeed, the Panthers' attempt at political integration has been less than successful, though they were equipped with what seems to be a correct view of American politics. Eldridge Cleaver was chided by officials of the California Peace and Freedom Party when he chose Jerry Rubin as his Vice-Presidential running mate, rather than one of the more doctrinaire leftists available to him. He was patronizingly described as ignorant of the significant trends in white radical politics. As it developed two years later, Rubin and his political orientation were closer to the center of white radical political activity than that of any of the gaggle of respectable leftists made available to Cleaver.

This political prescience is of little comfort to Panthers at this juncture. They see themselves as being maneuvered once again by whites intent on implementing a program that is only peripherally concerned with effectively eliminating racism. Seale's problems with Judge Hoffman, and the resulting inability of his co-defendants to challenge, at peril to themselves, the singling out of Bobby for unusual treatment, created a breach that is difficult to heal.

With Huey out of jail, a number of these problems may well be solved. He has had the benefit of twenty-two months of thought, and emerged from prison with an obvious determination to strengthen the Party. But now blacks have to settle for themselves whether they ever want to see Huey back in jail.

Judge Hoffman was also assigned the task of trying the Chicago Twelve, the Weathermen, who described themselves as a white vanguard orientation. None of them made the necessary preliminary court appearances, and all are underground. Panthers must compare their willingness to perform their vanguard function by submitting themselves to judgment by courts in which they had no confidence to the actions of their white counterparts, who disappeared.

Panthers must watch trial after trial take place involving their brothers in revolution, most of whom spend jail time waiting for a court date, while at the same time they see white revolutionary examples, such as Hayden, out on the streets.

Panthers are forced to balance the deaths of a few white revolutionaries, through what seems to be carelessness in handling explosives, with the death of black revolutionaries who never had the opportunity to contain or control the eruptions of police.

Under these circumstances, alliance with whites must suffer, Panther leadership must go underground, and the possibility that they have committed themselves and the rest of America's blacks to race war rather than revolution must weigh heavy on men who, in the last analysis, must return to the ghetto only to have shoved down their ideological throats the fact that Marx and Lenin were white.

V

The Race War

THE PANTHERS are in the middle of a race war for which their ten-point platform and program has not totally prepared them. While they are called racists by whites (some of them professed liberals), Panthers in turn attack other black revolutionaries as racist. In the meantime, Panthers have been killed by police, murdered by other blacks, and demeaned by ex-supporters for falling short of being supermen. It seems that the organization is having difficulty dealing with both the realities and the rhetoric of racial conflict, and has experienced setbacks as a result. Meanwhile, the pace of the war against people of color is stepped up.

Much of the Panthers' difficulty comes from taking an essentially courageous political stance, within a social framework which demands that decisions be made more and more along racial lines. They walk an ideological tightrope between the demand for black power and the ideal of people power, devoid of racism. Having adopted the slogan of "power to the people," they must at once attempt to secure revolutionary black power while forming alliances with whites seeking power through revolution. A politics based on the slogan "the enemy of my enemy is my friend" is tricky at best. Within the context of racial problems, class-war distinctions and clearly heavy-handed attempts to suppress the Party, their essential point concerning the need to cooperate with those who identify with the principles of the Party, regardless of color, is subject to misinterpretation, nonunderstanding, or just plain derision.

Panthers experience difficulty in clearly setting out their position partly because they spend a lot of time ducking bullets, but also because they operate in a rapidly shifting field of political alliances that finds them using the same rhetoric in different social and political situations with varying, and sometimes unpredictable, responses to their arguments.

To begin with, the architect of the Panther position regarding coalition with whites is Stokely Carmichael. He has never exhibited an interest in developing coalitions with white groups, though he has not repudiated his past pronouncements. He has denounced the Panthers as dogmatic, dictatorial and irresistibly seduced by a vision of revolutionary integration. Stokely, in turn, has been rejected by the Panthers, who accuse him of racism.

On the other hand, many whites who seek some form of alliance with Panthers are put off by their *de facto* rejection of whites, particularly in situations that seem conducive to mutual exchanges of information, opinions or tactics.

White radicals can understand and appreciate the Panther view of themselves as black liberation fighters, and seem willing to respect the Panther position that whites can have no voice in determining the posture or tactics of blacks in matters concerning blacks. They do grow uneasy when Panthers proceed to dictate the action whites should take in areas that do not seem to bear directly on black concerns. Some white disenchantment was perfectly obvious following the National Revolutionary Conference for a United Front against Fascism, held in Oakland in July, 1969.

Although the conference call clearly stated that the "primary objective will be community control of police to end fascism," the announced program listed several workshops that would be held covering a variety of subjects. Actually, there were no workshops, relatively little real exchange of ideas, a preponderance of whites, an almost total withdrawal by Panthers from any activity with whites (other than sharing the speakers' platform), and total control of the flow of the conference by Panthers. A United Front was formed at the conclusion of the conference.

It is difficult for observers to differentiate the domineering style of the Panthers, relative to whites, from that arrogant behavior dubbed racist with which earlier generations of whites controlled Negro participants in white-dominated freedom movements. Panther attitudes probably do not reflect racism. The leadership repeatedly rejects racial bigotry, and often when speaking to all-black audiences points out those racist attitudes that should be resisted. Panthers do not use a vocabulary that implies racism. They invoke hatred for the pig, identify with the class war, and condemn capitalism and imperialism, usually by pointing out how racism is an inevitable product of these orientations.

Moreover, Panthers are quite frank about the racial rules of the game they play. Blacks organize in black communities, whites organize in white communities, and both unite around issues upon which they can agree, and which have been developed in the separate organizational efforts.

Under these conditions Panthers define, at the outset, the area of mutual agreement that can lead to cooperation. Their seemingly overwhelming arrogance toward whites, then, is probably more a function of their belief that they are the vanguard, and therefore possessed of the truth, than a tendency to structure a situation favorable to the airing of their racial hatreds.

But there is a very apparent aspect of Panther behavior that does have racist overtones. Youth recruited into the Panthers joined, for the most part, with the belief that one day it will be necessary to go down against the man. Many of them viewed the statements of their leaders disavowing racism as a politic effort to keep a cool public image. An angry black youth accepting a role in the revolutionary politics of liberation knows that when the shooting begins his target will inevitably be white. His attitude during the prelude to armed revolution is partially formed around the idea that there is no law made by whites which black people are bound to respect. The subtleties of this position, including the observation that most white-made laws operate to the disadvantage of blacks, are not lost on these youths. They tend to extend this definition to include bourgeois customs regarding etiquette, social dialogue, and equalitarian-sounding phrases as part of white tricknology. "Get Whitey," was the ambition, and it followed that a "good white" represented a contradiction in terms.

The establishment of a politics of coalition with whites did little to curb the racial misunderstanding of most youthful party members. They assumed that the talk of coalition was simply a cover-up for the real phenomenon—the use of the rhetoric of revolution to foster dissension within the white community.

The idea was to get whitey to fight in his own community, thus freeing blacks to conduct their own war of liberation against a weakened and seriously divided white America.

Much of the subject matter of political-education classes in the Party deals with correcting racist attitudes. They have attempted to counter the somewhat natural tendency of young and hostile blacks to lump all whites in the same ideological bag. The effort is not totally successful, primarily because there is an element of divide-and-conquer in Panther tactics which can accommodate the view that whites should be exploited politically by being maneuvered into a position of viewing other whites as enemies.

Actually, to speculate about possible racism among the Panthers is to invite a tremendous amount of confusion. Even in defining their enemy as a capitalist, or a member of the ruling class, or a pig, Panthers know that their adversary is white. The most dominant environmental fact of black existence is the inability to define their own destiny because of whites who fashion the parameters of black life. Racism is at best an inexact term that most often describes the willingness of a society to concentrate the evils within it among an easily identifiable group. When blacks move to better their condition they are stuck with the racial distinctions that made their lives less than ideal. What can be said about the Panthers is that they are preparing blacks to take an active role in a race war, if that necessity ever becomes evident. And evidence that blacks have been losing the race war for a long time is all too depressingly clear.

Very possibly the beginnings of our present racial hassles are to be found in the three-century effort of Europeans to get the Moors off the Iberian peninsula. The Crusades are often presented as an extreme example of the determination of European Christendom to return the holy land to the rule of the cross. From the perspective of some black commentators on history, the Crusades represent little more than a series of retaliatory attacks against a darker people who exhibited the effrontery to violate white-owned soil. True, this view represents an oversimplification of the issues involved. The truth is, however, that the religious issues involved in the Crusades automatically carried racial overtones along with them.

Arnold Toynbee, in remarking on the development of racism in Europe,* points out that medieval painters, who normally included a black person among the Magi, gradually changed the racial identity of these gentlemen so that Christ was ultimately attended by three wise men who were white. A minor point, but one that has major implications.

---

* Arnold Toynbee, *A Study of History*, Oxford University Press, 1962, p. 224. Toynbee himself made modern contributions to the elimination of blacks from history. While specifically denouncing European racism, he contributes to its perpetuation by insisting that blacks have not had any part in forming or helping to form civilizations as we understand them.

The elimination of blacks from the cultural history of Europe is just one step removed from separating blacks from their own history. An intriguing aspect of this tendency is the fact that American students are taught a great deal about the history of European wars, but seldom about the Moorish invasion of Europe, which actually contributed a great deal more to European history and culture than a few buildings in Spain.

It was the Europeans who actually developed the concept of race, and who equated their accomplishments with their assumed racial superiority. Ethnicity has always been highly regarded among Europeans, and until fairly recently their racial classifications (with accompanying implications of superiority) divided European whites into racial hierarchies. People colored differently didn't stand a chance of faring better at the hands of racistly oriented people who managed to make something of importance out of differences which most non-whites cannot detect.

Toynbee shares with other historians the idea that the development of protestantism in Europe, with its emphasis on individual superiority, further helped establish European racial practices. But he doesn't mention that racism reached its full potential when Europeans began taking over the world.

Soldiers conquered, missionaries brought their own versions of why non-whites should accept a white god, and also why they should prove themselves true Christians by not fighting the man that bleeds them. Mining executives satisfied themselves that natives had no real appreciation of the way mineral resources could be used, theologians began to argue (sometime around the time of the slave trade) that black people did not really have souls, and all the while they congratulated themselves and each other on the marvelous discoveries they had made. Imagine, nothing went on in the world until Europeans discovered it—a fact they almost made stick.

The idea that whites have been systematically conducting a

race war has not been enthusiastically accepted by most people. Blacks are not most people, and even they want to reject the idea that they have been selected for genocide.

Panthers differ from other blacks only to the extent that whites attacking Panthers dream up reasons for persecuting them that they do not use toward the ordinary black. But Panthers, except for the outsized publicity devoted to their difficulties, are only the latest targets in the steadily escalating war that is being waged against blacks. They deserve to be judged only by their peers—people who can appreciate the fact that institutionalized racism must, in the long run, express itself by destroying black people.

Increased social action on the part of blacks has increased direct attacks on their persons. More significantly, these attacks come from official sources: police, national guardsmen, and sometimes the army. Proponents of the backlash theories see cause and effect in city riots and increased police repression. There is another possibility, primarily that the social consciousness of blacks has reached a level that makes nonviolent control of Negroes passé. The conclusions of the Kerner report are inaccurate in at least one respect: The nation is not moving toward two societies, one white and one black; it has always been organized this way. Moreover, blacks have never had the opportunity, however law-abiding they might have been, to secure for themselves the right to control their own affairs. The inability to establish a measure of self-determination, coupled with repeated attempts to secure it, led people into the street in 1965 when Watts exploded.

Detroit, Rochester, and a hundred other cities erupted soon after, and everyone described the incidents as riots. Riots, of course, are considered to be irrational mob exercises. These are precisely the terms that were used to describe the race riots in Chicago, when turn-of-the-century light standards were decorated with the bodies of hanging Negroes. Also, the lynch mobs, the KKK-conducted executions, and the excesses of southern bully boys attacking well-disciplined nonviolent protesters were also classed as riots—senseless, nonproductive and without support of the larger mass of respectable people. These earlier riots in our history did have purpose. They were nothing more than the white citizenry proclaiming itself capable of controlling black people.

Black rioting was something else again. Blacks did not go out of their communities, did not begin by attacking people, and could point to conditions which made riot a more attractive alternative than doing nothing to protest the racism constricting their lives.

Nonviolent protest earned blacks the right to vote in the south, but not the right to vote for someone or something that could make their lives more livable. They won the right to eat in restaurants they could not afford, take unsegregated trips on trains running between bigoted towns, and hold properly de-powered public office. These well-thought-of, and widely publicized, victories did nothing to change the lives of blacks. In fact, black unemployment went up, black income, while increasing, could not catch up with white income, and the black poor proliferated, grew angrier, began to organize, and thereby earned for themselves increased policing.

In March, 1968, Tennessee blacks, some of whom were organized by Martin Luther King, sent protests to the National Guard Bureau in Washington, Governor Ellington of Tennessee, and Mayor Briley of Nashville. They were upset because the National Guard had chosen several black communities in Tennessee, including the North Nashville section, in which to conduct riot-control maneuvers. The mayor was never heard from, Washington notified blacks that the scheduling of Guard training was left to the judgment of state officials, and Governor Ellington said, "Martin Luther King is training 3000 people to start riots, and when we say we are going to train the Guard to protect the lives of people and their property, there is a big hullabaloo about it."

On April 1, 1968, Martin Luther King predicted that a

fascist state would arise in America by 1970 if Congress did not do more for the poor. On April 5, Stokely Carmichael announced, from the police-filled city of New York, "We must avenge the death of Dr. King." On April 6, the maneuvers of Oakland, Berkeley and Emeryville cops killed Bobby Hutton and started Eldridge Cleaver on his journey into revolutionary exile. The race war was being intensified.

National Guardsmen, under pretext of looking for forty-six rifles, had already marched into an all-black housing project in Plainfield, New Jersey. All were armed, some with .45's and others with carbines. They overturned furniture, spilled belongings on the floor and then trampled over them to get to the next living unit. When questioned about it, the anglo-arrogant commander of the unit insisted that the blacks had destroyed their own belongings just to get on television.

It was in July, 1967, that two white girls were beaten and three unarmed black men killed in Detroit's Algiers Motel. Huey was ripped off in October.

By August, 1968, official killings were commonplace, and seven Miami blacks lost their lives, lending excitement to the otherwise plastic Republican Party presidential nomination convention. No particular notice was taken of these deaths. Blacks usually die quietly, and not all from gunshot wounds.

This official violence did not represent a new policy; rather it demonstrated the capacity of American government to meet a crisis.

The Kerner Report conservatively set the 1967 black riot-connected death rate at 87, with most of those deaths dealt out by peace officers. They documented the racist nature of riot control in Newark in a footnote:

"The damage caused within a few hours early Sunday morning, July 16, to a large number of stores marked with 'Soul' signs to depict non-white ownership and located in a limited area reflects a pattern of police action for which there is no possible justification. Testimony strongly suggests that

State Police elements were mainly responsible with some participation by National Guardsmen." *

The armed forces (and when it comes to riots, the Pentagon directs the show and gives orders to every troop from five-star general to fallen-arches traffic cop) are being deployed against black people, and are not being restrained in the expression of their racial bias. That's war on a most elemental level.

In theory, blacks, perhaps some Panthers, are racist and, therefore, are pushing for a race war. There is an acceptance of the fact that black anti-Semitism is reaching new heights. Both Jews and non-Jews are busy deploring the fact of black racism, particularly as it applies to Jews. Jews, it is pointed out, have suffered for six thousand years, a record that makes blacks newcomers to the bigotry ball game. Moreover, they were slaughtered by the millions just a generation ago, a trauma that makes Jews fearful of Nazism in any form, black or white.

From there it follows that the increasing sound of black anti-Semitism heralds for Jews the direction from whence might come their next racial antagonist. They have lots to point to. There is the long-standing open put-down of Israel by the Muslims, all of whom are pulling for Egypt in her frequent and unequal battles with the smaller and whiter nation. And then, there is the alleged harassment of Jewish businessmen, who find their commercial lot in the ghetto seemingly encircled by black-tinged hostility. Comes a riot, his shop is invariably hit. In New York, there was an open breach between blacks seeking control of local schools and the Jewish-dominated UFT. At almost the same time, the Metropolitan Museum of Art, exhibiting an essay accompanying the photo-exhibit "Harlem on My Mind," found itself accused of running an exhibit that masqueraded black anti-Semitic attitudes as art.

* Governor's Select Commission of Civil Disorders of the State of New Jersey, *Report for Action*, February, 1968, p. 304.

New York has been particularly sensitive to black-Jewish antagonisms, primarily because so many of each group have an opportunity to have contact with each other.

At Queens College a number of Jewish students, angered at what seemed to them to be the impending domination of the campus by anti-Jewish black militants, actually formed groups to do physical battle with blacks. A more formal organization, the Jewish Defense League, has taken a self-defense posture toward blacks and clearly state their intention of repelling black aggressiveness toward Jews. About thirty members of the league stood by police barricades set up outside Temple Emanu-El in May, 1969. Helmeted and carrying clubs, the members of the league were preparing to defend a synagogue in response to the rumor that James Forman would appear and repeat the claim for reparations that had been made to Protestant churches. Forman didn't show.

Anti-Semitism does come in handy for hostile blacks. For one thing, WASPs tend to get monumentally insulted when a black accuses them of being Jewish. The black involved may or may not know better. Most often, he's translating an anti-white bias into terms that put down Jews.

But there is a measure of black anti-Semitism, and one should place it in perspective. Jews play a special role in the Negro community. Communists, radicals, liberals, philanthropists, fighters for Negro rights and proponents of black causes have always included a goodly number of Jews. Moreover, Jews could always explain to blacks, in contemporary terms, that they too have suffered and that blacks, however ill treated, did not have to look at the recent past and mourn for six million of their brethren.

Unfortunately, that argument fosters hostility in blacks more often than it leads to understanding. The truth is that blacks expect more of Jews. They fail to understand how people who have known genocide can tolerate the development of conditions which would possibly lead to the demise of blacks. Blacks also are convinced that if Jews can still identify with the mass of whites, even though they are intensely aware of the six thousand years of Jewish wanderings, that the Jewish adjustment to potentially oppressive practices constitutes a menace to blacks.

Jews are second-class whites, and whether they want to hear it or not, the threat of anti-Semitism is immeasurably greater coming from the white community than from the black. Anti-Semitic whites have both numbers and power, a fact which helps to explain why Jews, with or without money, are limited in the number of places to which they can aspire in this society. Essentially, they are the Uncle Toms of the oppressed. What they should have learned from Germany was that Jews, who thought of themselves as Germans first and Jews second, even during the time that specific racial laws were being passed, volunteered for genocide. They could not believe, they did not resist, and one day there were six million atrocity stories.

Some of that slaughter can be directly attributed to American racism, for there was a time, before the ovens went into operation, when thousands of Jews could have been saved if America had offered refuge to some of Germany's racially oppressed.

They did not, and the rest is history, a lesson that should not need repeating. These white anti-Semites are also against blacks. They are the ones who find security in the warm relations between the United States and Rhodesia or South Africa, and who feel comfortable with the fact that America has openly supported every right-wing racist dictatorship that ever existed, as long as it made proper anticommunist noises.

There is only one fault with the observation that blacks constitute ten percent of the nation, and are therefore not in a position to successfully carry out a revolution which ultimately involves the use of arms. It is a racist construction. Those who extend the argument assume that, given sufficient black bellicosity, the nation will of necessity divide along race lines and take care of those non-whites who hate them. Those non-whites who are crying for revolution are insisting that whites have just as much reason to fight bigotry as blacks, in fact more. Blacks recognize, by virtue of their very low status in the country, that the fact of racial division is a weapon in the hands of a bigot. It forces people to interpret the behavior of blacks as threatening, rather than assume that conditions exist which should inspire any normal person to vigorous protest.

The theoretical position of the Panthers is, therefore, that racism in the hands of a class-conscious, capitalistic population becomes a weapon of control. They reject the idea of forming organizations which are philosophically committed to an idea of brotherhood which makes race irrelevant. Race, they insist, is a basic fact of our society.

Since racism is completely a part of the normal fabric of the society, all efforts to restructure the society must take into account the effects of racism on the populace and develop techniques to combat these effects. In developing these techniques it is becoming clear that some of them had best be military.

The 1968 Louis Harris Survey indicated that there were guns in 54 percent of American homes before Martin Luther King was shot. Since there are more whites than blacks, and further since whites control much more of the money to buy guns than blacks, there is little question that an outsized proportion of those guns are in white hands. If white backlash has any meaning it can be found in the reported statistic that gun ownership in the United States increased by 25 percent in the two-year period ending December, 1967, corresponding to the two years of black urban explosions, none of which were directed against the white community.

Guns aren't the only thing whites own. The governor of Georgia, Lester Maddox, prompted an increase in ax handle production when he was passing them out by the gross to whites who wanted to help him deny Negroes the right to eat in his restaurant. He went to Washington, D.C., and passed the ax handles out on the Capitol steps and in the Capitol restaurant. Minutemen arms caches have turned up all kinds of exotic equipment from fancy tear gas to heat-sensing rifle scopes to howitzers. In Cicero, Illinois, two men were arrested after sending arrows from a crossbow into a church-run coffeehouse. The arrows were stamped with a "Minutemen" inscription, and indicate the dedication that some people bring to the gathering of weapons.

In Cairo, Illinois, a right-wing group called the White Hats acted as an armed vigilante organization to keep blacks in line. The organization was officially known as the Cairo Committee of Ten Million, a somewhat pretentious name for a group originating in a city of fifteen hundred. They patrolled Cairo streets with dogs, used two-way radios in their cars, and apparently had the cooperation of the city police. Chief of Police Carl J. Clutts, who resigned after months of open warfare between blacks and whites, claimed that the group was formed for "any disaster where they could help." Evidently the disaster for which the White Hats were best prepared was that of blacks asserting their rights.

Panthers must be considered the prime targets in a race war, primarily because they have become the symbol of black assertiveness. The moment their rhetoric became belligerent, all of the states' institutions went to work in the attempt to discredit, disarm, eliminate and tame the Panthers.

Panther plots were discovered all over the country. In New York, Panthers were accused of planning to bomb department stores and botanical gardens. A bizarre murder charge came out of Hartford, Connecticut. Illinois Panthers had their offices raided on several occasions by different groups of law officers. In October, 1969, the entire Illinois office was destroyed by law enforcement officials who claimed that Panthers had been sniping at them from the roof of the building where their offices were housed. Imagine—a group with enough sophistication and political know-how to build a nationwide organization in the period of a couple of years could not develop a sense of tactic sufficiently refined to avoid shooting at policemen from their own headquarters.

Official sanction for Panther-hunting comes down right from the top. Congressional internal-security committees have found the black militant orientation to be dangerous to the country. J. Edgar Hoover himself has stated on repeated occasions that black nationalist groups (the Panthers in particular) constitute a serious threat to internal security. With such august backing, all that is necessary is that citizens, police, National Guardsmen, or anyone interested in the suppression of subversion identify a Panther, discover a Panther plot, and act patriotically. Bad niggers are un-American, and Panther-watching has become a favorite sport.

The first and most significant incident arising out of Panther-watching occurred October 28, 1967. "I've stopped a Panther vehicle," said a message radioed to Oakland Police headquarters by Patrolman John Frey. Fifteen minutes later, John Frey was fatally wounded, Huey Newton was on his way to a hospital with a bullet in his abdomen and Robert Heanes, the officer who answered Frey's call for assistance, was headed toward another hospital with two bullets in him, one in his right arm.

Newton was released on $50,000 appeal bail after serving twenty-two months of a two-to-fifteen-year term for manslaughter. His conviction, apparently a compromise, is viewed by blacks as one of the items which describe the parameters of racism. Panthers insist that the Newton incident was one which clearly demonstrated the willingness of the society to quiet revolutionary blacks by force.

Frey's death represented the first on-duty killing of an Oakland police officer in twenty years. How Newton got into a position to break this record is one of the mysteries of the case, as Oakland police have developed techniques to avoid the sudden embarrassment and loss of pay that accompanies getting shot and killed. Obviously, the ability to identify a car driven by a Panther was the first step in self-protection for police.

Inspector Roland Forte, of the Oakland Police Department, revealed in an interview the day after the shooting that the Intelligence Unit was aware of the license numbers of all cars driven by Panthers, and that a back-up procedure had been instituted to eliminate the possibility of an officer finding himself alone, facing an armed and hostile Panther.

Blacks who have been arrested in Oakland say that as a matter of routine, and before any information is exchanged, police spread-eagle them against a car or a wall, and carry out a thorough search for weapons.

Officer Robert Heanes, who came to back up Frey, implied that he was ignorant of the search procedures usually followed by Oakland police, as well as being unaware of the intelligence reports dealing with the identity of Panthers. Officer Robert Fredericks, who arrested Newton at the hospital, testified before a Grand Jury that "I observed a male Negro that I knew as Huey Newton lying on the movable gurney in the emergency room."

But Frey, who asked for help because he was stopping a Panther vehicle, and Heanes, who answered the call, supposedly did not recognize Newton, and had accepted a driver's license indicating that he was LaVerne Williams. This intelligence is somewhat suspect because LaVerne Williams, the owner of the car, was Huey Newton's girl friend. To accept the license from Huey as his own, the officers would have to have overlooked the F (for Female) which is prominently displayed on the license.

Huey was arrested, reportedly after volunteering his real name to Officer Heanes. John Frey arrested him, however, allegedly for refusing to identify himself and for giving false information to an officer. It was also Frey who directed Huey to walk from the front of the car he had been driving, past Frey's vehicle, and almost to the back of Heanes' patrol car. It was at this point that Newton was supposed to have suddenly spun around, grappled with Frey and also presumably shot at Heanes.

To further complicate matters, Newton had been accompanied by a man who disappeared after the shooting. Heanes testified that this unidentified male was standing to his left when the shooting started. In the midst of what must have been a hail of bullets Heanes was supposed to have looked toward the mystery man, who in turn responded to this official inspection by standing in the rain of flack and raising his hands. Apparently, this demonstrates that even a Panther will risk being shot and will quietly surrender when confronted with the stern glance of the law.

Prior to being arrested, Huey Newton had been a most unpopular figure with the Oakland Police Department. The attempt to arrest him, however, was somehow mishandled, resulting in the canonization of a black liberation fighter. The theory that police seem to be operating under is that militant black leadership must be identified and isolated, generally behind bars. And, where that cannot be accomplished, a few blacks ought to get shot. This is a pattern that is obvious when it comes to Panthers, and the accompanying shooting and attempts to isolate are engaged in by police, on and off duty, along with an occasional private citizen and with the full support of the institutions, particularly the courts. The most racist aspect of the move to handicap Panthers are the simplistic and rabble-rousing motives assigned to Panthers, which serve as excuses for police to act.

Bobby Seale was arrested in February, 1968, and charged with conspiring to murder someone who was never identified. Evidence of this conspiracy was supposedly uncovered by listening through a door. There might have been some connection in the fact that just a week before this arrest the Panthers had raised over $9000 at a fund-raising rally in Oakland. During that week over twenty-four Panthers were jailed and charged with various and sundry crimes. The charges were dropped soon after bail was posted, and the aggregate amount of the bail pretty much accounted for the $9000.

The arrests not only harassed Panthers, but also fit in with the economic racism that exists by denying black people the right to hang onto money. Essentially, the bail bond system discriminates against the poor, who do not have the funds to afford to post a cash bond. More directly, it discriminates against Negroes, primarily because they are arrested and charged with crimes out of proportion to their presence in the population. With the Panthers it has been used as a political tool.

After the long battle to release Huey Newton, it developed that no bail bondsman was willing to put up the money for the excessively handsome fee they usually extract. Huey was released only because his attorneys bailed him out with cash from their law firm's bank account.

After Bobby Seale's arrest, Newton issued an order from his jail cell.* Black Panthers, under threat of lifetime expulsion from the Party, were ordered to secure guns and to use them against any and everybody who attempted to come into the home of a Panther without benefit of an invitation or a search warrant. Newton pointed out that the infamous St. Valentine's Day massacre occurred because hoodlums obtained entry into private premises by disguising themselves as policemen. The only way to tell the difference, he reasoned, was to respond to actions. Everyone, in or out of uniform, who acted like a hoodlum was to be considered one.

Most of the white community, and all top-level military men, fail to recognize that the Panther message is directed to blacks and seeks responses only from blacks.

Remarks that are calculated to affect a white audience also often have "for black only" components. Included in this category are the more harsh and hostile statements about whites that are more often limited to conversations between

* See Appendix D—Executive Order #3.

blacks. Any black, at this stage of the political development of the ghetto, who would lay a claim to militant or revolutionary leadership, must of necessity publicly direct toward whites a measure of the hostility that exists within the community.

This need to seek legitimacy within the black community by being openly hostile to white power represents both an emerging black style, and psychological preparation for the time when blacks might find it necessary to act out some of these aggressive convictions. But extreme-sounding statements do not necessarily define a black person as an extremist. Moreover, the classification of responsible Negro vs. irresponsible Negro has meaning only to whites, who have a terrible need to classify superficial behavior as having in-depth meaning.

The Uncle Tom of old has pretty much left the scene, primarily because his obsequious manner raises anger in the blacks he purports to represent. The Uncle Tom function still remains, but it has been taken over by a new breed of Toms, individuals who can manage to sound militant while acting according to the same old "white is right" script. Actually, Uncle Tom was never totally the white man's boy. However misguided, his bowing, scraping and bootlicking often hid his hostility, an emotion which was satisfied by maneuvering some white with power into doing what Uncle Tom wanted him to do.

Many of the blacks who loudly brand Panthers as extremists or troublemakers are actually more hostile (not to mention more bigoted) toward whites than all black militants and revolutionaries combined. Their protestations seem to be inspired by an intense reluctance to expose themselves and their true feelings to the weight of white disapproval. This became obvious at an all-black meeting held in Oakland in March, 1968, presided over by Stokely Carmichael. The occasion was Stokely's attempt to build a Black United Front. His eloquent pleas for black unity were often interrupted by cries of "Kill! Kill!" mouthed by middle-class Negroes, some of whom had been chosen to administer poverty programs, federal and state agencies, and black self-help operations.

In the anonymity of an all-black forum it was these pillars of community who came out with emotion-laden proposals for black people to embark on a campaign of destruction. This is the kind of thinking that police prefer to believe goes on in the Panther inner circle.

The variety of stereotypes held by police regarding criminal types, coupled with their tendency to concoct explanations to account for their actions, are prominent aspects of the Bobby Hutton killing. The Oakland Police Department claims that the Panthers deliberately attempted to ambush two patrolmen. That proposition only makes sense if one is willing to accept Panthers as totally irrational people who have no regard for their own lives, and who further act with a total lack of responsibility toward the program they articulate to blacks.

It also presumes that Panthers have nothing to do with their time but lie in wait on an obscure ghetto street, on the off chance that an unsuspecting policeman might happen by. Bobby was killed during a week when Panthers actively began to suspect that there was an informer in their midst. Law enforcement people seemed incredibly knowledgeable about Panther whereabouts. A few days before the killing, a church where Panthers were holding a meeting was raided immediately after a handgun had been exhibited by a person who was not authorized by the Panthers to carry a gun, and who was considered a potential traitor.

A similar raid occurred in Detroit a year later during a Republic of New Africa meeting at Detroit's AME Church. In that incident police shot into the church wounding six or more people. Then they arrested more than a hundred people, claiming that police had been fired upon as they tried to enter the church. Two policemen were shot in this incident, one fatally.

Apparently, there had been a scuffle between blacks and police after patrolmen Michael Czapski and Richard Worobeck stopped Negroes they thought were carrying guns into the church. Czapski was shot seven times in the head and chest and killed, and Worobeck was wounded in the back and right leg. No clear connection was made between the group stopped by the officers and the people in the church. The evidence was sufficiently flimsy to prompt a black judge, George Crockett, to carry on an impromptu hearing at the police station, and to release 101 prisoners on the basis that the police description of the incident did not include proof that would link the members of the Republic of New Africa with the killings.

The raids are part of a pattern which finds police, supposedly involved in crime prevention, predicting, on the basis of police fears, where and when black insurrectionists will assemble. It seems clear that there is a national commitment to keep blacks in the place reserved for them and at the same time to frighten churches and churchmen back into the old familiar role of conservative, establishment-oriented institutions. By raising the specter of armed black revolt, the military avoids having to deal with whether or not such a revolt is justified, or even whether it exists at this time.

Panther and police versions of the April 6 shoot-out vary considerably. There are some commonly accepted facts, however, which help to suggest that the Panthers were the victims of police repression, racism and the desire to make examples of bad niggers.

The shoot-out occurred two days after the murder of Martin Luther King. Oakland was tense, and many sources credit the Panthers, particularly Cleaver, with calming black youth both in the neighborhoods and at predominantly black high schools in Oakland. Huey Newton, then in jail, had just announced that the name of the party had been changed from the Black Panther Party for Self Defense to The Black Panther Party, in order to emphasize the political nature of the Party.

In less than six months the Party had formed a liaison with SNCC, established a working relationship with the Bay Area's white radical community, begun publishing a newspaper regularly, and had gone through the mechanics necessary to run candidates for office, including Huey, Bobby Seale, and both Cleavers.

Ambushing police was foreign to the message Panthers preached to ghetto dwellers. The cry for armed self-defense was not a call for attacking policemen, but rather a device for organizing blacks around the concept of the sanctity of their homes. "We're not ready, we've got to get our shit together," was the standard response to the youngster advocating, "Burn now." Even when talking of a time when everything would be together, Panthers did not advocate a move to the barricades. "Think political," they demanded, and political action, unorthodox perhaps but political nonetheless, characterized most moves made by the Panthers.

An ambush would have hurt their image in the ghetto. Panthers could have justified Huey Newton shooting at two policemen in self-defense, if that justification ever became necessary. They could never convince Negroes that lying in wait for a police officer was anything other than criminal. Panthers seek approval first and foremost from the black community, and despite their angry rhetoric must limit their actions to those which less-revolutionary blacks can accommodate, appreciate and support.

More directly, the Panthers were not in a position to threaten their own leadership. Huey Newton had been locked up for six months and Bobby Seale was walking around with pending multiple felony charges. Dave Hilliard was still developing his potential for leadership, D.C. was busy overhauling office practices and procedures, and the rest of the party, including Kathleen Cleaver, was busy circulating petitions, making political speeches and trying to organize the community to recognize the absolute lack of black representation at all levels of government.

Eldridge was experiencing some difficulty in getting his parole officer to consider Panther activity as evidence of having been rehabilitated. He accommodated his parole officer by sticking to the letter of the law. His first book, *Soul on Ice*, had been released in March and was generally enjoying good reviews. He had recently been married, had hit his stride as a writer and as a public figure and seemed to be avoiding a return to jail or an introduction to death.

Cleaver filed an affidavit following his arrest claiming that the Panthers had been fired upon. What actually happened may never be known, despite the pile of testimony, statements, repudiated confessions, fleeting impressions and eyewitness accounts of the shoot-out. Six of the eight Panthers arrested were in custody before the real shooting occurred. Moreover, police, who managed to effect most of the arrests within minutes after the first shot rang out, were present in sufficient numbers to circle and search four square blocks.

Terry Cotton and Donnell Lankford were arrested at curbside by Officers Roy Hooper and Angelo Cannizzaro, who responded to a 904B radio call (emergency, officer in trouble) with such speed that the two Panthers did not have time to leave the scene. The policemen testified that when the sound of gunfire could be heard they discovered two Negroes crouched in parked cars who turned out to be Lankford and Cotton. Hooper said he handcuffed both men, after searching them. He then investigated the damaged police vehicle, parked in the center of the street, from where the emergency call presumably originated. He saw Officer Jensen there, wounded and lying on the seat of the patrol car. Jensen's service revolver was on the floor of the car.

Hooper left Jensen in the car and followed a trail of shotgun shells around the corner. He found a rifle on the ground, picked it up and then noticed a hedge moving. Behind the hedge was Warren Wells, who had been shot in the leg.

Oakland police officers Nolan Darnell and Richard Jensen were reported to be the intended victims of the Panther ambush. They said that at about 9 P.M. after turning onto Union and 28th Streets, they noticed a man (presumably Eldridge

Cleaver) ducking behind a Ford with Florida license plates. Darnell said that as he stepped out of the car to investigate, he was shot, causing him to fall to the ground. He then crawled back to his vehicle through a barrage of bullets.

Approximately 45 seconds after the firing stopped he put in a call for help. Darnell then noticed two men heading toward 28th Street. He took aim and fired, noting that he had wounded one suspect. Either it was Wells that Darnell shot or else someone, with a bullet in him, managed to get away from the scene. Cleaver, Hutton and Wells were the only Panthers reported as having been wounded in the action.

Officer Jensen also reported that the initial investigation was prompted by seeing Cleaver hiding behind an auto. He said that as the patrol car stopped in the middle of the street it was passed by a carload of blacks heading toward 29th Street, the same direction that the patrol car was moving. Jensen said that the first gunshots came from this car, at almost zero range. He was only superficially wounded, however, and had the distinction of being the only witness who saw the mystery auto.

Another officer, Daniel Lewis, arrested three more Panthers at 1267 30th Street. The owner of the house, Mr. Taylor Jackson, heard shots ring out at about 9 P.M., looked through his window, and saw four armed men running across the street. As he was telling passing officers about the men, his children notified him that three men were in the house. Officer Lewis entered and arrested John Scott, looked under a bed and pulled out Charles Bursey, and then went outside and found Wendell Wade.

Wade signed a confession, which he repudiated after being released on bail. According to this document, Wade and several other Panthers ran to hide after seeing a police car driven by Officer Darnell appear on Union Street. Wade said that he jumped over a fence after hearing shots and ran into the also-fleeing John Scott and Charles Bursey. The three vaulted another fence and ran into the back door of the Jackson house when a young boy opened the door. Wade said that he saw a policeman at the front door, turned around and hid under the house, where he was later found by police.

Charles Bursey denied all knowledge of the fracas. He said that he was hit on the head and knocked out in another part of Oakland. When questioned for the reason of being at the shoot-out site, at 30th and Union Streets, Bursey said: "I was running from the robbers. I ran out of my shoes because they were a size and a half too big. . . . I hid in the house because of all the shooting." He was sentenced to one to fifteen years in prison. His story apparently was not believed.

The three confessions were all similar in that they were in two parts. The original statements generally described alleged Panther activities immediately before the shoot-out. The second set of confessions, delivered hours later, all uniformly identified Eldridge Cleaver as the prime architect of the incident.

There is a kind of mushiness of detail in all of the confessions. They indicate that the Panthers went out to patrol, and that they had planned later to hide their guns in a house near where the shoot-out occurred. In his confession Cotton identified the proposed cache as David Hilliard's house. Hilliard lived a short distance away at 35th and Union Street. Cotton's original statement also identifies Cleaver as saying: "Let's go out and scout around, and if the cops stop us we'll have a shot [sic] out with them."

Cotton, in his second statement, was quoted as saying that Cleaver wanted to go out and kill a policeman for nothing. "I seem to remember hearing Cleaver say something like let's kill one of them." Cleaver, according to this statement, started shooting at Jensen and Darnell as soon as the police car appeared.

Wells also identified Cleaver as the ringleader, while claiming noncomplicity in the shooting. According to his statement, Wells was high on heroin during the entire event. He was convicted of attempted murder and sentenced to one to fifteen years, after his first two trials ended with hung juries.

Wendell Wade also implicated Cleaver, identifying him as the person who organized the patrol, and who had issued automatic weapons to Panthers.

Cleaver insists that the Panthers were themselves victims of a police ambush. He said that the incident began with a police car driving up as he was urinating behind a hedge. He did not immediately interrupt himself, except to seek the comparative privacy afforded by the side of his own vehicle. Cleaver said that a spotlight was thrown on him and he was ordered to move to the center of the street. He was a little slow in obeying the order and he states that almost immediately one of the policemen began to fire.

Diving to the pavement in front of his car, Cleaver saw what he thought to be Panthers pinned down in a cross fire. He saw one of the bullets hit Warren Wells. As the shooting continued, Cleaver crawled across the street, following two Panthers who ran between two houses, and were in turn followed by a shotgun-shooting policeman.

He leapt a fence, landing on Bobby Hutton. Both got to their feet, and ran to a backyard shed. The shed faced a passageway between two houses that was beginning to fill up with cops. Bobby had a gun, according to Cleaver, and he used it to make the officers take cover. As police ducked, Cleaver and Hutton sprinted down the passageway, and dove without pausing into the basement door of 1218 28th Street, where they were immediately pinned down by return fire.

"It was like being the Indians in all the cowboy movies that I had ever seen," said Cleaver. And 1218 28th Street ended up looking as if it had been a set in all of those movies.

Every single wall of every room of that building had been filled with bullet holes. Police had entered the building adjacent, 1226 28th Street, and stationed themselves at a window overlooking Cleaver and Hutton's hiding place. They proceeded to fire both down at Cleaver and straight across, into the main part of the house.

Across the street, a detachment of officers was firing from the roof of a brick industrial building. Spotlights were turned toward the hideaway, and still more policemen arrived and took positions behind parked cars. A weapons van was on the scene, issuing long guns and ammunition to officers who wanted a change of weapon.

One officer, Ronald Danielson, who had taken a position in 1226, could see the basement hiding the Panthers and the unit above. Noticing that no return fire was coming out of the unit he managed to contact a police command and had the two female occupants evacuated.

Mrs. Nellie Pierre, one of the two women, was escorted out while gunfire was still being directed at the basement. She recalls throwing herself down on the floor soon after hearing windows crash from gunfire. Police apparently knew that the house was occupied, according to Mrs. Pierre, as someone gave instructions to them over a loudspeaker asking them to lie on the floor.

Finally all firepower was concentrated on the basement, in what was described as a ninety-minute shoot-out. Some of the shells went through two and three walls. On the west side, immediately under the roof, several splintered holes appeared —documenting the passage of bullets through the entire width of the structure. Inside walls were plaster versions of Swiss cheese. A drainpipe on the east side of the house was perforated on all sides with various-sized holes, some almost an inch in diameter.

A portion of the house above the basement door ended up burned from a fire that had started in the basement hideout. Forty-eight hours afterwards, the residual pall of tear gas prevented anyone from staying in the house for more than a few minutes. One of the visitors stayed long enough to crayon a question on the bullet-pock-marked wall: "Is this how it is in Vietnam?"

Hutton and Cleaver had flattened themselves behind the eighteen-inch high cement foundation running along the outside wall. Eldridge estimated that they listened to bullets barely miss their backs for about thirty minutes. At one point Cleaver sat up momentarily, only to be hit in the chest by one of the tear-gas canisters that had been lobbed into the basement. Thinking he had been shot, he removed his clothing and had Bobby help him look for the wound.

"In my mind I was actually saying goodbye to the world and I was sure that little Bobby was doing the same thing. . . . They shot firebombs into the cellar turning it into a raging inferno and we could not stand the heat. . . . We had to get out of there, to flee from certain death to face whatever waited us outside. . . . Little Bobby helped me to my feet and we tumbled out through the door. There were pigs in the window above us in the house next door with guns pointed at us and they told us not to move—to raise our hands. This we did, and an army of pigs ran up from the street and started kicking and cursing us. . . ."

Officer Jerry Noble remembered that it was the gas canister which he shot through the open door of the wooden building that set the house on fire. A short time later Noble saw both men come out of the basement and fall to the pavement.

Robert Coffman, another Oakland policeman, was looking into the alleyway when the fire started. Holding a carbine issued to him from the weapons van, he saw Eldridge, nude, as he "dove or fell" out of the house. Coffman was one of the officers who ordered both men to stand and raise their hands, saw them make staggering attempts to comply with the order, and then moved to assist them.

It was also Coffman who responded to what he identified as shouts of "Watch for guns! He's running, watch out!" by releasing Cleaver, throwing up his carbine, and firing three shots toward Bobby Hutton's back from a distance of ten to twelve feet.

"The pigs told us to stand up," Eldridge continued, "pointed to a squad car parked in the middle of the street and told us to run to it. I told them that I couldn't run. And then they snatched little Bobby away from me and shoved him forward telling him to run to the car. The most sickening sight. Little Bobby coughing and choking on the night air that was burning his lungs. . . . He stumbled forward as best he could. And after he had traveled about ten yards, the pigs let loose on him with their guns. And then they turned to me. But before they could get into anything, the black people in the neighborhood, drawn to the site by the gunfire and the commotion, began yelling at them."

Another officer, Robert Fredericks, saw the naked Cleaver come out of the basement and fall prone to the pavement, next to a kneeling Bobby Hutton. He watched as Hutton, supported by two officers, came toward him. Fredericks turned around and walked to the middle of the street. He then wheeled, only five feet away from Hutton, after hearing "Look out! He's running! Hold it!" and fired twice at the moving figure.

Owen Brown, an officer from neighboring Emeryville, with a carbine issued at the site, describes Hutton as being "in sort of a crouching position. . . . He rolled, he hit the ground going in a southerly direction and rolled completely over." Then Brown saw Hutton come up in a springing position, as though "running a hundred yard dash."

Brown's description of Bobby's movements, including the racing stance, is compatible with Cleaver's vision of Bobby coughing and stumbling forward. Brown responded to the shouts by adding his gunshots into the volley that cut Hutton down.

"Why am I alive?" asked Eldridge. "Why did little Bobby die? It was not a miracle. It just happened that way. I know my duty. Having been spared my life—I don't want it! I give it back to the struggle. Eldridge Cleaver died in that house on 28th Street, along with little Bobby. And what's left is a force, fuel for the fire that will rage across the face of this racist country and either purge it of its evil or turn it into ashes. I say this for little Bobby, for Eldridge Cleaver (who died that night), for every black man, woman or child who ever died here in Babylon. I say it to racist America. That if every voice of dissent is silenced by your guns, by your courts, by your gas chambers, by your money, you will know that as long as the ghost of Eldridge Cleaver is afoot, you have an enemy in your midst." And why not?

Police poured sheets of fire into buildings occupied by innocents. Several officers, including some who shot at Bobby Hutton, were incapable of saying with certainty that they ever saw gunfire coming from the houses. Actually, there couldn't have been very much coming from Panthers. Six of the nine Panthers later connected to the incident had already been arrested one block or more away. The only Panther other than Cleaver or Hutton who managed to get to 28th Street was David Hilliard, who was found hiding in 1226, a house from which policemen were shooting.

Cleaver and Hutton, once they entered the basement, could not both shoot and hug the ground. It was a ninety-minute shoot-at, in which police managed to display the image of the fascist troops Panthers claim them to be.

Hutton became the Panther's first martyr. His death also guaranteed the future growth of the Panther organization. Verdicts of guilty, long prison sentences, Cleaver's exile, and the repeated assertion of police that they are combating banditry convinced black folk of one thing. Even those who hesitate to think of policemen as their enemies know that a line is drawn at the point that bullets come crashing through houses.

Essentially, a race war is going on as long as the force of arms is used to control the political expression of blacks. Blacks have to react by seeing a direct threat to the race when they become aware of white policemen shooting at black men in black neighborhoods, without regard to the danger presented to black bystanders.

Most of these Negroes are not yet candidates for the Black Panther Party, but they do have the word. It's Black Liberation. They are reacting to police actions on their streets by recognizing each other as the next possible victims. Even those who might agree with police that some of the Panthers are criminals find that the severity of police repression of Panthers issues from a police commitment to criminality that is of more danger to the black community than any number of armed blacks can be.

Realistically, black politics will either be controlled by blacks or else distorted by whites. The distortions introduced by police, in their condemnation of Panthers, is racist in the extreme. As the mass of blacks begin to become obviously angrier, even the small numbers of comfortable Negroes develop an increasing intolerance for racial practices they once took for granted. The knowledge that white citizens are stockpiling guns is added to black awareness of the increasing resistance to social change on the part of those white citizens who exercise political power. Now that police all over the country are routinely shooting up Panther offices, Blacks are seeking ways to combat this obvious force-supported racism.

The politics of black self-defense are developed in response to physical attack by police and others. Panthers, in moving to convince blacks that self-defense is both a necessity and an inalienable right, are attempting to organize the community around the basic human reflex which seeks survival. Self-defense, the blowing away of a cop, under appropriate circumstances is then not an exercise in the discharge of anger. It is a calculated political move, that of fighting racists while hoping that the race war doesn't get started in earnest. Policemen, at this point, seem to be trying to work toward bringing the war to an early conclusion. They represent that not-so-silent portion of the majority who support local police.

Panthers believe that conflict has to be waged on a broader

front than that specifically defined by race. Revolution in the mother country and liberation for the colony satisfies only their domestic political goals. They don't want a race war, and in fact at this point are not enthusiastic about moving to fight policemen. "We understand that we will have to move on the pigs. But now is not the time . . . To spontaneously go out against thousands of armed pigs shows not only a lack of revolutionary theory, but it shows a lack of good sense." *

Middle-class Negroes have only recently discovered a fear and hatred of that police authority which can casually justify killing blacks and now are considering how to react. They form all sorts of committees, even as they are being driven toward revolution by the Panthers, and being pushed toward being the defenders in a race war by the police. Inevitably, each black, in his own way, on his own time, in answer to a threat interpreted solely by himself, and completely without organizational affiliation more rigidly defined than being black, will begin to accept and respond to one of the Black Panther Party assertions:

"We say that we have had enough of black men and women being shot down like dogs in the street. . . . We have reached the point in history where we must claim that a black man, confronted by a bloodthirsty cop who is out to take his life out of hatred for the black race, has a right to defend himself— even if this means picking up a gun and blowing that cop away." †

* *The Black Panther*, October 18, 1969.
† *Ibid.*, November 23, 1967.

VI

Law and Order Equals Justice?

IN 1966, BOBBY SEALE and Huey Newton were arrested, in a case which began when Berkeley police tried to stop Bobby from speaking. Both claimed that the arrests were illegal, unjust, unfair and politically motivated. Also, they claimed that the courts, as constituted, were incapable of delivering the justice to which they were entitled.

Four years later, after scores of court appearances, dozens of arrests and what must amount to over two million dollars spent in bails, fines and legal fees, Seale and Newton are still involved with the courts. Their speaking styles have improved, the Panthers have expanded, and the legal arguments are presented in long elaborate briefs. The complaints are the same. Some of them are what prompted the articulation of Point 8 of the Panther Platform and Program, "We want freedom for all black men held in federal, state, county and city prisons and jails," and Point 9, "We want all black people when brought to trial to be tried in court by a jury of their peer group or people from their black communities as defined by the Constitution of the United States."

The Panthers can hardly be accused of not taking their case to court. They've been in a lot of them. In doing so, they have

197

inferentially answered the question, "If you seek to overthrow the courts, what would you have in their place?" For their arguments are not based in a concept of removing the courts, but rather to revise them in a revolutionary manner, to conform better with what Panthers believe a Constitution that protects all folks should guarantee.

Their attempt is to forcefully counsel those who make judgments that their authority, legitimacy and institutions were created through a revolutionary rejection of a government that did not afford justice. The goal of freedom for all black men held in jail is not a blanket assertion of their innocence, but rather, the reflection of a belief that because of color, class, ignorance, malice or custom, blacks could not receive a fair trial. Moreover, they insist (Point 9) that the "courts should follow the United States Constitution so that black people will receive fair trials." They demand trials in a court by a jury of their peers, defined as persons "from a similar economic, social, religious, geographical, environmental, historical and racial background."

Huey Newton commented on this portion of the Panther program at the time that the jury trying him for murder was being selected. He said that he did not object to whites serving on the jury, and could in fact conceive of an all-white jury conceding him justice, providing that they were from his peer group. An example would be whites who lived in West Oakland, particularly whites with similar economic status and analagous language habits. He considered these people, along with black people similarly situated, to be his peers.

Newton's arguments regarding the courts are not in themselves revolutionary. They do, however, provide a rationale for working toward revolutionary change. An article written by a U.S. Court of Appeals judge * points out that there are biases built into court practices which guarantee legal victories

---

* J. Skelly Wright, "The Courts Have Failed the Poor," *New York Times Magazine*, December 20, 1969.

for the propertied over the propertyless. Even in cases where it is obvious that fraud, sharp practices, or questionable moral values originated the claim, rentors, debtors, welfare recipients, installment buyers, or other categories of the poor cannot prevent court-sanctioned seizure of their property, their assets, or their future earnings. Even such reforms as small-claims court, created to enable the little man to collect debts without incurring the expense of an attorney, has been used to his disadvantage. Small-claims courts are used mainly by agencies that are in business to collect debts. "Business concerns are aware of their rights," says the judge, "and the poor are not."

Panthers say that rights are a higher order of legal authority than laws. "Not only do they have more laws on the books than they need, but they are considering passing other laws," Eldridge Cleaver pointed out in a speech made in Syracuse in July, 1968.*

"Does anybody know what the situation is?" he asked. "Do you know what we can do and what we can't do? Or what we can say and what we can't say? I don't know that anymore. And I don't have enough time to go and research all the laws. So I'm in the position that the only thing I can say about that is fuck it. . . . The legislatures, the congress—and even the courts of this country have become nonfunctional for the people."

Huey Newton had researched a lot of the laws. He walked around West Oakland with a gun in one hand and a lawbook in the other. On occasion, when observing an arrest, Huey would, at the top of his lungs, read the law covering that situation for the benefit of the person being taken to jail. This lawbook showed up as evidence in his murder trial. It had been dropped at the scene of the shooting, and was thrown in the trunk of a patrol car by a policeman who assumed that the book belonged to one of the wounded officers.

Huey's law research made him aware that Cleaver was right, there were far more laws than anyone could keep up with.

* *Dig*, recorded by More Record Company, 1969.

More important was the discovery that laws, supposedly neutral and impartial, operated to the detriment of black people.

In April, 1966, Bobby Seale and Huey Newton were arrested on Berkeley's Telegraph Avenue, a few blocks from the site of the 1969 People's Park confrontation. Bobby had chosen to make a speech, standing on a chair located outside of a campus hangout named, significantly enough, The Forum.

The sidewalk outside The Forum had become a free-speech center and many speeches had been made from that spot. But when Bobby spoke, police found that he was breaking a few laws. He was accused of blocking the sidewalk, of using offensive and vulgar language, and ultimately of resisting arrest. One of the officers who arrested him was off duty at the time, and out of uniform. He admitted at the preliminary hearing that he had drunk at least two quarts of beer immediately before he decided that Bobby was breaking the law. The other policeman was in uniform, and had started out to break up the gathering, primarily because he objected to Bobby's choice of language.

No one, outside of the police officers involved, testified that the sidewalk was effectively blocked. In fact, it was pointed out that people were capable of walking past the group that was listening to Bobby without undue inconvenience. The prosecution also failed to come up with anyone other than the arresting officers who had been offended by any of the words Bobby used. They could demonstrate that both Bobby and Huey resisted arrest.

The two officers attempted to arrest Bobby by each grabbing a sleeve of his coat. As they pulled, the back seam of the coat split, leaving each officer with one half of a coat and sending Bobby scurrying across the street. Bobby was followed by Officer George Williamson, who had left his date and another couple waiting in a car while he chased Bobby Seale. Williamson had never identified himself as a policeman, and found himself in quite a scuffle with both Bobby Seale and a black man named Gerald Horton, who identified himself as Huey Newton's cousin. (Horton was not related to Huey, but a deep feeling of identification made him act out the role of protecting a family member. In many respects, the relations between Panthers very much resemble the emotion-linked ties that more typify family than members of a political party, albeit revolutionary.) Horton had gone to Seale's aid, after trying to help Huey, who had been wrestling with uniformed Officer Sabitini and two white bystanders. Huey had been standing on the sidewalk, next to Seale's chair, when the attempt to arrest Seale was made. Officer Sabitini reported that Huey punched him several times, interfering with his attempt to place Seale in custody. Huey denied striking the officer first, but says that Sabitini attacked him.

There is agreement that Newton and Sabitini ended up wrestling in the street. Sabitini claimed that Newton attempted to take his revolver from him. Newton denied this, saying that he was trying to save his own life by preventing the officer from completing his draw. Two white bystanders joined in the fray, and helped Sabitini subdue Newton. One of them, Melvin Viers, was handicapped in his attempt by Horton, who jumped in and attacked him. Sabitini and the other bystander succeeded in quelling Newton, whereupon Horton gave up trying to help Huey. He ran to where Bobby and Williamson were struggling, only to be arrested by another Berkeley policeman named Eaton, at the same time that Bobby was being handcuffed by Williamson.

Viers and the other bystander who helped the officers subdue Newton, accompanied the officers and their prisoners to the Berkeley jail, where they made statements as witnesses to the events leading up to the arrests. They explained that they had helped the officers because they did not believe that anyone had the right to physically resist arrest. At the same time, they made it clear that they believed that the attempt to arrest Newton was totally improper.

The outcome of this episode was that Huey, who had resisted being arrested by a uniformed police officer, had the charges reduced to disturbing the peace, possibly because the District Attorney did not want to prosecute a case in which two white witnesses, who helped effect the arrest, testified that the officer had no grounds on which to apprehend Newton.

Huey claims, however, that he was punished by police for resisting arrest. He said that he was handcuffed and walking down the corridor accompanied by Officer Sabitini, when he tripped and stumbled because his belt snapped, causing his trousers to fall around his ankles. According to Newton, Sabitini tripped also, but fell on top of him. Newton said that the officer then proceeded to administer a thorough beating.

Officer Sabitini's report includes mention of the faulty belt, and also quotes Newton as lying on the floor and yelling, "police brutality" at the top of his lungs. The report did not refer in any way, however, to the police-administered punishment which Newton swears he received.

Bobby, on the other hand, who had been confronted by someone smelling of alcohol, and who was not otherwise identifiable as a policeman prior to the arrest, ended up being sentenced for resisting arrest, after his lawyer negotiated with the District Attorney's office.

An interesting sidelight to this episode was that Huey, at the time of his arrest, was on probation as the result of being found guilty of disturbing the peace in May, 1964. He had been sentenced to six months in jail and three years' probation as the result of superficially wounding a man with a dull steak knife following an argument at a party where both had been drinking. The District Attorney did not attempt to seek penalties based on Newton's probationary status following the 1966 arrest, nor did the court take official notice of the terms of his prior sentence.

In 1968, however, when Newton was being tried for shooting at cops, the fact of the 1964 conviction with the subsequent probation was used by the District Attorney. The prosecution argued that Newton was motivated to shoot it out with the policemen from fear of having his probation violated. Huey,

he explained, was afraid of being searched after being stopped
for a traffic-law violation, fearing that a small quantity of
marijuana that was hidden in his car would be discovered.
This discovery would be clear evidence of a violation of probation, and would result in additional jail time.

Huey denied ownership of the marijuana, pointing out that
he had been driving a borrowed car at the time of arrest, and
further stating that his probation had ended the night before
he was stopped. It turned out that Newton had one day more
of probation on the books, but that there was reason for him
to believe that his probationary term had come to an end.

The three-year-old conviction affected the sentence he received after being found guilty of voluntary manslaughter. In
addition to the manslaughter verdict, the jury determined that
Newton had been convicted of a prior felony. This finding
meant that Huey was sentenced to a two-to-fifteen year term
in prison, rather than the one-to-fifteen customary for first
offenders.

In deciding that Newton had been convicted of a prior
felony, the jury demonstrated the existence of another problem connected with the ability of the poor and the black to
guarantee themselves all of their rights. Judge Wright noted
that the poor, "despite the presumption of innocence . . . is
prima facie guilty. . . . He is almost always uncounseled and
sometimes he is not even informed of the charges against him
until after the so-called trial. Often, no records are kept of the
proceeding, and in the overwhelming majority of cases, these
courts are, in practice, courts of last resort." * The judge was
referring to police and magistrate courts, where it is not un-
common to find individuals having no connection with each
other, except the fact that they were charged with the same
offense, tried and sentenced en masse. But municipal and
superior courts are often just as bad; and beyond that, de-

---

* Wright, *op. cit.*

fendants, even when represented by counsel, are not guaranteed all the benefits legal counsel presumably provides.

The inability of many defendants to obtain adequate legal representation after being charged with a crime has been well documented. An aspect of this general unavailability of legal talent to the poor that is not as widely circulated is that lawyers, as a group, have been lax in condemning the injustices they know to be in existence at all levels of the judicial apparatus. They have never seriously challenged bail practices, even though they are aware that many of their clients spend more time in jail awaiting trial than they would have served if found guilty immediately after arrest. The criminal process, according to Michael Meltsner, Staff Attorney for the NAACP Legal Defense and Educational Fund, "greets an accused with a money requirement for him to remain free before trial. . . . There is still a cash register in the courthouse."

Bail, all too often, represents an informal fine. Power to extract this fine rests almost exclusively with law-enforcement officers. In most criminal cases the amount of bail is determined by the charge. This means that every officer who arrests a person automatically sets bail by writing up a series of assumed violations of the law.

All or most of the charges might be dropped before the defendant makes his first court appearance. But if he desires freedom, he pays a premium to a bail bondsman of at least ten percent of the amount of bail.

In February, 1968, Bobby Seale and his wife Artie were arrested and charged with conspiracy to commit murder and riot. Almost a year later, the case was thrown out of court by Lionel Wilson, a black Superior Court Judge. (Wilson is one of five black judges in the entire San Francisco Bay Area, and the only one on the Superior Court bench.) He severely criticized the arresting officer, and suggested that his actions were apparently motivated by a desire to improve his reputation by arresting Bobby Seale.

The evidence against Seale was so flimsy as to be nonexistent. Wilson found that the police lacked probable cause for the arrest, which was supposedly prompted by an officer—who may or may not have been tipped off by an anonymous neighbor—who stood outside a closed and locked door and heard the sound of automatic weapons along with plans to murder some unidentified person. But if a bail bondsman had not been paid $2000 to effect the Seales' release they might have remained in jail the year it took to have the charges dropped.

Panthers call bail ransom, and for good reason. Take the case of the New York Twenty-One, who were charged with conspiring to dynamite five department stores, the New Haven Railroad tracks, four New York City police stations, and the New York Botanical Gardens. By the time the trial rolled around, there were only thirteen defendants. They had spent ten months in jail because their bail had been set at $100,000 each. One of the Panthers, known to be suffering from a serious case of epilepsy, was without medical attention for almost seven months, presumably because a Panther, even in the midst of a grand mal seizure, is considered a danger to the state.

The police establishment feels that bail provisions need tightening. Delegates at the International Conference of Police Associations held in Montreal during July, 1970, representing 125,000 American and Canadian policemen, attacked easy bail. They called for outright repeal of all laws allowing accused criminals to be released on their own recognizance. The Conference also went on record as opposing what they termed organized cop-killing. They called on governments and judges to help put an end to this by appropriately harsh laws or else be faced with striking policemen. The other menacing alternative offered by the policemen was "all out retaliation for these senseless killings even if it is in the form of on-the-street justice."

Most criminal lawyers know that the jail conditions under which their clients serve their "debt" to society conform to the constitutionally proscribed description of cruel and unusual punishment. Almost every jail has a "hole," similar to those in which Bobby Seale and Huey Newton have spent time. They are usually windowless concrete boxes with a hole in the center of the floor that serves as a toilet. Also on the floor is vomit and excrement, proof that some prisoners either missed the hole, or had been reduced to a mindless psychological state where it made no difference. Sometimes there is a filth-encrusted mattress in the jail cell; often there is not; but almost always, as in Bobby's case, a prisoner confined to the hole is required to perform all bodily functions within the cell, usually completely nude.

Lawyers are also used to the general conditions of jails and penitentiaries, and can argue validly that the threat of homosexual rape, the increased possibility of being attacked by another inmate, the reduction of a person to a number, and the imposition of petty rules, of relevance only to jailers, constitute cruel and inhuman punishment.

Attorneys have not lifted their voices in protest. They have not pointed out that criminal penalties in the United States are the harshest of all western nations. The bar has also not moved vigorously to inform the nation that less is spent on the rehabilitation of American criminals than is spent in almost any other industrial nation.

Attorneys are also privy to other kinds of information. They know who the incompetent judges are, are aware of the extent that influence, prejudice and sometimes dishonesty guide decisions. They are also completely aware of the unfair or illegal practices engaged in by District Attorneys.

J. Frank Coakley, when he was the District Attorney of Alameda County, once boycotted a superior court judge. He absolutely refused to bring any criminal matter before Judge Spurgeon Avakian, who had a reputation for being liberal. The District Attorney successfully insisted that the judge would not grant the prosecutor his version of fair and impartial treatment. This forced the judge, who was assigned to the criminal bench, to try routine civil cases, therefore making it necessary for judges assigned to civil cases to preside over the trials of criminals. Criminal lawyers in Alameda County cannot so easily avoid trying cases before judges they believe would be unfair to their clients.

Lawyers more than anyone else, except the hapless subjects who pass through the courts daily on their way to jails, know that on a purely physical basis our courtrooms and jails are slums. They are understaffed, overcrowded, noisy, confusing and infinitely depressing. The very conditions under which lawyers work make it impossible for them to fulfill their potential for their clients. Courts are really rigged to the disadvantage of lawyers. Their atmosphere breeds the kind of mistakes that send clients to jail.

Black attorneys in this situation become doubly victimized. Their rights as attorneys, even as members of Bar Associations, are as easy to nail down as warm Jell-o. They have a choice of working for black people, most of whom cannot afford legal help, or working in the name of all the people, somewhere in the apparatus of government.

Black law practices are generally overworked and underpaid. Fees are often high enough, to the anger and discomfort of their clients, but their ability to collect those fees is substantially less than that of their white counterparts.

Black lawyers are expected to contribute some of their legal talent advancing black causes through court action. Many of them have. A few are members of civil-rights-oriented organizations, and more volunteer to defend cases arising out of civil rights protests. Almost none are in a position to accept an important case in the beginning stages and follow it through every legal avenue up to and including the U.S. Supreme Court. And that is where the second increment of disadvantage comes in.

Black lawyers live legal lives that whirl around the walls of a descending vortex of constitutional violations. They are often reviled in a court by judges who hide their racism behind a strict interpretation of the law and a particular penchant for order when black defendants are in their courtrooms, but they are not unique in having to absorb racial slurs from judges.

In San Jose, California, a Mexican-American Public Defender took issue with Juvenile Judge Gerald Chargin, when the judge's racism was hanging right out front. An obviously mentally disturbed seventeen-year-old had allegedly raped his fifteen-year-old sister, making her pregnant. The Judge started out assailing the youth's morals. "You are just an animal. You are lower than an animal. Even animals don't do that. You are pretty low. . . . I don't have much hope for you. You will probably end up in State's Prison before you are twenty-five."

The judge was not far off there. Dr. Alfred Blumstein, Executive Secretary of the President's Crime Commission and an official at the Institute for Defense Analysis, estimated that there was a 50-50 chance the average American ten-year-old boy would be arrested for a non-traffic offence during his lifetime. There was a 60 percent chance of like arrest if the boy lived in a city. The likelihood of arrest increases for non-white youth to a high, for city-dwelling black youth, of 90 percent. So that defendant, and numberless other non-whites passing through courts run by men like Chargin, are very prone to becoming convicts before twenty-five.

Chargin had been warming up. He next commented on the victim, the fifteen-year-old pregnant girl. "Well, probably she will have a half a dozen children and three or four marriages before she is eighteen." Then returning to the defendant, Chargin said:

"We ought to send you out of the country—send you back to Mexico. You belong in prison for the rest of your life for doing things of this kind. You ought to commit suicide. That's what I think of people of this kind. You are lower than animals and haven't the right to live in organized society—just miserable, lousy, rotten people.

"There is nothing we can do with you. You expect the County to take care of you. Maybe Hitler was right. The animals in our society probably ought to be destroyed because they have no right to live among human beings. If you refuse to act like a human being, then, you don't belong among the society of human beings."

Mr. Lucero, the public defender, objected.

> MR. LUCERO: Your honor, I don't think I can sit here and listen to that sort of thing.
>
> THE COURT: You are going to have to listen to it because I consider this a very vulgar, rotten human being.
>
> MR. LUCERO: The Court is indicting the whole Mexican group.
>
> THE COURT: When they are 10 or 12 years of age, going out and having intercourse with anybody without any moral training—they don't even understand the Ten Commandments. That's all. Apparently, they don't want to. . . .
>
> MR. LUCERO: The Court ought to look at this youngster and deal with this youngster's case.
>
> THE COURT: All right. That's what I'm going to do. The family should be able to control this boy and the young girl.
>
> MR. LUCERO: What appals me is that the Court is saying that Hitler was right in genocide.
>
> THE COURT: What are we going to do with the mad dogs of our society? Either we have to kill them or send them to an institution or place them out of the hands of good people because that's the theory—one of the theories of punishment is if they get to the position that they want to act like mad dogs, then, we have to separate them from our society. . . .

This outburst did result in charges being brought against Judge Chargin before the California Judicial Qualifications Commission.

Judge Chargin's outburst was evidently accepted as a temporary aberration by the Commission, which mildly rebuked the Judge and sent him back to the bench. Judge Chargin's explanation to the Commission was probably the same as that he expressed in a letter to the San Francisco Board of Supervisors, who considered censuring him:

> Every person is properly entitled to expect justice to be administered by one completely free of bias, prejudice or hatred toward any person because of his race, ethnic origin or religious or political beliefs.
>
> In view of the intemperance of my remarks, it may be difficult for you who do not know me personally to realize that during my entire life I have been dedicated to these beliefs.

Blacks and Mexicans would find little to argue about in the letter, and some might even concede that the judge was perfectly sincere in making his statement regarding the rights of "persons" before him. But they also know the judge called the defendant an "animal—lower than an animal," automatically defining him as a nonperson.

The California State Supreme Court voted to publicly censure Chargin, nine months after his remarks, the first censure of any judge in its history. The court acted on the unanimous decision of the State Commission on Judicial Qualifications, noting that it could not find any other similar incidents in the judge's career.

Mexican-Americans in the San Jose area, particularly those who have been personally affected by Chargin's decisions, think otherwise. For them, the incident which led to censure represented one of his few moments of total truth. The censure was not received as an indication that the judge had been disciplined. Rather, considering the fact that Chargin was allowed to continue to pass judgment, the Supreme Court's action was looked upon as a judicious judiciary warning—cool it Chargin, don't shake up the natives.

The rigors of surviving in their position tend to isolate black attorneys from the fundamental legal battles that contribute to black liberation. Actually, few attorneys are of a temperament or disposition to specialize in cases with heavy political implications, even when they can afford the luxury.

With the possible exception of the National Lawyers Guild, professional civil-rights-oriented legal associations are legally cautious to the point of timidity. They either press legal points they think the courts are ready for, or represent model persons, obviously responsible citizens, who seek constitutional relief.

On the other hand, there is ACLU, which pursues the goal of abstractly defending civil rights with seeming total objectivity. Anatole France's observation that the law, "in all its majestic equality, forbids the rich as well as the poor to sleep under bridges on rainy nights, to beg on the streets and to steal bread," has been updated and put into legal practice by ACLU, which has made certain that George Wallace and Klan Wizard Shelton had civil rights representation equal to that ACLU gives to blacks.

Timid, overobjective, conservative, or just plain cautious, it doesn't make much difference; professional civil liberties legal organizations traditionally seek to oppose the injustice that is legally sanctioned discrimination with a delicate gentlemanliness that borders on the apologetic. They handle a lot of cases, and in as noncontroversial a mode as possible.

Lawyers by training and tradition are not radical, even those who delight in using unorthodox courtroom tactics. The few lawyers who are genuinely radical—Arthur Kinoy, Gerald Lefcourt, William Kunstler and Charles Garry among them—are products of identification with the politically and racially oppressed. They may not have lost their faith in the courts, but they know full well that there has been little in their experience with these institutions to inspire anything other than intense hope of drastic future change in the way that justice is administered.

Ideological draft-evaders, peace-movement celebrities, white revolutionaries, and southern civil rights activists are all defended by an incredibly small number of radical lawyers.

Panthers also use these lawyers, primarily because black

radical attorneys are hard to come by. There is no radical black firm, and the approximately 4000-member National Bar Association, the Negro answer to the American Bar Association, does not seem inclined to encourage its membership in that direction. Two hundred and fifty of their members withdrew at the organization's 1969 convention, noting with considerable force that the National Bar Association was not meeting the needs of black people: "The systematic suppression of black people continues, notwithstanding the plethora of court decisions, civil rights laws, antipoverty legislation, human relations commissions, enlarged political representation, and other symbolic promises to blacks which serve as this society's substitute for true equality."

The solution, they said, was "To create a permanent and on-going body of all black lawyers determined to join the black revolution and committed to taking all steps necessary to assist black people attain the goals to which they are rightfully entitled by the most fundamental principles of law, morality and justice."

The decision to form a radical black legal caucus might have been encouraged by the recognition that black law students, anticipating the need for a black revolutionary legal perspective, had formed their own organization before graduating from law school.

The need for such a group became apparent in 1968, when a symposium of black lawyers on Racism and The Law was held in San Francisco. The attorneys adopted a lively rhetoric in attacking white racism, and on the way delivered a few choice criticisms of black revolutionaries, particularly the Panthers. Specifically, their gripe was the defense of Huey P. Newton, which they contended should be in the hands of black attorneys. Essentially, the lawyers challenged the integrity of blacks who took their black revolutionary business to white lawyers. Panthers retaliated immediately.

The May 18 issue of the *Black Panther* featured the text of a press release written by Bobby Seale, and a Kathleen Cleaver article titled "Black Power, Black Lawyers and White Courts," under the headlined statement, "Black Lawyers are Jiving."

Bobby took off on attorney John George, who had in the past represented Seale, Newton, and a number of other Panthers.

"I, Bobby Seale, know for a fact, when without my knowledge, John D. George, who was handling three misdemeanor cases for me, sold me out by waiving a jury trial for me where I would possibly be railroaded off into jail. . . . He has been one of the advocates and foolish black racists running around talking about we should have a black lawyer. HUEY P. NEWTON'S [sic] life is in danger and these ignorant, stupid, life-sucking, petty minded fools, who call themselves black lawyers, have done nothing but harm the black community. The first thing they can do, those so-called black lawyers, is to begin filing massive appeals for every black brother in prison. . . ."

George had confessed over a year before his doubts about his capacity to represent black revolutionaries adequately. In January, 1967, George attended an informal meeting between young Bay Area revolutionaries and Stokely Carmichael. A portion of the conversation was devoted to a consideration of the attitude expected of lawyers defending black revolutionaries. George's only contribution to the discussion was to question his own ability to discard much of what he had learned of legal practice in order to accommodate the styles of men prepared to give new meaning to the concept of adversary proceedings.

"Black Power," wrote Kathleen Cleaver, "would never be attained if the burden of achieving it were in the hands of black lawyers. . . . During the non-violent stage of the resistance movement, black lawyers did not rush to defend the jailed students and freedom fighters. . . . Thousands of people were jailed and beaten and denied their rights, but the bulk of the legal work was done by white lawyers, regardless of whether or not they could be paid. . . . The vast bulk of legal service given to the struggle has come from white lawyers dedicated to the establishment of social justice, and the vast bulk of that legal service has gone unpaid. . . . James Forman, Stokely Carmichael and Rap Brown of SNCC have all been indebted to the services of white lawyers—without too much complaint from the black lawyers or the black community. Neither has there been much of an outcry from Muhammad Ali's use of white lawyers in his draft case. However, all of a sudden . . . an outcry has been raised about the fact that Minister of Defense Huey P. Newton has a white lawyer."

Kathleen identified four attorneys who, "in the entire span of Afro America . . . are prominent in the struggle: Floyd McKissick, National Director of CORE, Howard Moore, Jr., General Counsel for SNCC, C. B. King of Southwest Georgia . . . and William Paterson, of Scottsboro Boy fame. Undoubtedly, there are others that I do not know of, working in their own ways for the liberation of black people. But again, their number is small compared to the number of black lawyers working for the aggrandisement of their personal wealth and prestige, which within the racist and exploitive legal structure of America means bootlicking. . . . The point has been made that for Huey P. Newton to go to court with a white lawyer weakens the argument for black liberation. Seeing as how the entire legal system is white, the logic of this complaint escapes me. . . . White resources at the disposal of black people, a white legal firm defending the Minister of Defense of the Black Panther Party is a defense, an example of black power. Black skin is not—as our black lawyers, politicians, doctors, teachers, and other professionals highly attest in their mad scurry for white power, white values, white acceptance and white hostility to black power. . . . Are these people onlookers of a liberation struggle being waged for their benefit who just generally dislike white people and don't like the way it looks in court? Are these people black lawyers and their friends who want to cash in on the prestige associated with this historic case? Whose benefit are they concerned with, Huey P. Newton's or black lawyers'?"

The debate seemed to end there, and just as well. There was more to Panther disenchantment with black lawyers than Bobby Seale's three misdemeanor cases. The only lawyer the Panthers could get to accompany them to Sacramento in May, 1967, was Beverly Axelrod. In almost every subsequent case involving Panthers, black attorneys represented them sporadically and then restricted their commitment to actions at the lower court level. The most consistent legal support came from white radical attorneys.

Charles Garry, whose firm includes a black attorney, and who has successfully defended over a score of cases involving possible imposition of the death penalty, committed himself, the resources of his firm, and his legal reputation to the defense of the leaders of the Black Panther Party.

He is providing a service unobtainable from the black legal community at this point in time. Undoubtedly as he continues to represent the Party, Garry will attract and contribute to the dedication of the black attorney, who needs to learn, in the name of black revolution, what Garry can teach him about revolutionizing the practice of law.

Garry says that he has learned more from his association with the Panthers about the essential duty of lawyers, than from any comparable group.

"I knew about Negro America. I had known about Negro America for over thirty years, and had been active in civil rights work for that long. But I never really know the black ghetto or its problems. I was probably more conversant with the problems of the ghetto than most white people, but I found out after spending half an hour with Huey that I was totally ignorant of the cries and needs and aspirations of men and women in the ghetto today." *

During the same thirty-year period, Garry had represented

* *Minimizing Racism in Jury Trials, op. cit.*

politically unpopular defendants. The defense of Huey Newton required Garry to draw on all of his experience and to develop new ways of handling his defendants in court.

Garry made a singular contribution to courtroom procedure by developing an approach to the selection of juries calculated to expose latent racism or prejudice of potential jury members.

Prior to the trial, both prosecuting and defense attorneys, along with the judge, examine the jury panel in a structured series of questions called the *voir dire*. Garry explained to one panel member that "*Voir dire* means in plain English, you speak. This is your chance to speak so that we lawyers can get an evaluation of your state of mind."

Garry's problem was to structure his questioning of a prospective juror so that the response would reveal whether the panel member's state of mind could be detrimental to his client. Another purpose of the *voir dire* is to soften the shock of the details of the prosecution case, and therefore, condition the juror to hear more than the sensational portions of the prosecution's case. Of particular importance is the necessity to educate the jurors about the law, the rules by which courtrooms are run and the assumptions that underlie the American jury system.

A member of Garry's defense team, Professor Robert Blauner, wrote an introduction to the *voir dire* pointing out some of the contradictory assumptions used in selecting jurors. District Attorney Jensen's concept, he said, was that the case had two sides—that the interests of the defendant should be taken into account, but also the constituency and values of the dead policeman. No! says Dr. Blauner.

"From the philosophical tenets of our legal system—as I understand them—only the individual Huey P. Newton was entitled to a fair trial. The 'justice' received by the deceased and his family, the wounded officer, the Oakland Police Department, and the white racist community should have been totally irrelevant to the trial that took place. For this reason I cannot subscribe to the argument that a jury representative of the county's actual racial attitudes would serve our ideals of justice and the elusive but still to be pursued goal of a 'fair trial.' " *

The questions raised by Professor Blauner regarding the possibility of a fair trial for Newton cropped up repeatedly. Garry had decided that to seek a change of venue in the Newton case would be futile. "The question was whether there were more racists in Alameda County than in the rest of the state. No matter how much white racism permeated Alameda County, it voted for fair housing by 54 percent. Obviously, we should not file a motion for a change of venue unless we could do better in some other California county." He related a conversation between himself and an Alameda County judge.

"I said, 'Judge, where do you suggest that Huey Newton could get a fair trial in the State of California?'

"Laughingly he said, 'If you make a motion for a change of venue, I'll transfer the case to Orange County,' which is famous for its reactionary majority.

"I replied in the same vein, 'I was thinking about someplace in Cuba!' "

Garry faced a problem other than that of racism. Many of the prospective jurors did not actually understand the idea of a man being innocent until proven guilty. In one instance this attitude actually masked the conviction that Newton was guilty. Early in the questioning, one prospective juror, answering whether Huey P. Newton, in his opinion, was guilty or not guilty replied:

> Well I don't know for sure whether he shot the officer or not, but the officer is dead.
>
> Q. And by the same standard, just because the officer is dead, you are going to say that Huey Newton did it; is that right?
>
> A. Well, that's got to be proven.

* *Ibid.*, p. 70.

> Q. Well, my question is: As you sit there right now do you believe that Huey Newton shot and killed, stabbed, whatever it was, Officer Frey?
>
> A. I don't know whether he shot him or not. That I can't say.

The judge proceeded to explain to the juror about the necessity to assume that the defendant was innocent and elicited from him the belief that he could adopt that attitude. Another series of questions and answers followed.

> Mr. Garry: Well, do you really believe that as Huey Newton sits here right now next to me, that he is innocent of any wrongdoing of any kind?
>
> A. No. That I don't believe.
>
> Mr. Garry: See? There you are, Judge. I challenge this juror for cause.

The judge refused to dismiss the juror, insisting that semantics rather than a negative attitude on the part of the juror caused Garry's discontent. The judge again questioned the juror, and received a seemingly satisfactory response. The juror said that he could make up his mind solely from the evidence presented him and that he would not bring any preconceived notions to bear on his judgment.

Garry again persisted:

> Mr. Strauss, again I ask you that the same question which you have answered three times to me now—
>
> The Court: No. Please ask the question without preface.
>
> Mr. Garry: As Huey Newton sits here next to me now, in your opinion is he absolutely innocent?
>
> A. Yes.
>
> Q. But you don't believe it do you?
>
> A. No.
>
> The Court: Challenge is allowed.

A total of ninety-nine prospective jurors were examined before the regular jury was selected, and fifty-three others in order to have four alternate jurors.

In October, 1967, the Panthers did not look too much like the threat to internal security that J. Edgar Hoover finds them.

Bobby Seale was in jail serving a six-month sentence resulting from his visit to Sacramento in May, accompanied by twenty-two armed Panthers. Eldridge Cleaver had not emerged as the Minister of Information. He was still establishing in his own mind the degree to which he could hassle his probation officer and not have his freedom threatened. The Panthers seemed to be demoralized, leaderless and without a great deal of future promise. The only thing they appeared to have going for them was a jailed leader who apparently had put his theory into practice and successfully defended himself. But Huey, in jail, Huey defendant, Huey who overnight became the baddest man ever to walk through West Oakland, Huey who faced the pig and survived, Huey who took a gun and a lawbook into the streets with the knowledge of how and when to use either or both was a morale factor that helped build the Panthers from there.

The police and the courts helped, by persisting in acting just as the Panthers described them.

The grand jury met to consider indicting Huey for murder and assault with intent to murder, just two weeks after Huey had been arrested in a hospital with a hole in his midsection following the killing of Officer Richard Frey and the wounding of Oakland Patrolman Herbert Heanes. J. Frank Coakley, the District Attorney, had explained, on October 31 to a California State Legislative Committee, the kinds of charges that he felt should be presented for grand jury consideration. Three volumes of testimony were taken at the hearing, and not one of the district attorneys, judges or grand jurors who testified could say with any precision the reasons that prompted referrals of particular criminal cases to the grand jury.

Coakley explained that he presented the grand jury with cases involving sexual molestation "of a child of tender years," consumer fraud and abortion cases. Garry insists that Coakley was lying, and that the 4 percent of criminal cases presented to the grand jury every year represented instances where the District Attorney wanted to guarantee an indictment. Since then, Garry has stoutly maintained that Huey would never have been indicted at a preliminary hearing by the evidence that convinced the grand jury.

What the grand jury heard was that a minimum of five shots had struck the dead officer. Two shots had come from the front, two from the back, and one had grazed the officer coming from a direction that could not be determined.

Heanes, the wounded officer, described answering Frey's call for assistance, and of following behind Frey after Huey had been placed under arrest and was walking away from Newton's car. He remembered seeing Newton whirl around, heard gunfire, and discovered that he had been wounded. Heanes apparently lost consciousness momentarily, regained it, shifted his gun to his left hand, looked around to see what the passenger who had been in the car was doing, and after satisfying himself that the passenger was unarmed, aimed at Newton's midsection using his left hand, and fired what he remembered to be one shot. Heanes lost precise awareness of events again, but did come to long enough to see two male Negroes running away.

Two policemen testified to the facts in the case. One responded to a call from Kaiser hospital, recognized Huey lying on a gurney, and arrested him. The other described the position of Frey and Heanes at the scene of the shooting.

Dell Ross, a black witness, said that he and a friend were sitting in Ross's car, just around the corner from the shooting. Ross's friend ran away leaving the door open. Before Ross could close the door, two men came in, one with a gun, and forcefully persuaded him to drive away. He identified Huey as one of the men, but could not be made to say that Huey had told him that "he had just shot two dudes."

By the end of the day, Huey Newton had been indicted for murder, assault with intent to commit murder, and kidnapping. The only evidence offered linking Huey with the shooting came from a policeman who could never place a gun in Newton's hand, who testified that there was someone other than Newton on the scene, and who clearly indicated that he was not in full command of his faculties throughout the entire episode.

Garry says that the "Grand Jury gave but fleeting moments, if that, to deliberation."

After hearing the evidence, the Grand Jury went to lunch, then reconvened at 1:43 P.M. Twenty-seven minutes later, at 2:10 P.M., the Grand Jury was excused by the court after returning the three-count indictment.

Garry noted, "Thus with no time whatever allotted for deliberation, proceedings normally requiring more than 40 minutes at a reasonable pace were accomplished in 27 minutes.

"The transcript eloquently shows that the Grand Jury had no more time than to shut the door and open it again to accomplish its statutory and fundamental duty to weigh the evidence.

"The Grand Jury did nothing of the kind, but swiftly returned the indictment at the District Attorney's bidding without the slightest consideration or deliberation upon the evidence.

"The defendant was held to answer without reasonable or probable cause."

Garry's legal offensive had begun. Briefs, memoranda, causes of action, pleadings, appeals and numerous other forms of legal dialogue flowed out from his office, headed toward every court that Garry thought might have jurisdiction. He assembled a research team composed of some of the lawyers from his firm, volunteer lawyers, law students, and other interested parties. Nationwide communication with other attorneys, particularly those who specialized in civil rights cases, was begun in an effort to discover every law that remotely touched upon the issues relating to the Newton case, and every court decision that ever modified any of those laws. He directed a movement-wide effort to research all the laws. A significant part of his interlocking series of arguments in defense of Huey was devoted to an examination of the practices of both grand and trial juries.

A memorandum was filed declaring the statutes which governed the selection of grand juries as unconstitutional because they lacked standards which assured that grand juries would be composed of a fair cross section of the community. In doing so he cited a U.S. Supreme Court finding that held that all state statutes affecting the basic rights of citizens must, in order to be constitutional, have clearly stated standards of procedure. He further asserted, that the California statutes governing the selection of grand juries allowed judges unfettered discretion, which in turn led to the systematic exclusion of low-income people, including Negroes, from grand jury panels.

Basic to his argument was the position that the grand jury route to indictment was anachronistic and arbitrary, therefore directly violating the rights of that minimum of the accused who were indicted by the grand jury route, rather than by the preliminary hearing. The grand jury, said Garry, shields a district attorney from his duty to subject his evidence to the scrutiny of judicial review.

He then cited sections 939.7 and 939.8 of the Penal Code which requires the grand jury to weigh all the evidence submitted to it, to order further evidence to be produced if it has reason to believe that there is other evidence that will explain away the charge, and to find an indictment only "when all the evidence before it, taken together, if unexplained or uncontradicted, would in its judgment, warrant a conviction by a trial jury."

It seemed obvious that the evidence presented to the grand

jury in the Newton case did not exclude the possibility that the unknown person who had been with Huey could very easily have fired the gun that Heanes, the key witness, could not place in Newton's hand.

On April 22, 1968, Garry filed a complaint with the Clerk of the U.S. District Court in San Francisco, against the City of Oakland, Mayor Reading, Oakland Police Chief Charles Gain, Patrolman Heanes, District Attorney J. Frank Coakley, and the Alameda County Superior Court, on behalf of Newton, the Reverend Neal, Bobby Seale, Eldridge and Kathleen Cleaver, David Hilliard, and eleven other Panthers. It was a class action representing black citizens and residents of the Northern District of California.

Garry set out the Panther ten-point program and platform, and asserted that the Panthers, in the attempt to accomplish their program, had a fundamental right to free speech, press, assembly; the right to petition the government for redress of grievances and to "undertake mutual aid and protection of the black people from illegal and unconstitutional discrimination against, attacks upon and harassment of them by white society, and in particular by police departments, police officers, including the Oakland Police Department." The defendants' actions "are motivated by the white racism that infects American society generally, that has as its objective to perpetuate the second class citizenship suffered by plaintiffs and black Americans generally." He then itemized a bill of particulars.

He said that the charges against Newton were without foundation in law and, in fact, that Newton had been harassed by policemen on numerous occasions in the year preceding October 28, 1967, and that on that date, the police attempted to murder Newton.

The February 25, 1968, raid on Bobby Seale's house, in which officers burst in although they did not have a warrant, was described as illegal. Also associated with the arrest of Seale and his wife was the arrest of three Panthers, one of them David Hilliard, in a car.

A raid on Eldridge Cleaver's place on January 15, 1968, was described, in which San Francisco police entered with drawn guns and without a warrant, ransacked the apartment, cursed out the occupants, and left.

Bobby Hutton was described as being illegally and unlawfully shot to death on April 6, 1968, and the arrests of Cleaver, along with six other Panthers, was characterized as without reasonable, probable or any cause.

A raid on St. Augustine's Episcopal Church, disturbing a Panther meeting, the handcuffing of Newton to his hospital gurney, the regular harassment by police of the Panthers and all the other events listed in the complaint were evidence that the purpose was to harass and intimidate the plaintiffs and members of the class they represent, black folk, from the exercise of their constitutional rights. They're all racists, said Garry, and let it go at that.

The complaint is a remarkable document in that it contains the seed of every legal argument used in every case where Garry represented the Panthers. Attached were affidavits of Panthers describing police harassment and alleging that police illegally extracted false confessions from them. Particular attention was paid to Garry's argument that the entire grand jury procedure was illegal, and that the provisions of the California Constitution and Statutes allowing the procedure were on their face unconstitutional.

Garry did not succeed in winning all of his arguments, and in fact was accused of using the courts as a forum for spreading Panther propaganda. He did succeed, however, in pinpointing a number of legitimate complaints about the uses to which laws are put, and he has succeeded in winning victories of sorts.

In July, 1968, Alameda County Superior Judge George Phillips, Jr., dismissed an all-white jury, to the extreme discomfort of J. Frank Coakley. The judge declared a mistrial and ruled that Deputy District Attorney Frank Vukota had used his peremptory challenges to exclude non-whites from the jury. Coakley's response to this action was to say that the decision "impugns the character and integrity of white jurors and their ability to render a fair and impartial verdict in the case of a non-white defendant."

Judge Phillips had anticipated him. "Courts must proceed," he said, "on the assumption that in a case of class exclusion on the basis of race, some prejudice does result that will not be subject to precise measurement. That prejudice is so subtle, so intangible that it escapes the ordinary methods of proof."

In August, 1968, President Johnson signed a law that eliminated the "key man" procedure in which federal juries were picked from among persons recommended by leading citizens. New procedures required that federal juries be empaneled entirely at random, and, therefore, also eliminated the generally accepted practice of using telephone subscribers or voting lists to obtain the names of potential jurors, a process which declares that politically apathetic citizens, along with those who prefer the privacy of an unlisted phone and those citizens who cannot afford phone service, are not eligible to serve on juries. Garry's arguments may or may not have influenced national legislators; they certainly anticipated them.

The grand jury selection system in Alameda County is a variation of the "key man" procedure. Each of the twenty superior court judges nominates three candidates for a panel from which the nineteen members of the grand jury are chosen. In 1968, there was only one Negro member of the grand jury, a professor at one of the local junior colleges. The system is still in use, but the 1970 grand jury contained a number of surprises. Four of the grand jurors are black. By a strange coincidence, one of them is Father Earl Neal, spiritual advisor to the Black Panther Party, and the other is Mrs. Betty Smith, the wife of the president of Merritt College, where Bobby Seale and Huey Newton first began organizing the Black Panther Party.

The presence of black people on a grand jury might not prevent all the mischief of which such panels are capable, but it offers the possibility of exposing those bodies to what black people think is justice. At the very least, grand juries will have to begin considering an idea novel to their tradition—that black and poor people expect such bodies to serve their interests.

"Those not involved in making laws are not legally bound by them," is a basic tenet of the revolutionary stance of the Panthers. H. Rap Brown's rhetoric, however, is not solely or necessarily a call to disobey existing statutes. It is also a call to black people to begin seizing control of the apparatus of lawmaking which affects their lives. "It should be perfectly understandable," continues Brown, "that we, as black people, should adopt the attitude that we are neither morally nor legally bound to obey laws which were not made with our consent and which seek to oppress us. Nor can we be expected to have confidence in courts that interpret and enforce such laws. The white man makes all the laws, he drags us before his courts, he accuses us, and he sits in judgment over us."

Implicit in Brown's description of the fact that whites judge blacks in court is the recognition that whites also judge whites. And it is also in this area, the inability of blacks to sit on juries in judgment of whites, particularly when the accused has damaged the quality of black life, that tells blacks where it's at.

The San Francisco grand jury is all white, and is chosen by the key man system in which distinguished citizens suggest possible candidates. Those non-whites who even bother to think about that grand jury had their low estimate dropped another notch when it was revealed that two off-duty tactical squad men attacked Mexican teen-agers without provocation, and very much in public, accompanied by an observer, a member of the grand jury.

A quick legal move extricated the juror from being exposed as a witness to the crime, but the damage was done. A number of minority persons reinforced their belief that grand jurors are friends of cops, even those who viciously pick on minority youth. The more objective non-whites, those slow to condemn the barrel because of one very funky apple, got around to this way of thinking after the grand jury treatment of a case in which an off-duty police officer shot and killed a black man. Robert O'Brien, the cop, like the other two friends of the grand jury, had been drinking just prior to the event.

He was the officer who was transferred from one San Francisco precinct after black residents complained about O'Brien's wearing of a tie clasp saying "Gas Huey."

O'Brien had explained that his wearing of the pin was in the nature of a joke, and that at no time in his life had he ever personally wished that harm come to Huey Newton. It followed that O'Brien was totally without ill feelings toward blacks, and could certainly not be considered a racist. He was just a good cop, who did an excellent job, who on occasion drank a lot, and had been known as the man who chased a topless waitress into her dressing room, and then threatened to shoot the lock out—just a fun-loving segment of that thin blue line who was blessed with a sense of humor. Besides, said O'Brien, it was a water pistol.

George Baskett, a black man, was killed with O'Brien's real gun September 29, 1968, just three weeks to the day after Huey was found guilty. O'Brien is proof that for some people rehabilitation is possible after being a juvenile delinquent. He had been convicted at seventeen for auto theft, and again at eighteen for petty theft. His first-hand knowledge of the ways of crime apparently was valued by his employers at Macy's department store, who hired him as a security guard. A couple of years later, O'Brien joined the S.F. Police force. He managed to earn a meritorious award by being one of four police officers who talked a drunken black man out of killing himself. On such is the claim to being liberal, or perhaps unbiased, parlayed into a bid for the kingdom of heaven.

The killing of Baskett erupted after O'Brien parked his car, and the fifteen-foot boat it was towing, in the middle of a narrow alley, whose residents were primarily black. O'Brien and one of his companions, another off-duty policeman, Willis Garriot, had rented a garage in the alley in which they kept the boat. A municipal bus driver, Carl Hawkins, who lived near the rented garage, scraped the boat slightly with his car when attempting to maneuver around the 35-foot-plus car-and-trailer combination, by trying to drive partially on the sidewalk and avoid both the close walls of the nearby buildings and the blockading bulk of the policeman's car and boat.

Hawkins asked, "Did I hit you?"

O'Brien replied: "Yes, you hit the trailer. If you hit the car I'll shoot you."

Marilyn McLean, a girl who had accompanied O'Brien that weekend, testified that the officer had been drinking wine on the way home, and had found it necessary at times to stop the car so that he could suck at the wine bottle. She described O'Brien as immature, and quoted him as saying that if she didn't "put out" that she would have to walk home.

Brush Street is located just a few blocks from the Hall of Justice, and policemen, accompanied by a television camera-man, arrived there scant minutes after the shooting. Later, the cameraman was to complain that two film sequences were missing. One showed the ambulance arriving to take the soon-to-be-dead Baskett away, the other was a shot of O'Brien falling to the ground.

The recovered portions of the film showed O'Brien holding his gun on three black people who were backed up against a garage, Baskett lying unattended on the street, with a gaping and bleeding chest wound, and finally O'Brien, sitting on the pavement, surrounded by helpful and sympathetic policemen who understood O'Brien's problems and arrested four of the black residents of the alley.

Carl Hawkins, driver of the car which brushed O'Brien's boat, was charged with conspiracy and assault with a deadly weapon. Hawkins's wife Elizabeth, the dead man's brother Otis, and Richard Dickerson, Mrs. Hawkins's son, were all charged with conspiracy, assault with a deadly weapon and assault to commit murder. Eight hours later, police officially decided to call the shooting justifiable homicide. This decision was reached on the basis of a police report that was prepared without consulting any of the black witnesses to the shooting and which was later demonstrated to have been changed several times to meet the specifications of the lieutenant then on duty.

Howls from the black community effected the release of the four witnesses, the dropping of the charges against them, and the subsequent arrest of O'Brien on suspicion of murder. Some of the pressure came from black officers of the police community-relations bureau, who went down to Brush Street and heard descriptions of the killing that differed drastically from the official version.

O'Brien was booked, and then, incredible as it might sound, released on his own recognizance. Black reaction to this development was predictably angry, and O'Brien was again put in jail, only to be released again, this time on $25,000 bail, half of which was put up by a wealthy hotel owner and a prominent Democrat.

The case then went to the grand jury, which did not hear the testimony of Otis Baskett, the victim's brother, who had witnessed the entire event and who was waiting to testify. The all-white panel indicated its responsiveness to the need of black people for equitable justice by indicting O'Brien for manslaughter.

O'Brien was rebooked, the bail was reduced to $3,000 and his attorney, Jake Ehrlich, called the indictment a vindication. Ehrlich had just finished defending another policeman, Robert Main, who had shot at a cat out of his back window, missed, and instead hit an Oriental lady who was his neighbor. Ehrlich called that shooting unfortunate. He said, "It could have happened to you or me. It doesn't amount to anything. . . . Of course, the woman was hurt, but the officer has been sufficiently punished by the torture he's gone through."

Ehrlich apparently understood cops. Earlier in his career,

he had won a case where his policeman client had been accused of taking bribes. Ehrlich convinced the jury that the policeman in question, who had never earned over $300 a month in his life, had been extremely thrifty, and therefore was able to save $50,000. His defense of O'Brien went far beyond that. Ehrlich conducted a defense that was racist in the extreme.

There was general agreement about the facts in the case. After the auto accident, a shouting match between O'Brien and Hawkins ended with O'Brien coming into the street with his gun. There are claims that O'Brien shot two or three times down the street, and others that Mrs. Hawkins leveled a gun at O'Brien and shot also. O'Brien's essential story was that he killed Baskett in self-defense. Originally, he claimed that Baskett had struck him repeatedly on the head with a club, and that the gun went off accidentally. Police laboratory findings indicated that O'Brien had shot Baskett from further away than an arm's length, a finding consistent with the stories of the witnesses. O'Brien, at 6'5", weighting 235 pounds, was five inches taller and 75 pounds heavier than Baskett, who had picked up a stick and was apparently attempting to disarm O'Brien with it.

All the blacks testified that O'Brien was particularly nasty. Mrs. Hawkins said that O'Brien started niggering everyone in sight. He called Mrs. Hawkins a nigger bitch, waved his gun around, yelling, "I want to kill me a nigger so goddamn bad I can taste it," told Baskett that he would give him until the count of three to drop the stick, counted "One-two-three," and shot. Baskett groaned, causing O'Brien to walk over and kick him, yelling all the while, "Shut up!"

A prosecution witness was an eighteen-year-old white student named David Anderson. Anderson testified that he watched the shooting from a rooftop, after his attention was drawn to the commotion by the sound of shots.

He corroborated other witnesses who said that O'Brien had yelled at the onlookers to get their heads in the windows, threatening to shoot them, kicked one of the men standing at the garage, saying, "Just give me an excuse—give me a reason and I'll shoot you," and then went back to Baskett and kicked him.

Anderson had given a report to police the night of the shooting. The following night, several policemen burst into his room. Anderson's father had been visiting him, but left just before the policemen arrived. They were ostensibly searching for persons who were sniping at firemen answering a call in Brush Street. A friend of Anderson's, John Coate, was in the apartment at the time. He testified that he and Anderson were held up against the wall for about fifteen minutes while Anderson's roommate was being questioned elsewhere.

Two of the officers who conducted the raid testified that revolutionary posters were on Anderson's wall at the time of the raid. Anderson's father said nonsense, that only travel posters, his gift to his son, were on the wall September 30. Further the police insisted that a black, Richard E. Brown, also described as a Panther, was in the apartment. Both Coate and Anderson denied that Brown was in the apartment. Ehrlich actually attempted to prove that Brown was Anderson's roommate. He attempted to demonstrate that Anderson was a member of SDS, and that he was involved in rioting on the San Francisco State College campus. The defense ploy was obvious, to discredit Anderson's testimony by demonstrating to one and all that he was a left-wing SDS activist nigger-lover.

During the record five-day filibuster that summarized his defense, Ehrlich took off on Anderson: "This boy is a member of SDS and hates police as sure as I'm standing here. He hates them and would shoot them if he had a chance." Ehrlich played rock music to demonstrate Anderson's decadence, tried to connect Anderson with the Black Panthers, and even implied that the antipolice graffiti on the walls of city prison was somehow connected to Anderson. His nigger-lover dismissal of Anderson was classic. Referring to the fact that the other prosecution witnesses were black, Ehrlich opined: "I can realize our black brethren sticking together. They do things

I don't approve of, but I can understand. What I can't understand is Anderson, coming apparently from a good home, and
selling his soul to destroy a policeman." Good old white-
folks-*über-alles* Ehrlich.

Ehrlich saved his best insults for blacks. Earlier in the trial,
Tactical Squad member Donald Hansen, who had arrested
Richard Brown twice, testified that Brown was Anderson's
roommate and indicated that he was also in the courtroom.
Ehrlich spun around, located Brown and spat out, "What's
your name? Stand up, boy!"

Brown remained seated, saying, "My name is not boy. My
name is Richard Brown."

Next Ehrlich harangued the deputy district attorney, demanding that Brown be locked up. This oration was interrupted by the judge (who had also let fly at Anderson for his
assumed political affiliation), who opined, "I'm sure you never
meant to offend anyone, Mr. Ehrlich."

> EHRLICH: Some black people think its disgraceful
> to be called boy. I don't understand their childish, in-
> fantile feeling. My father and mother called me that. I
> don't like this feeling that someone is trying to offend
> these people. I've fought for these people, I've defended
> them without fee. I have no hatred for these people, no
> feeling for them at all. But I don't understand these
> people, and I certainly don't want any back talk out of
> them either.

That's where Ehrlich was at all the way. He didn't understand black people, didn't care to understand them, but did
know and understand that race baiting before an all-white
jury, in defense of a policeman accused of killing a black man,
is a tried and true technique.

"This is strictly a white and black fight. This man Anderson
is an unmitigated liar. Any man who would sit here and lie a
man's life away is not entitled to a fair trial. I say he should
be taken out and shot."

He called Carl Hawkins "a sanctimonious liar," "old Mr. Prayer Meeting" and "the deacon." Otis Baskett, the dead man's brother, was described as "a smart aleck," "a plain liar."

"Those people would have killed . . . O'Brien, and they would have killed you too, if you'd been there," he said to the jury. "They have absolutely no respect for an oath, the truth, or for common decency. . . .

"O'Brien could have shot Baskett any time. But he didn't, he was backing away," when the gun discharged. "If it had been me, I don't know but what I would have shot him immediately and gotten myself out of that alley." Brush Street he described as "a hell hole with some 200 hyenas in there."

O'Brien was acquitted.

The Huey Newton trial had been completed six months before. Judge Monroe Friedman, the presiding judge, seemed scandalized when it had been suggested to him that a predominantly white jury might not be inclined to treat a black defendant fairly.

"Are you trying to say it is your opinion that a white jury is more likely to convict a Negro?" Friedman asked a witness in the outraged tones of an angry man defending his system of belief from heresy. Friedman is one of the few Jews allowed to join the Elks, an organization which specifically excludes all Negroes and most Jews from membership.

The witness, a professor of law who had made extensive studies of the sources of jury bias, replied, "It is rumored that it has happened."

Friedman expressed doubt about the accuracy of the statistics the defense offered to demonstrate that bias resulted from using voter-registration rolls as a device for impaneling juries. The figures were based on the U.S. Census Report of 1960, the last census year. They showed that 82 percent of eligible voters in Alameda County were registered to vote, but that highly black West Oakland had only a 53 percent registration. "If there is any physical interference with the registration of voters in Alameda County, whether black, white, yellow or brown, I want to know about it," he said importantly. The judge failed to mention what he might do, were such evidence placed before him.

Garry made much of the procedures which helped to eliminate blacks from juries, a practical point that was not touched upon by Walter Guibini, the San Francisco deputy district attorney who later prosecuted O'Brien before an all-white panel. Garry subpoenaed Alameda County Jury Commissioner Scharr, who testified that he first selected 7000 names for consideration, and that this list was later whittled down to a six-months panel of 1800.

Edward Keating, a publisher and attorney who had worked with the legal team preparing Newton's defense, testified that he had found that a large percentage of the 5200 names that were eliminated from the jury panel were those of blacks living in West Oakland. As it turned out, the jury which tried Newton included one black, who subsequently became jury foreman. He was one of two bankers on the jury, which contained not one person who could be considered Newton's peer. Jensen, the prosecuting attorney, had dismissed twenty-one of the twenty-two Negroes who had been impaneled.

The prosecution's case against Newton was based on the assumption that the Minister of Defense knew when he was stopped, for a yet-undisclosed violation of traffic laws, that there was marijuana in the car, which if discovered could send him to prison for violating probation. Huey, therefore, in desperation whirled around just before he was to be placed into a patrol car, pulled a gun from his shirt, and wounded Officer Heanes, who was standing at least a car's length away. Almost simultaneously, Huey grappled with Officer Frey. He succeeded in removing the policeman's gun from the holster, and killed him with it. He then, with the assistance of an unknown person presumed to be the man who was in the car when Huey was stopped, ran around the corner and commandeered, at gun point, a car belonging to Dell Ross.

Garry introduced a surprise witness, Gene McKinney, who

acknowledged that he was the man who had been with Huey the night of the shooting. McKinney refused to give out any other information and was subsequently cited for contempt. The fact is, however, that Garry had introduced what should have been considerable reasonable doubt that Huey was the only person who could have shot the policeman.

Heanes's story was essentially the same one he gave before the grand jury. He testified to being wounded, to missing essential facts connected to the shooting, and could not with any precision give an account of McKinney's movements, except to note that at one point McKinney was standing on the sidewalk with his hands in the air. The policeman also contended that he did not recognize Newton and was unaware that he was a Panther.

This testimony seemed surprising, considering the fact that Newton's face graced a number of back rooms at the police stations, and that the Oakland police were keeping a close watch on the movements of known Panthers. A recording of that night's police radio calls was introduced, which contained a call, presumably from Frey, stating that he had stopped a Panther vehicle. Moreover, Robert Fredericks, another Oakland policeman who arrested Newton in the hospital, recognized him immediately.

The prosecution's key witness was Henry Grier, a bus driver, who testified that he had seen Newton shoot both officers, after drawing a gun from under his coat. Grier had not appeared before the grand jury, but had made a previous report to police. Garry demonstrated that there was an inconsistency between Grier's statement to the police and his testimony in court. The bus driver, who positively identified Newton as the killer by moving across the courtroom and placing his hand on Newton's shoulder, had originally told police that he did not see the gunman's face.

The discrepancy in his testimony was not discovered until after the jury had retired to consider the case. Garry successfully obtained the original recording of Grier's statement, and demonstrated that subsequent copies had been either altered or coincidentally flawed in a manner that changed the original statement saying he "did not" see the face of the assailant to one saying that he "did see" the man's face. Judge Friedman noted the discrepancy. He in no way altered his instructions to the jury, even to the point of bringing their attention to a particularly significant fact of Grier's testimony. He did order the typed statement to be changed without calling the jury's attention to the change.

There was another inconsistency in Grier's story. His original statement described a person smaller than Newton, who was wearing clothing of an entirely different type than Huey actually had on that night. Grier also said that there were three passengers in the bus who might also have seen the shooting, but that they refused to sign cards listing themselves as witnesses.

Garry produced one of the passengers, Henry Miller, who said that he did see a police officer with a man, but that it was too dark to distinguish any features. Other defense witnesses included two blacks testifying that Frey had a reputation as a racist cop, and who described humiliating experiences to which Frey had subjected them.

One interesting piece of evidence came from a worker in the police criminal lab who testified that the Oakland police, in conducting their investigation, never asked him to subject Newton to the usual routine tests which would have proven whether or not he had fired a gun.

Newton himself took the stand, and insisted that Officer Frey attempted to kill him. He said that he remembered being shot, experienced a sensation in his midsection similar to the feel of boiling soup, and passed out. Newton said that he did not regain consciousness until he woke up in the hospital.

A doctor testified that Newton's description of his loss of consciousness was entirely compatible with the type of wound he received.

The verdict was completely illogical. Newton was not

convicted of murder, but of voluntary manslaughter. At the same time, the jury acquitted him of the charge of shooting at Officer Heanes. The kidnapping charge was also dismissed, but that was a foregone conclusion, since Dell Ross, whose car was allegedly commandeered by Newton, testified at the trial that he had no memory of the events transpiring the night of September 28, and that he could not recall his testimony to the grand jury.

Newton was sent to jail immediately, even though an appeal was pending.* The contrast between Newton, who was denied bail on appeal of a manslaughter conviction, and O'Brien, who was allowed to walk the streets although charged with murder, presents to black people a gigantic legal bas-relief which graphically portrays the picture of the color-coded face of justice.

The appeal brief covered every phase of the trial, but did not raise many issues (other than the conduct of the trial itself) that were not presented in the civil suit filed in April, 1968. Garry did point out in his appeal that Judge Friedman, when confronted with the important discrepency in Grier's testimony, simply ordered the typed statement to be changed without calling the jury's attention to the change. This he did, after denying Garry's motion to reopen the trial to consider new evidence.

---

* Huey's conviction was reversed by a unanimous decision of the State Court of Appeals, after he had served twenty-two months of a two-to-fifteen-year term. California law allows the Adult Authority to release a convicted felon after serving one-third of the minimum sentence. In Newton's case that would have been eight months. Such early releases do not fit in with the concept of rehabilitation held by the authority, which estimates that approximately 3 percent of prisoners are released after their first parole hearing. This hearing is not usually held until the entire minimum sentence has been served.

The Court of Appeals ruled that Judge Friedman was in error when he refused to instruct the jury that unconsciousness if proved is a complete defense to the charge of criminal homicide— ". . . if they fully believed his [Newton's] testimony with respect to his asserted unconsciousness, they had been given no basis upon which to acquit him if they found it to be true."

Garry's appeal also dealt with the repressive police atmosphere of the trial, where Newton's family and fiancée had to be fingerprinted before being allowed in the courtroom, which was dominated at all times by a squadron of curt, helmeted policemen.

Authoress Kay Boyle, who attended the trial, wrote:

"Tension in and around the Alameda County Courthouse was so high that, by order of the presiding judge in the case, seventy-two-year-old Monroe Friedman, even members of the press were frisked before they were permitted to enter the courtroom on the seventh floor. Since the opening day of the trial July 15, an array of sheriff's deputies, silver helmeted and with revolvers and handcuffs at their belts, were stationed inside both the 12th Street and 13th Street entrances of this building to which the general public usually has free access. All other doorways were barred. From the sixth floor to the tenth, the stairway was sealed off. On the tenth floor, Huey Newton and other prisoners were held in maximum security.

"During the entire day, anyone seeking to enter the courthouse had to be cleared by sheriff's armed deputies who stood inside the glass doors, stoney-jawed, with helmet straps clamped rigidly under their chins. Irritation, anger and outrage were the prevalent reactions to the massive display of armed security, and there was a good deal of all of these emotions in the voice and eye of the brilliant, hard-hitting defense attorney, Charles Garry, when, on the opening day, he called Judge Friedman's attention to the fact that the sensational security measures being taken were creating an atmosphere of fear and intimidation prejudicial to Newton's case. 'Every time I enter this court, I feel I am in a police state,' Garry said, and Judge Friedman tartly admonished him to confine himself to the issues and not interject personal matters." *

* "Notes on Jury Selection in the Huey P. Newton Trial," *The Progressive*, October 1968.

Garry managed to get one victory in a subsequent court action, the almost miraculous release of Eldridge Cleaver from prison in Vacaville, California, where he had been sent following his arrest in connection with the shoot-out when Hutton was killed.

Cleaver was sent to jail by the Adult Authority, who automatically revoked his parole based on police reports of the incident. Garry successfully argued before Solano County Superior Judge Raymond Sherwin that a writ of *habeas corpus* was in order. Judge Sherwin ordered the release June 12, 1968, saying that Cleaver's parole was revoked not from any "failure of personal rehabilitation, but from his undue eloquence in pursuing his political goals, goals which were offensive to many of his contemporaries." Sherwin also noted that the two-months' delay of the Adult Authority in granting Cleaver a parole hearing was unconscionable. Cleaver had this decision reversed September 27, 1968, by the State District Court of Appeal. The State Supreme Court upheld the Appeals Court decision on November 20, and a week later Cleaver was off to Cuba.

Generally, Panthers don't do too well in the cycle of arrests, trials and jail sentences. According to *Newsweek* * there is a sixteen-page confidential memorandum going the rounds of the federal intelligence community which says that 350 Panthers were arrested in 1969 on charges ranging from robbery, burglary, auto theft and narcotics violations, as well as the illegal-weapon charges that almost invariably accompany a Panther arrest.

Supposedly, since 1967, Panthers have killed five policemen and wounded forty-two, but the toll of Panthers seems to have been higher. There appears to be an unwritten agreement that Panthers are wrong in the eyes of the law, under any and all circumstances.

In January, 1969, two Panthers, John Huggins and Al-

* February 23, 1970.

prentice Carter, were killed at UCLA. The next day, seventeen Panthers were arrested at Huggins's home and twelve of them were charged with conspiracy to commit assault with a deadly weapon, and violations of the deadly-weapons-control laws. Police explained that they had no suspects in the killings of Huggins and Carter, but that they believed the Panthers might have been preparing to seek vengeance for the deaths of their comrades.

In Berkeley the national headquarters was heavily patrolled by Berkeley cops. Oakland policemen found it necessary to have a stream of police cars make a turnaround just two blocks south at the Oakland-Berkeley border.

Another conspiracy charge involved six members of the Illinois Panthers, including Fred Hampton. The State's Attorney was quoted as saying that the indictments were not a systematic attempt to break up the Panthers' Illinois organization, but did not deny that convictions would seriously disorganize the party, because half the persons charged held administrative positions.

Hampton himself was killed December 4, in a before-dawn raid conducted by fourteen Chicago policemen. The State's Attorney released a photo indicating what was purported to be a wall scarred by a shotgun blast. Curious reporters chased down that bit of evidence and exposed it as a photograph of a wall with exposed nail heads. The Coroner's Jury investigating the death found it to be justifiable homicide, despite the fact that Hampton had apparently never risen from the bed in which he was killed, and that no evidence was produced to indicate that any of the nine Panthers who were in the apartment when it was raided ever fired a shot.

Erika Huggins, John Huggins's widow, was one of eight Panthers arrested in New Haven, Connecticut, and charged with murder and conspiracy to commit murder in the slaying of Alex Rackley, a member of the New York Panther organization. Rackley had supposedly been kidnapped in New York, taken to New Haven, beaten, tortured, stabbed with an ice-pick, shot, and then tossed into a shallow river. The arrests in Connecticut led to a raid on the Chicago Panther office, where several Panthers were arrested and charged with conspiracy to harbor a fugitive.

The fugitive in question was George Sams, Jr., who was not found in the Panther headquarters when it was raided. Further, any Panther headquarters would be a strange place for Sams to hide, considering that he was the State's main witness against the Panthers. In December, Sams pled guilty to murdering Alex Rackley, but he did so, Sams said, on orders from Bobby Seale, who had been in New Haven two days before the murder fulfilling a speaking engagement. In his trial testimony, Sams reported that he actually took orders from Stokely Carmichael, an apparent contradiction.

Bobby Seale finally was indicted and charged with conspiracy to commit murder, based to a large extent on Sams's testimony.

By contrast, the almost nationwide uniformity of approach to Panthers is not viewed by law enforcement officials as conspiratorial, or even smacking of law-enforcement cooperation. The façade is beginning to break down, however. Cecil Poole, a Negro U.S. Attorney who was replaced in his job by a Nixon appointee, said that there was a definite government attempt to get the Panthers.

The mayor of Seattle publicized the fact that he had turned down a request from the Treasury Department to conduct a raid on Washington Panther headquarters, under cover of searching for guns of a type prohibited by federal law. He subsequently complained that federal authorities, specifically the FBI, in an apparent retaliatory move, refused to investigate a rash of bombings that was terrorizing the city.

A case can be made charging that law-enforcement officials, in conjunction with judges, juries and respectable citizens, have, through racism, conspired to systematically deprive blacks of their right to a fair trial. Severe criticism was directed toward Detroit's criminal courts for their handling of 7231

persons arrested during the six-day riot in 1967. According
to a study conducted by the University of Michigan Law
School, vital guarantees were lost as a result of the arrests.
The Recorders Court, which handles all city criminal cases,
made a basic policy decision to aid the executive branch in
breaking the back of the disorder. In doing so, the court
followed a uniform high-bail policy designed to keep those
arrested off the street and in jail. Bail as high as $200,000 was
set for some of those arrested during the disturbances, and
$10,000 to $25,000 bail was common. One judge set 161 bonds
out of 175 at $10,000. The most telling description of the
state of mind of city officials was given by the Executive Judge
of the Recorders Court, Vincent J. Brennan.

He said that the court was reluctant to release arrestees,
because "We didn't know what people we were arraigning—
whether they were on probation or parole. Within two or
three days records started coming through"—and many of
the prisoners were released. Immediate release of those arrested
might have had a bad effect on police and National Guard
morale, explained the judge. "If a policeman arrests a man at
2 P.M., and then at midnight runs into the same guy again,
he'll just say, 'What's the use.'

"We know that there must have been incidents when some
rights were violated somewhere along the line. We only hope
it was a minimal amount."

Courts are, in the discharging of their duties, supposed to
protect rights, rather than hope that violations are kept to a
minimum. One black judge sitting on the Detroit bench, Judge
George W. Crockett, Jr., was praised in the University of
Michigan Law School report as being probably the only judge
who kept his head during the riots and administered justice
impartially.

Judge Crockett is considered the finest constitutional expert
on the Detroit bench, but has been the target of a campaign to
remove him from office, headed by the *Detroit News*, the
city's largest newspaper. The paper, which saw nothing wrong

in the acquittal of the policemen charged with murder in the widely publicized Algiers Motel incident, lost all patience with the judge because of his actions in a mass arrest.

One hundred forty-seven black men were arrested on March 30, 1969, after a gun battle in which one policeman was killed. Some of the blacks involved were members of a revolutionary organization called the Republic of New Africa. On 5:30 of a Sunday morning, Judge Crockett walked into downtown Detroit police headquarters and asked for a list of the men arrested.

He couldn't get one; none had been made out. Less than an hour later, the judge had set up an impromptu court right there in the station. He heard testimony, and released most of the prisoners. The county prosecutor tried to hold one of the men in defiance of Judge Crockett's order. He was promptly charged with contempt.

Judge Crockett's attitude is probably the result of his expertise on the Constitution, coupled with the fact that he has spent time in jail. In 1952, he went to New York to defend a communist charged with teaching the overthrow of the government. He was cited for contempt in his conduct of the defense, and spent four months in an Ashland, Kentucky, federal jail.

In the opinion of Detroit's blacks, Judge Crockett is a strict constitutionalist. He believes in the Bill of Rights. In this regard, the semantics of President Nixon and that of black people are in conflict. For the President, when seeking what he called a strict constitutionalist for a spot on the Supreme Court, nominated two people who blacks felt were out and out racists. Black judges such as Crockett do more to establish the conditions under which orderly justice can exist than all the commission, laws, and high-court token-black appointments that have come into being since the republic decided that the differences which led to the Civil War could be settled by freeing slaves and creating second-class citizens.

Judge Crockett's value to America's system of justice is

derived from the fact that he acts as a judge, and speaks as a black man. He is not integrated in the sense that integration requires prior identification with the racist-tolerant attitudes that govern American institutions. There is a white judge in North Carolina, for instance, who sentenced five young blacks to twelve years in prison for setting fire to a KKK headquarters. Less than $100 damage was done to the door of the dilapidated service station which also served as the Klan office. The incident occurred in Benson, South Carolina, apparently in response to an armed trip that Klansmen made through the Negro district immediately after Martin Luther King was buried.

"I might have been wrong with it," said Superior Court Judge William Y. Bickett, "I don't mind admitting I might have made a bad judgment—a mistake.

"But I used my best judgment at the time. I was sitting on top of a red-hot situation over there. What I did was a deterrent to the situation rather than punishment for the individual defendants." The judge said that he had no plans to alter his judgment, even though he recognized that the severity of the sentence "might now work to the detriment of the individuals involved."

Judge Bickett was speaking from his position as a cracker, tarheel, state representative of white superiority on the Superior Court bench. His racism, if not understandable, is detectable, and is obviously representative of the kind of justice wanted by those with power in South Carolina. There are other judges on the bench, variants of white, anglo-saxon persuasions, who, even when polishing up their liberal image, essentially vibrate judicially with a sympathetic appreciation of the needs of racists, and the necessities of the rich and powerful.

But there are other judges, who come to their positions from another social bag. Some have backgrounds of poverty, others have family origins in European countries that have been and are still somewhat regarded as producers of an inferior stock of white men. And then there are the Negro and Jewish judges, who in performing their duties, lean over backwards to demonstrate that they are just like everybody else—white, that is. These judges, by denying their backgrounds, rejecting their personal knowledge of the manner in which disadvantage is distributed in this nation, by neglecting to appreciate the fact that the product of a melting pot is a superior metal only when the superior properties of the constitutents to the alloy are preserved and used, are placing a rubber stamp on the conspiracy of racism and repression which is now using the courts full-time, in the search for law and order.

Judge Julius Hoffman is a Jew, a fact he was constantly reminded of by at least two of the defendants in the conspiracy trial in which Bobby Seale was one of the original eight defendants. He presided over what is probably the most chaotic trial ever conducted in modern times. Hoffman is a legal technician, with a reputation for knowing everything about courtroom procedure and the ability to demonstrate that he knows little about justice, unless it is the brand of justice dispensed by his German Jewish counterparts in the days preceding Hitler's decision to get Jews off the bench completely.

Abbie Hoffman (Did the judge ever ask himself: Does his name have to be Hoffman?) and Jerry Rubin, two of the defendants, must have shook the judge right down to the roots of his juridicial-christian ethic. They threw gibes at him in English, German and Yiddish. Hoffman's a "shonder for the goy," they intoned, an expression which was decorously translated into "a front man for white supremacists."

The defendants did not restrict their remarks to Hoffman's ethnic background; they in fact conducted themselves in a wildly unorthodox fashion, expressing their contempt for the entire process in which they were involved. Wisecracks, insults, obscene and objectionable language, flying paper airplanes, a defense table that was used constantly as a footstool, maddening delays caused by the inability of the defendants to get themselves into the courtroom at the same time, an im-

promptu birthday party for Bobby Seale, only partially describes the antics that went on at the trial.

But Hoffman and Rubin could not help but get to the judge
as they tore into him from the vantage point of 5000 years of
Jewish history and culture. There he sat, a judge, a big man
in the community, facing two men who obviously came from
good Jewish families. They persistently blamed Judge Hoffman for every evil that ever befell Jews, particularly those
of the past fifty years. Eichmann, white supremacist, whatever the Yiddish equivalent of bootlicker might be, second-
class goy and other descriptions—that must have strung Hoffman out. Hoffman was a white man as far as the defense was
concerned, a Jew pretender, a fascist turncoat whose token
presence in the halls of government was helping to fashion
procedures that would contribute to the future elimination
of those Jewish brothers he had abandoned, in favor of the
assimilatory honor of making judgments about people in the
name of the law.

And if they weren't enough, there was the nigger, Bobby
Seale. Bobby, who had been spirited from a San Francisco jail
and secretly transported to Chicago by car, and for no apparent reason other than the paranoia or sadism of federal
law-enforcement officials. He refused to be silenced, attempted
to cross-examine every government witness who mentioned
his name, and regularly accused Judge Hoffman of acting in a
racist manner by denying him the right to an attorney of his
own choice, or, alternately, the right to defend himself.

Bobby and Hoffman were in conflict over the business of
legal representation before the trial began. William Kunstler,
the defense attorney whom Hoffman sentenced to four years
in jail for contempt, had asked for a delay in the trial, so that
Charles Garry could recover from surgery and represent
Seale. Not only did Hoffman deny the motion, he told Seale
that Kunstler would represent him.

The Judge evidently based his decision on the fact that

Kunstler, who had replaced Garry as chief lawyer for the eight, had filed a general appearance in behalf of Seale in order to visit him in jail.

Seale had been out of touch with everyone, including his attorney, because of the antics of the federal marshals, who announced to all and sundry for a week that they had no knowledge of Seale's whereabouts. Hoffman had already cited two attorneys connected with the case for contempt and ordered them to jail, and denied virtually every motion offered by the attorneys who he allowed to remain free for the duration of the trial.

Hoffman picked the jury himself, attempted to select the attorneys, told everyone what to do, and gave every indication of the quality of his impartiality by denying thirty-five of thirty-five defense motions offered in a pretrial court session. Both the judge and the government attorneys subjected the defense to a unified wall of opposition, and the entire trial was conducted in a courtroom filled with marshals, surrounded by federal security troops and infiltrated with FBI agents. Hoffman, a hanging judge, had a record of twenty-four convictions in his last twenty-five cases. Before that, there was an acquittal. Hoffman was reported to have been so mad that he sentenced one of the jurors to two years in jail, for reading a newspaper clipping about the case.

From the very beginning, Seale attempted to defend himself. He told Hoffman that he had never chosen Kunstler as his attorney and that he had no intention of doing so. During the pretrial hearings Bobby publicly fired Kunstler, saying that he could only be adequately represented by Garry. When the trial began, Hoffman refused to allow Seale to make an opening statement, after the defense lawyers had completed theirs, and the fight was on. Bobby received the first of sixteen citations for contempt of court.

Daily, Hoffman and Seale clashed on the question of legal representation.

MR. SEALE: What about Section 1982, Title 42 of the Code where it says the black man cannot be discriminated against in my legal defense in any court in America?

THE COURT: Mr. Seale, you do know what is going to happen to you—

Hoffman absolutely refused to accede that Seale had any rights other than those that he, in his judicial wisdom, would deign to grant him. While the judge sometimes lost his cool, he never lost that sense of righteousness that was anchored to his acceptance of this right to absolute power.

THE COURT: You know you do not have a right to speak while the judge is speaking.

MR. SEALE: I have a right to speak and make requests and make arguments to demonstrate the fact I want to cross examine. When you say I disrupt, I have never tried to strike anybody, I have never tried to hit anybody. I have never. You know that. And in my arguments and motions I called you a racist and a fascist and a pig, and that's what I consider you as and my arguments and my motions will always carry that as long as my constitutional rights are being denied. So it is a lie, and you know it.

THE COURT: You have a lawyer of record and he has been of record here since September 24.

MR. SEALE: I have been arguing that before that jury heard one shred of evidence. I don't want these lawyers because I can take up my own legal defense, and my lawyer is Charles Garry.

THE COURT: I direct you, sir, to remain quiet.

MR. SEALE: And just be railroaded?

THE COURT: Will you remain quiet?

MR. SEALE: I want to defend myself do you mind, please?

THE COURT: Let the record show that the defendant Seale continued to speak after the Court courteously requested him to remain quiet.

Hoffman, with all his arrogant reliance on the majesty of his orders, could not cope with Bobby Seale. The nigger had the effrontery to lecture him on the constitution: "After you've done walked over people's constitutional rights, the sixth amendment, the fifth amendment and the phoniness and the corruptness of this very trial for people to have a right to speak out, freedom of speech, freedom of assembly, and etcetera. You have did everything you could with those jive lying witnesses up there presented by these pig agents of the government to lie and say and condone some rotten racists, fascists crap by racist cops and pigs that beat people's heads—and I demand my constitutional rights—demand—demand; . . . I am not going to be quiet. I am talking in behalf of my constitutional rights man, in behalf of myself, that's my constitutional right, to talk in behalf of my constitutional rights."

He lectured in history: "Sixty-eight thousand nine hundred ninety-nine black men died in the Civil War for that right. That right was made during the Reconstruction period. They fought in that war and sixty-eight thousand of them died. That law was made for me to have my constitutional rights." And American culture: "We're hip to the fact that Superman never saved no black people."

The Judge could lash back at the white defendants and their lawyers with what he thought were telling points or intimidating threats. He might not have understood who they were, but he knew where they came from and could verbally and culturally return some of their fire and expect it to hit home. But with a nigger he was out of his culture. The only cultural artifact to fall back on was that of slavery. Niggers obeyed orders, that was all. And finally, when Bobby did not, he had him handcuffed, gagged, and chained to a chair. Hoffman did so using the oily, unctuous, unconscionable lie of the fascist blinded by the light of truth as he sees it, that Bobby was chained in order to assure a fair and impartial trial.

This honorary white man, dispenser of government opinions and prototype of the American fascist judge, had given Bobby the justice he thought a black man deserved. Law and Order? Slavery? Is there really a difference?

There is no question that Bobby Seale disrupted Hoffman's procedural approach. And it seems quite clear that the declaration of a mistrial in Bobby's case was an appropriate act.

Hoffman had warned Bobby at several points in the trial that he had the right to gag him, to place him in chains, a right that even his Nazi precursors had not exercised.

Hoffman seemed to have an emotional need to pillory Bobby. More to the point, he is a racist federal judge presiding in a northern and reputedly enlightened portion of the nation. He is an authoritarian and an insult to the sensitivities of anyone who values manhood, freedom, equality, the notion of community, the concept of humanity, or the preservation of human warmth, sympathy and understanding. He is the end product of the ability to succeed in America through the device of denying identification with his ethnic roots, his religious beliefs and his phantom dedication to the idea of justice.

When Hoffman chained and gagged Bobby Seale, he did nothing except to put a nigger in his place. That symbolic act brands him for all time as an enemy of that portion of humanity that is black, a threat to all men who righteously know that everyone's freedom is limited to the extent that one man's liberty is denied, and an omen to Jews, who must, against the lesson that history has taught them, see in Hoffman's conduct the reflexes of the Judas goat.

The Chicago Eight became the Chicago Seven. Bobby could not be silenced. He rattled his chains, moved his chair around, and managed to shout through the gag that was binding him that his constitutional rights had been denied.

And Hoffman, when he declared the mistrial, setting another trial date for Bobby, used his legal adroitness to deny Bobby more than the inability to be tried by a jury of his peers. Hoffman, by stringing out a list of sixteen alleged instances where Bobby was in contempt of court, and sentencing him for ninety days on each of them, avoided the U.S.

Supreme Court ruling that entitled a defendant in a contempt proceeding a jury trial whenever the possible penalty exceeded six months.

The main complaint is that Hoffman used his knowledge of the letter of the law to defeat the law's spirit. And in doing so, he trampled on the rights of those who were being tried in his court, and helped to mangle the hopes of those who still expect justice from the courts. The fact that he is Jewish is important, because somewhere out of the reservoir of cultural knowledge of the travail of Jews, Hoffman should have internalized the fact that the politically unpopular, those persecuted by society's institutions, have often been Jews. "Assimilation, yes! Revolution, no!" seems to have been his battle cry, and Hoffman, therefore, identified with those who, like Senator Stennis, believe that a situation can arise where a man forfeits his rights.

Rights can be ignored, rights can be unknown, and rights can also be trampled upon. Rights can wither because they are not exercised and rights can exist only on paper in those force-dominated societies which demand total loyalty from each and every citizen. But never, ever, under any conceivable set of circumstances, can an individual forfeit his rights.

Bobby Seale refused to be tried, unless and until his rights to legal counsel were satisfied in a way meaningful to him. When Bobby said that he had a constitutional right to talk about his constitutional rights, he was expressing an ultimate belief in the necessity of all public institutions to respect an individual's humanity.

The point which Bobby made was dramatized even further in the trial of the New York Twenty-One, a group of Panthers represented by a black attorney. For ten months the group had been in jail charged with conspiracy to commit acts which had never been consummated. When they finally came to trial, it was the defendants who disrupted the courtroom—who essentially refused to be tried under the conditions prevailing in that New York Court. These conditions included a distrust of the jury selection system, questions about possible racism on the part of the judge, doubts about the ability to receive a fair trial under the widely publicized circumstances surrounding the trial, and an absolute conviction that the trial, if entered into, would represent another railroading of blacks whose politics, not acts, have been declared criminal.

Judge Murtagh, like Hoffman, insisted that the group stand trial. When their courtroom antics made it impossible for him to conduct the trial according to his lights, he threw the Panthers back into jail, saying that he would release them only when they agreed to submit to the courtroom procedure that he deemed necessary. This is an Irishman now, who is of an age to know with precision the injustices heaped on Irish revolutionaries by a government intent on suppressing revolution.

He knows better than most that the concept of peer, descending as it does from the British experience, never included working-class Englishmen, let alone Irishmen.

Murtagh could have taken another tack, listened to the arguments and then proceeded to set up a courtroom situation in which the Panthers would have had to defend themselves before a jury of their peers. The move would have been unprecedented, and would have been subject to judicial review. But it would have established at his level the idea that one judge was sufficiently moved by the concept of what a fair trial was supposed to be, to go about the task of setting one up. Instead, the reflex was to throw the Panthers back in jail, to deny their arguments' merit, and, therefore, to penalize them for standing up for rights that transcend a judge, any system of jurisprudence, or any notion of what law and order is supposed to be.

Point Number 10 of the Panther Party Platform and Program summarizes: "We want land, bread, housing, education, clothing, justice and peace." These objectives are supported by an adaptation repeating the words of the Declaration of Independence. Particularly stressed is the phrase: "That to secure these rights, governments are instituted among men, deriving their just powers from the consent of the governed; that, whenever any form of government becomes destructive to these ends, it is the right of the people to alter or to abolish it, and to institute a new government, laying its foundation on such principles and organizing its powers in such form as to them shall seem most likely to effect their safety and happiness. . . . But," the declaration concludes, "when a long train of abuses and usurpations, pursuing invariably the same object, evinces a design to reduce them under absolute despotism, it is their right, it is their duty, to throw off such government, and to provide new guards for their future security."

The Panthers do not find any conflict between their battle cry, "All power to the people," and the words of the Declaration of Independence. In fact, they have not attacked the Constitution. To the contrary, most of the arguments they raise in court, however unorthodox might be the delivery, are based on constitutional questions. With American history as the justification for their political stance, and their knowledge of court practices as their reason for mass resistance to being judged by tribunals that seem to be biased against the poor, people of color, and the politically unpopular, the Panthers seem to be on firm ideological ground.

Law before order, and both before justice, is an impossible equation in a nation where slavery has been outlawed, and where blacks are beginning to be obsessed with the need for real and effective freedom. Law and order can conceivably be translated into a synonym for justice. But to look at the courts as they operate today is perhaps to recognize that blacks must interpret the call for law and order as a mandate for a black-directed change that at the very outset rejects the opportunity to be judged by people who have openly declared themselves to be superior to blacks.

VII

Who Will Civilize the Jungle?

THURSDAY, NOVEMBER 21, 1968. Eldridge
Cleaver, scheduled to return to jail and submit to a hearing
validating the move of the Adult Authority seeking to end
his parole, is speaking:

"I cannot relate to spending the next four years in the penitentiary, not with madmen with supreme power in their
hands. . . . I'm not afraid to walk into any courtroom in this
land with a lawyer like Garry. . . . But don't you come up
to me telling me that you're going to revoke my parole on a
charge for which I put in nine years behind the walls, and for
which I was supposed to receive my discharge next month.
Don't you come up to me talking that shit because I don't want
to hear it. . . .

"I just have to say that I didn't leave anything in that penitentiary except half of my mind and half of my soul and that's
dead there. I have no use for it. It's theirs. They can have that.
That's my debt to them. That's my debt to society and I don't
owe them a motherfucking thing! They don't have anything
coming. Everything they get from now on, they have to take!
I believe that our time has come. A point has been reached
where a line just has to be drawn, because the power struc-

ture of this country has been thoroughly exposed. There is no right on their side."

Sunday, November 24. The Cleavers are receiving visitors. At home Kathleen is Mrs. Cleaver rather than the gun-carrying Communications Secretary pictured in the revolutionary press. She and Eldridge pass wisecracks between them.

Much of the meaning is hidden from a visitor, because the private experience of marriage, with the intimate awareness that death, imprisonment or both are the only realistic expectations of any couple dedicated to bringing off revolution, is not subject to outside understanding.

Cleaver is showing off what he calls his slavemaster chair. It is a stuffed antique armchair whose wooden arms and legs are decorated with carved niggers. They are the frozen predecessors of the statues of pickaninnies that once decorated lawns, held veranda doors open and rigidly demonstrated the place that black folks had in this society. The chair, with Cleaver in it, backs on the open doorway between the small living room and the adjacent study where Cleaver's desk, library, record collection and sound system are located. Cleaver's living room looks smaller than it actually is. Two of the walls are completely covered with revolutionary posters from all parts of the world. One with a silhouette of Che comes from England, and features a poem, "To Eldridge," written by Christopher Louge, one of Britain's poetic voices of extreme disaffection.

There is a heroic-sized poster from mainland China, prominently displaying a large black man dressed in an orange and yellow robe. He is crouched, apparently running, holding a rifle in a manacled left hand. The chains leading away from the broad wristlet are broken, and the black is leading a revolutionary army of identifiably Third World people.

A one-foot-square likeness of Stalin, woven on silk in China, is obvious in its austere black and white, even though it is placed to one side of the multi-colored, postered wall.

"Why in hell do you keep Stalin's picture up there?" asks Kathleen, noting that Mao's picture was not in the room.

"I just keep it there to remind you, Baby, that Mao is a Stalinist."

When Kathleen jokingly threatens to remove it on grounds that a black revolutionary's wall should not be decorated with white people, Eldridge directs another placement of the likeness. In a few minutes, moving against desire, Kathleen relocates Stalin's picture so that it is now at the visual center of the wall.

Where the windows ought to be, there are more posters. These are placed on a floor-to-ceiling sandwich of half-inch sheet steel on three-quarter-inch plywood. All of the windows in the house are armored this way, as is the front door, and the back door located in the kitchen.

When Cleaver shifts in his chair, the butt end of a very large gun can easily be seen. There is no need to ask questions. If his speech of the previous Thursday did not convince anyone of his intentions, the armor plate and his armament does. Cleaver will walk out of that house with all the freedom he can muster or else die there, shooting at anyone who would attempt to restrict that freedom.

Cleaver interrupts his conversation to speak with Panthers coming in groups of three or four. Many of them are faces which memory does not place at any of the rallies, demonstrations, assemblies or political events where Panthers gather in force. They don't settle in the living room, but rather distribute themselves in other parts of the house.

Cleaver is mellow, relaxed, humorous and totally involved in his one occupation, advancing revolutionary consciousness. His talk ranges from reminiscenses of prison to side remarks directed toward Kathleen. At one point he gets up, goes upstairs and after about ten minutes returns dressed in an olive drab raincoat. With him is Kathleen, also dressed to leave, and still answering Eldridge's jibes.

He says that he has to leave and prepare for a radio show,

a necessity which prompts his visitors to leave. Walking down the wooden steps to the sidewalk, Cleaver's friends pass by a group of people, some carrying signs protesting the action of the Adult Authority. Across the front of the house is a narrow, red-lettered, eight-foot-long section of sheet saying, "We love Eldridge."

The protesters were the advance guard of a vigil composed of people who declared themselves ready to use their bodies in protection of Eldridge. They would be the first line of defense, and would block the steps leading up to Cleaver's front door if and when police came to drag Eldridge away.

They gathered in increasing numbers Sunday night and Monday, so that by Tuesday night the sidewalk in front of Cleaver's house was filled with people. Some were camped out in an area leading to the next-door basement. Still others walked in front, some carrying picket signs, and most speculating on what Eldridge would do and whether or not he was in the house. Most had correctly surmised that Cleaver had already vacated the premises.

The stairs leading up to the house were completely clogged with sitting people who left just enough room to allow a single file up the stairs. At least two Panthers always stood at the top of the small landing. These men challenged everyone they did not know, and sent quite a few people back down the stairs. When they could be convinced that the person seeking entrance to the house was legitimate, one would rap sharply on the door, always with the same staccato pattern.

"Who's there?"

"Sam." The guard always identified himself first.

"Who's coming in?"

"Joe," or "Ann with food," or "The doctor."

Occasionally it was necessary for one of those inside to come out and identify the person seeking entrance.

Every time the door opened, it was to the sound of weapons being cocked, rounds being shoved into the barrels of shotguns, and clips of ammunition reporting their readiness to shoot with a sharp metallic clack. A visitor entered facing a sea of guns. Halfway up the stairs, located to the right of a narrow corridor, was a Panther with a pointed 12-gauge shotgun. At the top stood another youth, with an automatic weapon. An alcove under the stairs hid a man lying prone; his 30.06 rifle, however, was clearly in sight and pointed toward the entrance.

Four feet behind him, and several feet above, was another pointed rifle. Its owner was also out of sight, hidden by the wall separating the alcove from the kitchen. In the center of the kitchen, on a direct line with the front door, was the short leg of an L-shaped counter that ran down the center of the room. Behind it was a large-caliber automatic rifle, pointed by a man who, while clearly in sight, had a totally unobstructed view of the front door.

All around the kitchen, and out of sight of the front entance, were more Panthers, all of them armed and each ready to jump to pre-set firing positions whenever it should become necessary. Their conversation was cut off in mid-syllable when the sound of weaponry announced someone's entrance.

In a remote corner of the kitchen, close to the barricaded back door, was a bag full of medical equipment. A motorcyle-riding MD, member of the Medical Committee for Human Rights, had made several trips to and from the house hauling in medical supplies. At one point he attempted to explain to one of the field captains how his makeshift hospital was organized and what first-aid techniques should be utilized in case of trouble.

"Oh man, come on," said the captain, attempting to explain the facts of life to what he perceived as a well-meaning but impractical liberal. The doctor was the only white person in the house, and seemed out of place with his white medical coat covered by a windbreaker and with a crash helmet on his head. "If the shit starts to fly, just who do you think is going to take time out to sew up somebody?"

"I will," said the medic, in a business-as-usual tone that

commanded instant respect. "But you know, somebody be-sides me should know what's going on with the medical sup-plies just in case. . . ." The objections stopped, and several of the Panthers attentively participated in a first aid lesson with special emphasis placed on gunshot wounds.

There was a kind of learning process going on in the other two main-floor rooms. Both the living room and the study were stuffed with men. One was sitting in an easy chair, his rifle beside him. The arm of the chair held a biology text, from which a student was preparing his biology assignment for the following Monday.

Somebody looked at Stalin's picture and asked, "Who the hell is that whitey on the wall?" It was explained to him by another college student. This student would occasionally look up from his book to read a passage which he found illustrative of racist educational purposes. "Check this out!" he would say, and often would start a politically oriented conversation, punctuated with quotes from the Red Book, held by many of the other Panthers.

The men filling the two rooms were the off-duty reserves. They rotated to the kitchen, or to the upstairs where still more Panthers filled the bedrooms, using everything, including a crib abandoned by a baby evacuated from the house, as a barricade between themselves and the steel-shuttered win-dows.

Combat ready, drilled by a thousand openings and closings of the front door; a thousand cycles of cock, aim, uncock, relax; a thousand reductions of response to the environment, to the single ability to shoot when necessary: the Panthers waited in defense of Eldridge's right to the sanctity of his home. All of the conversations, self-revelations, humorous ex-changes and, as the night wore on, the tense slumber of men waiting for an alarm, were governed by the metronomic cer-tainty of the clicking and clashing of firing mechanisms in response to a knock on the door.

Guns and personnel came in throughout the night. The

pieces were carried through a lumber yard, dropped over a fence, and later retrieved by their owners from Cleaver's yard.

When someone left for any reason, his piece remained behind. A number of handguns lay on surfaces, ready for anyone who might find himself in need. In the corners of the rooms and on the floors of the closets were extra rifles, shotguns and an occasional automatic weapon, all accompanied by a cache of appropriate ammunition.

Nothing happened Tuesday night. No one really expected trouble. The mobilization had been arranged in anticipation of the possibility that the authorities, anxious to get Cleaver back in custody, would show up ahead of schedule to press their claim.

Crowds began showing in earnest on Wednesday. Cleaver was scheduled to surrender at 1 P.M. By that time, both sides of the street were filled with people. It was one of San Francisco's bright days, and every detail of the street was sharply outlined by the clear and slightly cold atmosphere. A helicopter circled repeatedly, and every so often a private plane would fly by at a relatively low altitude. Work had stopped on a large construction project at the far end of the block, but large men wearing hard hats could be seen pacing up and down the unfinished building.

There were no uniformed policemen in sight, but the crowd, in fact the entire block, was thoroughly infiltrated by plainclothesmen. Taxicabs discharged white men, all tensely alert, in the middle of adjacent blocks. From there, properly dark-suited, wearing ties and ominous-looking bulges, they ambled down the center of the street, acting for all the world like tourists gaping at a landmark.

A telephone truck that was parked on the block for a long while would pull away, as a gas utility van pulled up on the other side. Neo-hippies, short of beard and long in questions, would wander through the crowd, attempting to get information. One of them was dressed as a cowboy, and came on hip.

About the time the first "I dig" was leaving his mouth, a young Panther walked by.

"Hey man. I haven't seen you around here before."

"Yea! Do you . . . ?"

"You a pig?" It was more a statement of accepted fact than a question or a challenge.

"Come on now, man. Do I look like a pig to you?"

"Right on!" said the Panther, and moved away without further comment. He was part of an early warning system, a number of young blacks who would walk along the street, gesture toward one of the white males integrating themselves with the crowd, and call, "Watch out, that's a pig. If anything goes down, be careful of him."

Cleaver did not keep his appointment with the parole officer. His attorney, Charles Garry, Kathleen Cleaver, and an army of newspaper men showed up on time. Kathleen said that she was hoping to meet Eldridge there, as she had not seen him for two days. Garry notified officials that Eldridge was aware that he was expected, but denied any knowledge of the whereabouts of the Minister of Information. When it became obvious that Cleaver was not going to show, his wife, lawyer, news corps, and sundry followers caravaned back to Pine Street to see if Eldridge was home.

If Eldridge had come home, he would have had to pass through about two thousand people moving around his block. It was an impromptu festival. Friends met, shook hands and speculated about Cleaver. A busload of children from the Martin Luther King School, a black-controlled private elementary school, sang songs.

Garry had declared to newsmen that Cleaver was not in the house, and that police should accept that fact and not bother to enter. The newsmen had been beguiled by the children's singing, and charmed by Kathleen, but not to the point of being oblivious to the discipline governing the opening and closing of Cleaver's front door.

They wanted to know what or who was in the house other

than Cleaver. Garry had taken one newsman in with him, a slightly bent, gray employee of the *Oakland Tribune*. The attorney had justified his choice with praise for the reporter's abilities, and respect for his employer, who demanded facts the right wing can make opinions about. The reporter, ashen, almost mute and very uncomfortable when leaving the house, answered no questions.

Finally Charley Garry answered: "There's people with guns in there." And the wide-open secret that had filled the block with poorly disguised police officers, was now given out to an audience who came expecting a stakeout.

Away from Pine Street, in every direction, uniformed police were conspicuous. Every surrounding intersection held its parked patrol car. They were passed every few moments by a battery of cruising vehicles which covered the surrounding territory relentlessly, but did not come within a block of the crowd. It was a military operation, prepared for in advance. If armed men were not in the house, police were prepared to find them there.

Few people walked on the police-dominated streets surrounding the house. For a time, in the morning, pairs of black-leather-jacketed youth could be seen on corners within a one block perimeter. Occasionally, one would pick up a walkie-talkie and say something. A pair of them were arrested, in clear view of a number of Panthers. No one resisted arrest, and the outlying lookouts came into the block. The day moved on. People watched the house, watched those they assumed to be Panthers, tried to identify police, chilled as shadows moved across the street, and left when it became obvious that nothing more was going on.

Volunteers showed up regularly. Ironically, the food that entered the house was bought in the all-night supermarket where a year before a supermarket guard had shot a black youth, resulting in minor disturbances.

The toilet wasn't operating properly, and fuses kept blowing out. The electrical trouble didn't develop until nearly dawn Tuesday, saving a number of nerves that might have had trouble surviving several night hours of intermittent light failure.

Someone figured out how to correct the lighting problem, but no one had plumbing skills. The general lack of plumbing know-how extended to a mutual ignorance of anyone connected with the trade. They consulted the yellow pages, found a plumber, and brought him through. Wednesday night came, and those in Cleaver's house were fed, could read if they wanted to, and were assured of the blessings of indoor plumbing.

This would be the bad night. A warrant had been issued for Cleaver, who was last known at that address. Police have a habit of promptly delivering warrants, particularly when they are for well-known revolutionaries. They sat and waited for a policeman to knock on the door and say that a piece of paper gave him the right to come in.

Someone circulated the information that the Panthers were willing to honor a warrant, provided one officer served it, and searched the premises after leaving his gun outside. Police would hardly have gone for such a deal, at least not at a time where a large crowd watched them go in. With or without a crowd, the thought of a policeman going anywhere without a gun is disturbing to police authority.

Would police challenge the house? They surely knew that Cleaver was not there, but how badly did they want to prove it? Everyone could see that the police activity during the day had prepared police for a night assault.

The house directly south of the Cleavers' had been filled with police. Panthers looking out of darkened bedroom windows could see weapons and milling men, in the short-lived but regular bursts of flashlight beam coming from the apartments. During the day, police had unobtrusively moved into selected apartments commanding some sort of view of either Cleaver's house or the streets in front.

Diagonally across from a corner building whose apartments

were suddenly frequented by males was an empty building, said to contain fifteen or twenty black volunteers, who had bivouacked there for two days. They were reportedly prepared to resist police who didn't believe the rusty lock on the downstairs door, or pigs who decided to shoot.

The neighborhood is integrated in the sense that people of all races live in the area. The night streets, however, were never before so mixed with walking black and white males, each very nervous of the other.

Two policemen drove their squad car half a block the wrong way up a one way street to cut off and question a pedestrian bearing a superficial resemblance to Cleaver. In front of the house a large group of teenagers danced, laughed and generally enjoyed themselves. Stretched out along the block were pairs of leather-jacketed youths. Some walked to Broderick Street, four houses west of Cleaver's, but they didn't wander too far down the block.

There, on a steady but irregular schedule, several white males found it necessary to walk from one building to the next. Whenever a black rounded the corner and came upon a plainclothesman, there was an instant of tenseness, the kind that comes from someone obviously prepared to shoot rather than make a mistake.

Blacks withdrew, wanting to respond only to attack, and deciding that waiting around the corner could be interpreted as inviting attack.

Inside, the house was closed. Traffic was reduced to a minimum, as Panthers and police probed toward each other.

The cowboy came back, accompanied by four other western-looking types. They parked their slightly dented Pontiac next to a fireplug, and sauntered up to the group in front of the house in order to talk with them. Earlier in the day plainclothesmen had limited success in joining the vigil, when many of the participants were white. But by 11 P.M. Wednesday night, there were only a few whites left on the steps, and they were well known to all the youths in the area.

The stakeout came to a sudden end at 4 A.M. The numbers of people in front of the house had dwindled. At the same time, white male visitors to the area were on the increase. Cabs still drove by filled with men. Two and three whites would stop, get out of their car, look around and get back in.

Patrol cars had begun to cruise through the block. When the first one pulled abreast of the Cleaver house, in slow motion, one of the black-jacketed youths on the sidewalk made a throwing gesture toward the vehicle. The startled officer first hit the brake, and then speedily accelerated out of the block.

It was soon after that the decision to abandon the stakeout was made. Some of the men who left the Cleaver house were apparently unarmed. But others, carrying long objects, some in rifle bags, walked to their cars, tossed them in and drove off. Apparently no one was stopped on the way home. The cowboy and his cohorts persisted, though. They lounged about the corner talking to each other as men left the house. Then Kathleen, directing a work crew, began cleaning up the area in front.

The cowboy moved in.

"Say, what's going on here?"

"It's all over, man. Everybody's going home," said the youth, turning around and wondering to no one in particular what it would take to convince the pig to leave everyone alone.

"Well, we might come back later and see if anything is happening," said the cowboy, sauntering back to the car along with his buddies.

Kathleen, who had been sweeping the steps with enough vigor to sooner or later cover the cowboy with sweepings, was just getting into range when the quartet walked off.

"Pigs are insane," she said, and went back to sweeping. She cleaned up, and went to stay that night at a friend's house, returning the next day, Thanksgiving.

A line had been drawn, a statement made. Panthers had

openly invited police to exchange gunfire. The revolution was on; only the battles remained to be fought.

A year later, with Cleaver in Algeria and every other prominent Panther leader in jail or under close police surveillance, Fred Hampton of Illinois and Mark Clark, another Illinois Panther officer, were killed by police. The shootings climaxed a year of incidents all over the country and of Panther arrests, raids and killings by policemen. Hundreds of members of the organization have been indicted and charged with crimes. Some of the arrests were undoubtedly motivated by political considerations. But politics cuts both ways.

A large number of blacks who are in jail are there for political crimes only in the sense that a politics of racism made criminality their only out. There are others, some of them Panthers, who enter a life of crime for political purposes. The seemingly fragile justification that it is an act of politics to take something back from whitey is sometimes shored up by the intention to organize in jail when arrests come.

Prison authorities have experienced their inability in past years to inhibit the growth of the Muslims within prison walls. Cleaver, who was himself politicized through prison conversion, believed that revolutions are hatched either in exile or in jail. To a revolutionary to be in or out of jail is only a description of the geography of oppression. Policemen, judges, bailiffs, collection agents, prison guards, generals, *status-quo*-oriented public officials, and citizens content with their lives are all pigs, and counterrevolutionary.

A University of Chicago law professor, Geoffrey G. Hazard, Jr., who is also Executive Director of the American Bar Foundation, attempted to alert the House Committee on Crime during hearings held in July, 1969, to what is happening in the ghettos: "Youth crime is becoming a self-conscious act of political rebellion." These youths, in or out of jail, are the stuff of which black revolution is made, and are the basis of a new politics.

The call for armed black revolution is hardly new. In 1843,

a Presbyterian minister, Henry Highland Garnet, delivered a speech in Buffalo, New York to a group named the National Negro Committee. His speech, "Call to Rebellion," included the exhortation: "Let your motto be resistance! Resistance! Resistance! No oppressed people have ever secured their liberty without resistance." Garnet, the first American black leader to call for a national liberation struggle, himself carried a gun (which he used to defend himself from a white mob on at least one occasion), called for the establishment of a black press as an effective means of promoting black unity while attacking institutional racism, and attempted to make the black liberation struggle a subject of international interest. He spoke several languages, was the American delegate to the World Anti-Slavery Convention, and was active in antiwar activity as well.

Garnet was a direct influence on John Brown, who not only reprinted "Call to Rebellion" at his own expense, but directly precipitated the Civil War by attacking Harpers Ferry.

History is repeating itself, and in doing so is underlining the fact that the inability of whites to understand the nature of the frustration of black people is no excuse for the failure to perceive the absolute necessity of developing resistance to all forms of human brutality.

Revolution is not necessarily guns. It is a state of political intransigence, a definition of community separate from that claimed by those who rule, a blueprint for unorthodox transfer of power and a gamble that success will convert, for the edification of historians, a potential traitor to a revered patriot. If every man, woman and child with a claim to black heritage stood up at the same time and loudly shouted, "NO! ! !" the revolution would be over. But such a commitment cannot be sought outside a political philosophy which recognizes that ultimately the right to independence, self-determination, collective self-respect, might have to be pursued through violence.

The Black Panther Community News Service reprinted a portion of Mahatma Gandhi's declaration on the question of the use of violence in defense of rights which was originally published December 16, 1938, in the *Manchester Guardian*:

"Where the choice is set between cowardice and violence, I would advise violence. I praise and extol the serene courage of dying without killing. Yet I desire that those who have not this courage should rather cultivate the art of killing and being killed, then basely to avoid the danger. This is because he who runs away commits mental violence; he has not the courage of facing death by killing. I would a thousand times prefer violence than the emasculation of a whole race. I prefer to use arms in defence of honor rather than remain the vile witness of dishonor."

The choices, then, are not between violence and nonviolence, legitimacy and nonlegitimacy, or even taxation, with and without representation. Ultimately, where mass oppression is concerned someone shows up to insist that the quality of life for the masses should be improved. It is of little importance whether past efforts have been successful. Recognition of the validity of truth demands that aggrieved people strike out and move toward defining their own destiny.

If it were possible for a group of people simultaneously to arrive at some common recognition of their discontents, there would be no need for revolutionary leadership. But such is not the case. All citizens are trained by the state to accept whatever comes their way. In the final analysis, however, it is the people, the masses if you will, who move toward change. It is doubtful that in the process the rhetoric of the revolutionary is actually incorporated in mass thinking. What is more likely is that some essential message that manages to illuminate a previously ignored fact of their life moves them toward revolt.

Black people are not revolutionaries at this point in time. It is fair to say that they are getting there. The move toward a revolutionary mass culture is coming about as the vision of repression becomes a little clearer to see. An oppressed people can determine the extent to which their lives are threatened by totalitarianism, by simply establishing the extent to which the government is willing to use force against its citizens. That's it. All other criteria are lies. Memphis, for instance, where Martin Luther King died at the very moment that his efforts were beginning to be perceived as revolutionary, even though nonviolent.

Newspapers all over the country carried photos of the picket line he devised. Hundreds of men marched single file, each wearing a placard stating "I am a man." Most of the photos were cropped, or else were taken at a point in the march where the political relevance of that event could not be fully appreciated.

Those picketers were walking through a corridor of death. On one side were National Guardsmen, with upraised, bayonetted rifles. On the other, a line of tanks. Official dicta justified that show of force as a deterrent to rioting. That is one of those government-sponsored half-truths. Any massive show of force directed against the citizens of a country is a mute and powerful statement of intent. The bringing of such force is predicated upon a contingency plan. Somewhere along the line of events, someone with authority knows exactly what it would take for the entire mass of armament to erupt into flames that would control the actions of the citizenry by distributing death.

Law and order is a farce if it is perpetuated by denying justice and peace. The problem posed by the Panthers goes further than black liberation. It embraces white liberation, national freedom and collective self-respect. Panthers, in describing themselves as the vanguard, insist that it is only by identifying with the need for black liberation that American whites can free themselves.

The politics of black liberation yield valuable insights about America. Black people are poor, but whites who think of themselves as affluent are to a great extent kidding themselves. By a quirk of statistics, it turns out that less than 5 percent of Americans control over 20 percent of the economy, and that the poorest 20 percent of citizens own less than 5 percent of the nation's wealth. Those in between are hardly well off. At least 10 percent of the nation is receiving public assistance, a figure which welfare officials admit could easily be doubled by the simple expedient of extending welfare to everyone who qualifies under the law.

A further comment on America's assumed affluence is revealed by government estimates which have established an annual income of $10,000 as the figure which would allow a family of four to live modestly. Over 75 percent of American families earn less than $10,000 a year, and whether they know it or not, have not succeeded in achieving a modicum of gracious living.

In sum, the institutions which serve Americans are less effective in achieving a reasonable standard of living for citizens than the organizations which serve stockholders, giant corporations and the economic empires called conglomerates. What is being termed as a taxpayers' revolt, illustrated by the increasing refusal of Americans to support bond issues and tax increases, seems to be nothing less than people who cannot afford to pay out more money saying so through the use of the ballot.

Whole educational systems are going bankrupt, colleges are not expanding to accommodate the public need for higher education, and welfare needs are hardly being met. Hunger is a real phenomenon in this rich land, and discontent is wider spread than just among non-whites.

Black discontent is not an isolated phenomenon. The entire nation is being niggerized. It is becoming a cesspool, a slum, a crumbling and eroding monument to the rapaciousness with which some who have power approach the rest of the nation. Beaches are covered with oil slick, undisposable garbage clogs overused sewers, the air we breathe is filled with man-made toxins, and whole rivers are being converted into receptacles for industrial wastes. Incongruously, one Ohio river was declared a fire hazard, so great was its pollution. The quality of all our lives is being compromised by the greed and insensitivity of a few.

Greed and oppression are major items in the history of this country, as is violence. H. Rap Brown was not at all facetious when he remarked, "Violence is as American as apple pie." Long before any college students thought of seizing an administration building, a group of American farmers occupied the courts and refused to let any justice be transacted. That was in 1786. The farmers were successful, the taxes which they were protesting were repealed and Shay's Rebellion became history. The middle of the nineteenth century produced a number of riots directed against Irish Catholics; the bloodiest occurred in Philadelphia, City of Brotherly Love, in 1844. Over 2000 people were killed in 1863, during a five-day riot protesting selective service for the Civil War. Rioters were white, and northern, and many of their victims were black.

Ten years later, the west coast experienced a series of riots which killed a large number of Chinese. There was also the genocide which accompanied the conquering of American Indian territory. Beginning in the 1890's, fifty years of labor violence were characterized by shootings, bombings, bloody clashes and virulent police oppression of working people. In the 1920's, there were still more riots, and these resulted in the death of several hundred black people.

Violence is apparently on the increase. Over 8000 people are shot to death annually, and on the average one of every four hundred Americans is either murdered, raped, robbed or beaten. Although Negroes figure in the crime statistics, the truth is that the overwhelming number of violent incidents are the result of white activity.

Much of this violence is the direct result of national policies; and police, who ostensibly fight crime, help to contribute to the figures. The tone for police departments is set in many instances by the FBI, which in numerous ways is both racist and right-wing. J. Edgar Hoover, despite evidence to the contrary, has repeatedly asserted that black militance is a major cause of social unrest. He has developed a list of subversives which is totally condemnatory of SDS, the Black Panther

Party, SNCC, the Revolutionary Action Movement and the Republic of New Africa. Significantly, the police action directed against SDS has been much less extreme than that experienced by the other four groups, which unlike SDS are all black.

The police party line on black militance was demonstrated before a subcommittee headed by Senator John McClellan, in early 1969. Policemen from Oakland and New York, testifying at sessions held two weeks apart, gave almost identical testimony on the Black Panthers.

Imagine, despite the different levels of activity throughout the country, policemen from San Francisco, New York, Chicago, Jersey City, Los Angeles and Oakland had essentially the same thing to say about the danger of the Panthers to internal security. In building their case, incidentally, extensive use of police arrest records was the rule. There was no attempt to note whether the individuals named were convicted or acquitted of the charges.

It is easy to understand the fact that Panthers are hassled uniformly by police in all parts of the country, when there is clear evidence that the police establishment has developed a monolithically unified stance against them.

The informed opinions of special investigating commissions have underscored police involvement in perpetuating violence. The National Commission on the Causes and Prevention of Violence issued a report tracing the history of violence in America. "The grievances and satisfactions of violence have so reinforced one another that we have become a rather bloody-minded people in both action and reaction. We are likely to remain so as long as so many of us think violence is an ultimate solution to our problems."

One psychologist, Dr. Philip G. Zimbardo, believes that the pressures of big-city life are transforming Americans into potential assassins. He noted the fact that an estimated total of 40,000 American youngsters were beaten and tortured by other family members, primarily parents, every year.

The National Commission on the Causes and Prevention of Violence, in the sixth policy statement sent to the White House since June, 1968, when the Commission was formed, noted that the American machinery of justice was fragmented, inadequate and archaic. Although the Commission did not make any specific recommendations about how the nation might go about correcting racial prejudice among policemen, turnstile courts and scandalous jails, they did state:

"Police carry not only the burden of law but also the symbolic burden of all government; it is regrettable, yet not surprising, that particularly the tensions and frustrations of the poor and the black come to focus on the police.

"The antagonism is frequently mutual. Racial prejudice in police departments of major cities has been noted by reliable observers. Prejudice compromises police performance. Policemen who systematically ignore many crimes committed in the ghetto, who handle ghetto citizens roughly, who abuse the rights of these citizens, contribute substantially to disaffection with government and disrespect for law."

Police actions are not isolated from other social phenomena. Police departments are part of a national organization with direct links to the Army. The Directorate for Civil Disturbance Planning and Operations (DCDPO) was created and incorporated into existing army operations at the Pentagon. A worldwide information complex, geared to give instant data to military leaders, maintains dossiers on 100 to 150 cities. This center retains a small standing army, ready to move into any city where disturbances occur. The army, however, gets most of its information on the potential danger to a city from local police officials.

The police establishment is also linked to big business in a somewhat bizarre fashion. A San Francisco export concern, Polak Winters & Company, filed a suit in United States District Court against Bangor Punta Corporation of Greenwich, Connecticut. Bangor Punta is a conglomerate that had an estimated $260 million income in 1968. The suit estimates that by

1972, public security and law enforcement needs in the United States alone will have a market of $1.5 billion. This revelation becomes shocking when one considers that Bangor Punta has a total of 65 percent of the law enforcement market and specializes in supplying equipment for an entire national police department.

In other words, police armaments that are tested out domestically are then exported to other countries (Japan is a leading customer). By exporting police technology, the Americanization of police practices all over the world is a distinct possibility. Of more immediate importance is the implication that the profit motive places up-to-date technological innovations for the control of a civilian population into police hands. With links to the army, big business and traditional conservatism, the police establishment gives every indication of being willing to limit the freedom of all Americans, in a search for law and order.

Even the American Medical Association, an organization that can live with contemporary notions of what law and order should be, has attacked police practices. A survey conducted by the Physicians for Automotive Safety condemned the practice of "hot pursuit" by police seeking to apprehend people suspected of committing misdemeanors. They concluded that "more than 500 Americans die and over 1,000 sustain major injuries each year as a result of rapid police pursuit of lawbreakers, most of whom are guilty of only minor traffic offenses." Police departments have ignored these findings and continue to chase whenever they feel it necessary.

Police, moreover, are involved in controlling categories of crime that require more subtle judgments than those available to many patrolmen. They are in charge of antiobscenity laws, have censoring units zeroing in on books, movies and plays, and enforce antiprostitution laws, usually by arresting the prostitute but not her customer. Most important, police departments generally have a political division, where officers decide what citizens are politically subversive, and what criminal charges can be brought to bear on some of them.

Police are not responsible for all of the ills of the nation, particularly those related to race. They are, however, in the position of being able to block effective amelioration of problems, by simply enforcing what they consider to be law, morality or both. Now that they have zeroed in on black militance, a crisis has been created.

Who shall civilize the jungle? It shouldn't be police; they don't know how.

The problem is fairly simple. People, a populace, get the kind of police activity they want, up to and including a police state. There are simply not enough guns, or more important, enough people willing to wield them against a population that insists on maintaining control of its police force.

There are enough policemen, however, to limit effectively the actions of those who express dissatisfaction with the quality of their lives, as long as a majority of citizens are satisfied with or uncritical of their life experiences. Unfortunately, the majority, whites, do not equate any unhappiness they might harbor with that articulated by blacks. One of the reasons is that proportionately fewer whites come into any form of contact with police. When they do, the contact is generally devoid of the racist leanings or class hangups that many officers display only to blacks.

The content, perhaps silent, toleration with which most whites approach the police function makes them vulnerable to the notion that blacks tend to attract police attention because of widespread criminality. Even when there is sympathy for the goals of blacks who in some organized fashion have run afoul of the law, conflict with police is not considered a critical issue. The white citizen might approve of the goals and put down the tactics. Or else, where he feels that police have acted unfairly, he places faith in the court system ultimately to dispense justice.

Blacks, on the other hand, who experience the loss of friends or relatives through police action, have no real recourse to the courts. The defendant is dead. Panthers report that twenty-eight of their members have been killed by police in a two-year period. Blacks have to assess that fact, all the while knowing that many more black men have anonymously gone to their deaths at the hands of police.

Blacks, who are disproportionately victims of the fact that "too often lower criminal courts tend to be operated more like turnstiles than tribunals," consider arrest nothing more than a one-way ticket to jail.

On one level a tremendous amount of black energy is directed toward erasing the race and class distinctions which result in disproportionate contacts with courts, welfare departments, policemen, and probation officers. But as long as police serve effectively to contain the boundaries of social protest, they must contend with a gut-level opposition to them as policemen. It is the black community that has pushed most vigorously for effective police reform, and it is this particular item with which the society has not seen fit to deal, even on a token basis.

Whites who really wish to effectuate law and order need to develop an appreciation of how that goal can be reached. Whites can determine the conditions under which black liberation will become a reality. In doing so, whites may discover that they too are being liberated from a slavery which they have been conned into believing is freedom.

The combination of white peonage and police killing upset San Francisco's black community in November, 1969. Someone, black, apparently attempted to fraudulently cash a check for $150 at a downtown branch of Bank of America. He presented the check to a female teller, who grew suspicious and presented the bogus document to one of her superiors. The suspect developed suspicions of his own and decided to leave the bank without the check or the money. He was followed out, by a policeman working as a part-time clerk.

This policeman was not an undercover agent. He was moonlighting. His life was governed by an inexorable economic situation which made it difficult for him to live in the manner he would like, simply by working for the relatively high-paid S.F. Police Department. He, therefore, picked up a second job.

The bank was delighted with the arrangement. Clerks earn less than highly trained guards, and in this moonlighting officer they had both.

It seems clear though, that the officer in question should not have had to take that job in any capacity other than guard. When he leapt over the counter to pursue the fellow he thought had attempted to bilk the bank, the officer was coincidentally defending his right to work a minimum of sixty hours a week, just to make ends meet. He was possibly fatigued; after all, the work week was fairly long, and he would, therefore, have been operating at less than optimum. But in accordance with accepted nationwide police practice, he was armed and authorized to discharge that gun under certain conditions, toward anyone suspected of committing a felony.

The officer followed the man he thought to be the suspect into the street, and reportedly kept track of him moving through thronged, downtown pedestrian traffic. The chase (conducted at the pace of a fast walk) ended with the suspect receiving a bullet in the back of the head, shot by an officer who said that the suspect had made motions indicating that he might be armed. The man was not. Result, one dead black man, and one exonerated policeman, who conceivably might be commended in the future for sharp off-duty work, but who has no immediate prospect of making ends meet through working at one job.

While the black experience is a concentrated distillate of the flaws in the society as a whole, police practices reveal the enormity of the problem which must be solved. The armed constabulary, in this context, accurately represents the extent to which government is flawed and is in desperate need of the corrective action of citizens who genuinely desire a government which seeks to improve their lives.

Policing involves much more than crime prevention, the apprehension of felons, or the regulation of driving behavior. The FDA, for instance, has police powers and represents more pillmakers than pilltakers. As a result, we have been subjected to a dreary procession of doubtful drugs that have taken their toll of American lives, mental health, and in some instances future generations.

Those policing agencies regulating mass media have not insisted on the public's right to be exposed to a variety of newsworthy informational items. The Panthers are a perfect example. In the main, the impact of their arguments have not reached the general public. What is known about them generally revolves about their position relative to the gun. The speeches of Eldridge Cleaver, the writings of Huey P. Newton, the rationale behind the ten-point program, the genuine humor with which Bobby Seale has approached the serious business of revolution, the appropriate strengths of Emory's art, the genuine tenderness governing many of the relations between Panthers convinced that an early death is their destiny, the desperate courage required of youth determined to face the overwhelming disapproving force of a society which has betrayed them, their families, friends and aspirations, and the real potential within black circles to unify ultimately behind a Panther-like political orientation, have been presented only in the underground press.

Even those newspaper or television commentators who oppose the excrescence that is the Vietnamese war never speculate on the ultimate racism of a nation that seeks through force of arms to convince a people that it is right that they kill each other. Under these conditions it is hardly to be expected that the media will seriously attempt to get the idea across that killing is an invalid expression of national interest.

The same internal revenue service that comes down heavily on wage earners who illegally try to save a few dollars in tax, openly bargains with the monied person whom they know has withheld hundreds of thousands of dollars from the public treasury. Despite the obvious fact that the automobile industry is befouling the air, burning up natural resources, creating piles of metallic garbage and producing unsafe vehicles that have, through deaths, injuries and property damage cost the nation more than the entire industry is worth, it is allowed to make profits rather than being made to pay reparations to those upon whom they have inflicted harm.

Somehow, it is against the law to shoot dice on a street corner, while at the same time the ultimate form of economic legitimacy is the well-heeled crap-shooting that goes on in Wall Street–dominated securities exchanges. There are agencies that go after the poor suspected of welfare cheating, and others that make sure surplus food is securely locked away. A cosmic form of obscenity is the concept of surplus food in a nation where there are millions of hungry people.

Democracy—functional, vibrant, participatory democracy—is revolutionary. But, it requires well-informed, concerned citizens, who know their rights and who have a capacity to become angry when those rights are violated. The dilemma which blacks find themselves involved with is the choice between violent assertion of their rights to be human, and a non-violent acceptance of a majority silently submitting to the ruination of their own lives. No one, regardless of ethnic background, is going to escape the political upheaval that is revolution. All that can be done is to determine the style of a revolution that is already in progress.

The Black Panthers can only be controlled by Black People. They can be maligned, killed, misrepresented, ignored, hated, offered bribes by whites, but they can only be controlled by blacks. Issues raised by Panthers do get to blacks, and the attempts to control the Party by force of arms only serves to illustrate to blacks the necessity of resisting the oppressive social inertia of a people who have, by failing to oppose injustices in their own lives, opted to deny their own humanity.

The young men who were prepared to shoot it out in protection of Cleaver's rights in San Francisco, the eleven Panthers who held off three hundred heavily armed Los Angeles police-men for five hours, the indomitable Bobby Seale, who—manacled, chained and gagged—managed to shout to a court that his rights were being violated, represented a politics of liberation that is impelling in its validity.

Panthers are an organization formed by politically oriented men, who because of their race, class, or opinions were denied the right to present their views as elected representatives of their peers.

Who is more valid? The judge who in sending Dred Scott back to slavery noted that Negroes had no rights that white men were bound to respect, or Bobby Seale, who in being denied his day in court, attempted to expose the system of justice as a fraud?

And then, there is Eldridge Cleaver, who informed his peers that "if God himself would wield such misery on the people that I love I say, let's move on him." It takes more courage and/or wisdom to move against an assumed good than an accepted evil.

Blacks are guided by their experience that the fact of a majority is not a guarantee of rightness. Their political necessity is coming from outside the area with which most whites identify. Blacks have assumed the task of completing the work begun by the revolution in 1776. They have managed to maintain a sense of humor, despite humorless enslavement, and create a vision of utopia through a lens formed from the detritus of the oppression which is their lives. In their frustration, and by virtue of being the most denied, blacks are attempting to point the nation toward a heightened appreciation of its own humanity.

That's who the Panthers are, an organization dedicated to discovering the remains of utopia, by challenging the chaos of Babylon. They have no question about who should bring civilization to the jungle which is America. Whites have demonstrated their inadequacy in this area.

Europe's history is devoid of a period where freedom was experienced. The closest it came was in Greece (Africa influenced Greece), where the idea, if not the practice, of the democratic state was conceived.

Red men were all but eliminated on this continent. Yellow men, needed for the future development of chop suey and the then present need to expand the railroad, were kidnapped and seduced into crossing the Pacific. Mexicans, mixed descendants of Europeans and Indians, were also systematically eliminated by a people capable of tolerating fantastic dimensions of evil in the name of racial superiority.

And whites who were never allowed to look over their shoulders at the demon who talked them into accepting oppression as normal, whites who came as prisoners to penal colonies like Georgia, who "freely" contracted as indentured servants for a life of slavery, whites who were taught to do unto others as it has been done unto them, who have been victimized by being denied access to the history of their oppression, have not yet come to recognize that their discontent, their anger, their frustration are symptoms of the disease they share with blacks—oppression.

A black time is upon us. "We shall gain our manhood!" shouts Cleaver, "or else the world will be leveled in our attempts to do so." That is the prophecy of this age, and the answer to those who question the intent of the Panthers. "By any means necessary," embraces both peaceful means and those which rise from the impelling necessity to counter unreasonable force with politically motivated violence.

The choice is civilization or civil disorder, extremes which Martin Luther King detailed as community or chaos. The black cats, born amidst white Americans, trapped between their heritage of a bloodthirsty history and a tendency toward soul-saving rhetoric, the nigger, despised, spat upon, considered a creation slightly higher than whale shit, is the natural heir of the American dream.

The black man, whose need for a sense of his humanity is so

compelling that he has produced great men under the most difficult of circumstances, is moving to bring greatness to the American Experience. His thrust toward freedom is an ultimate gift to America and the world. If he is denied the opportunity to contribute to the cleaning up of American politics, he will stand in the ghettos of America and evolve into the most determined resister of genocidal racist expression the globe has ever experienced.

The choice between white reactionary styles and a freedom-seeking, non-uptight-about-other-people orientation is what lies before us.

Who shall civilize the jungle? It is obvious. Those who know that the jungle is not a threatening place. Black people, whose ancestors foolishly succumbed to the ego trip, shouted, "Come out of those trees and fight like a man," now know that manhood could have been achieved within those trees and without experiencing the political vacuity essential to a culture that seems compelled to destroy the strange, the heretical, the different, all darker people, and then to characterize those efforts as opposing sin.

No one will civilize if whites fail to recognize, and identify with, the demands of blacks that they be treated in a civil and human fashion. To destroy black people, a process that began before the systematic attempt to repress Panthers, will demonstrate to the people of the world (most of whom are not white) what they must do in order to survive. And, during the ensuing struggle, ghosts of every murdered black will haunt the land, seeking the destruction of those who would assume rule without first seeking the power to rule that is freely conferred only by a free people. It is impossible to suppress freedom and simultaneously to control the urge of men to choose to fight for their humanity.

An often-heard Panther litany seeks black power for black people, red power for red people, yellow power for yellow people, brown power for brown people, white power for white people and all power to the people. Its lack is a necessary and sufficient reason for revolution. Either the race or racism will be eliminated, and that decision will be made by white Americans.

The Panther, the black cat, is preparing for the worst.

Appendix A

October 1966
Black Panther Party—Platform and Program

WHAT WE WANT—WHAT WE BELIEVE

1. WE WANT FREEDOM. WE WANT POWER TO DETERMINE THE DESTINY OF OUR BLACK COMMUNITY.

We believe that black people will not be free until we are able to determine our destiny.

2. WE WANT FULL EMPLOYMENT FOR OUR PEOPLE.

We believe that the federal government is responsible and obligated to give every man employment or a guaranteed income. We believe that if the white American businessmen will not give full employment, then the means of production should be taken from the businessmen and placed in the community so that the people of the community can organize and employ all of its people and give a high standard of living.

3. WE WANT AN END TO THE ROBBERY BY THE WHITE MAN OF OUR BLACK COMMUNITY.

We believe that this racist government has robbed us and now we are demanding the overdue debt of forty acres and two mules. Forty acres and two mules was promised 100 years ago as restitution for slave labor and mass murder of black people. We will accept the payment in currency which will be distributed to our many communities. The Germans are now aiding the Jews in Israel for the genocide of the Jewish people. The Germans murdered six million Jews. The American racist has taken part in the slaughter of over fifty million black people; therefore, we feel that this is a modest demand that we make.

285

4. WE WANT DECENT HOUSING, FIT FOR SHELTER OF HUMAN BEINGS.
We believe that if the white landlords will not give decent housing to our black community, then the housing and the land should be made into cooperatives so that our community, with government aid, can build and make decent housing for its people.

5. WE WANT EDUCATION FOR OUR PEOPLE THAT EXPOSES THE TRUE NATURE OF THIS DECADENT AMERICAN SOCIETY. WE WANT EDUCATION THAT TEACHES US OUR TRUE HISTORY AND OUR ROLE IN THE PRESENT-DAY SOCIETY.
We believe in an educational system that will give to our people a knowledge of self. If a man does not have knowledge of himself and his position in society and the world, then he has little chance to relate to anything else.

6. WE WANT ALL BLACK MEN TO BE EXEMPT FROM MILITARY SERVICE.
We believe that black people should not be forced to fight in the military service to defend a racist government that does not protect us. We will not fight and kill other people of color in the world who, like black people, are being victimized by the white racist government of America. We will protect ourselves from the force and violence of the racist police and the racist military, by whatever means necessary.

7. WE WANT AN IMMEDIATE END TO POLICE BRUTALITY AND MURDER OF BLACK PEOPLE.
We believe we can end police brutality in our black community by organizing black self-defense groups that are dedicated to defending our black community from racist police oppression and brutality. The Second Amendment to the Constitution of the United States gives a right to bear arms. We therefore believe that all black people should arm themselves for self-defense.

8. WE WANT FREEDOM FOR ALL BLACK MEN HELD IN FEDERAL, STATE, COUNTY AND CITY PRISONS AND JAILS.
We believe that all black people should be released from the many jails and prisons because they have not received a fair and impartial trial.

9. WE WANT ALL BLACK PEOPLE WHEN BROUGHT TO TRIAL TO BE

TRIED IN COURT BY A JURY OF THEIR PEER GROUP OR PEOPLE FROM
THEIR BLACK COMMUNITIES, AS DEFINED BY THE CONSTITUTION OF
THE UNITED STATES.

We believe that the courts should follow the United States
Constitution so that black people will receive fair trials. The 14th
Amendment of the U.S. Constitution gives a man a right to be
tried by his peer group. A peer is a person from a similar economic, social, religious, geographical, environmental, historical
and racial background. To do this the court will be forced to
select a jury from the black community from which the black
defendant came. We have been, and are being tried by all-white
juries that have no understanding of the "average reasoning man"
of the black community.

10. WE WANT LAND, BREAD, HOUSING, EDUCATION, CLOTHING, JUS-
TICE AND PEACE. AND AS OUR MAJOR POLITICAL OBJECTIVE, A UNITED
NATIONS-SUPERVISED PLEBISCITE TO BE HELD THROUGHOUT THE BLACK
COLONY IN WHICH ONLY BLACK COLONIAL SUBJECTS WILL BE AL-
LOWED TO PARTICIPATE, FOR THE PURPOSE OF DETERMINING THE WILL
OF BLACK PEOPLE AS TO THEIR NATIONAL DESTINY.

When in the course of human events, it becomes necessary for
one people to dissolve the political bands which have connected
them with another, and to assume, among the powers of the earth,
the separate and equal station to which the laws of nature and
nature's God entitle them, a decent respect to the opinions of
mankind requires that they should declare the causes which impel
them to the separation.

We hold these truths to be self-evident, that all men are created
equal; that they are endowed by their Creator with certain unalienable rights; that among these are life, liberty, and the pursuit
of happiness. *That, to secure these rights, governments are instituted among men, deriving their just powers from the consent
of the governed; that, whenever any form of government becomes destructive of these ends, it is the right of the people to
alter or to abolish it, and to institute a new government, laying
its foundation on such principles, and organizing its powers in
such form, as to them shall seem most likely to effect their safety
and happiness.* Prudence, indeed, will dictate that governments
long established should not be changed for light and transient

causes; and, accordingly, all experience hath shown, that mankind are more disposed to suffer, while evils are sufferable, than to right themselves by abolishing the forms to which they are accustomed. *But, when a long train of abuses and usurpations, pursuing invariably the same object, evinces a design to reduce them under absolute despotism, it is their right, it is their duty, to throw off such government, and to provide new guards for their future security.*

Appendix B

MAY 2, 1967

STATEMENT OF THE
BLACK PANTHER PARTY FOR SELF DEFENSE
ON THE MULFORD ACT NOW PENDING
BEFORE THE CALIFORNIA LEGISLATURE

The Black Panther Party for Self Defense calls upon the American people in general and the black people in particular to take careful note of the racist California Legislature which is now considering legislation aimed at keeping the black people disarmed and powerless at the very same time that racist police agencies throughout the country are intensifying the terror, brutality, murder, and repression of black people.

At the same time that the American Government is waging a racist war of genocide in Vietnam, the concentration camps * in which Japanese Americans were interned during World War Two are being renovated and expanded. Since America has historically reserved the most barbaric treatment for non-white people, we are forced to conclude that these concentration camps are being prepared for black people who are determined to gain their freedom by any means necessary. The enslavement of black people from the very beginning of this country, the genocide practiced on the American Indians and the confining of the survivors on reservations, the savage lynching of thousands of black men and women, the dropping of atomic bombs on Hiroshima and Nagasaki, and now the cowardly massacre in Vietnam, all testify to the fact that towards people of color the racist power

---

* See: *American Concentration Camps*, by Allan R. Bosworth

structure of America has but one policy: repression, genocide, terror, and the big stick.

Black people have begged, prayed, petitioned, demonstrated and everything else to get the racist power structure of America to right the wrongs which have historically been perpetrated against black people. All of these efforts have been answered by more repression, deceit, and hypocrisy. As the aggression of the racist American Government escalates in Vietnam, the police agencies of America escalate the repression of black people throughout the ghettos of America. Vicious police dogs, cattle prods and increased patrols have become familiar sights in black communities. City Hall turns a deaf ear to the pleas of black people for relief from this increasing terror.

The Black Panther Party for Self Defense believes that the time has come for black people to arm themselves against this terror before it is too late. The pending Mulford Act brings the hour of doom one step nearer. A people who have suffered so much for so long at the hands of a racist society must draw the line somewhere. We believe that the black communities of America must rise up as one man to halt the progression of a trend that leads inevitably to their total destruction.

(Signed)

_____

Huey P. Newton, Minister of Defense

Appendix C

10 POINT PROGRAM AND PLATFORM OF THE BLACK STUDENT UNIONS

We want an education for our people that exposes the true nature of this decadent American society. We want an education that teaches us our true history and role in the present day society.

We believe in an educational system that will give our people a knowledge of self. If a man does not have knowledge of himself and his position in society and the world, then he has little chance to relate to anything else.

1. WE WANT FREEDOM. WE WANT POWER TO DETERMINE THE DESTINY OF OUR SCHOOL.

We believe that we will not be free within the schools to get a decent education unless we are able to have a say and determine the type of education that will affect and determine the destiny of our people.

2. WE WANT FULL ENROLLMENT IN THE SCHOOLS FOR OUR PEOPLE.

We believe that the city and federal government is responsible and obligated to give every man a decent education.

3. WE WANT AN END TO THE ROBBERY BY THE WHITE MAN OF OUR BLACK COMMUNITY.

We believe that this racist government has robbed us of an education. We believe that this racist capitalist government has robbed the Black Community of its money by forcing us to pay higher taxes for less quality.

4. WE WANT DECENT EDUCATIONAL FACILITIES, FIT FOR THE USE OF STUDENTS.

We believe that if these businessmen will not give decent facilities to our community schools, then the schools and their facilities should be taken out of the hands of these few individual racists and placed into the hands of the community, with government aid, so the community can develop a decent and suitable educational system.

5. WE WANT AN EDUCATION FOR OUR PEOPLE THAT TEACHES US HOW TO SURVIVE IN THE PRESENT DAY SOCIETY.

We believe that if the educational system does not teach us how to survive in society and the world it loses its meaning for existence.

6. WE WANT ALL RACIST TEACHERS TO BE EXCLUDED AND RESTRICTED FROM ALL PUBLIC SCHOOLS.

We believe that if the teacher in a school is acting in racist fashion then that teacher is not interested in the welfare or development of the students but only in their destruction.

7. WE WANT AN IMMEDIATE END TO POLICE BRUTALITY AND MURDER OF BLACK PEOPLE. WE WANT ALL POLICE AND SPECIAL AGENTS TO BE EXCLUDED AND RESTRICTED FROM SCHOOL PREMISES.

We believe that there should be an end to harassment by the police department of Black people. We believe that if all the police were pulled out of the schools, the schools would become more functional.

8. WE WANT ALL STUDENTS THAT HAVE BEEN EXEMPT, EXPELLED, OR SUSPENDED FROM SCHOOL TO BE REINSTATED.

We believe all students should be reinstated because they haven't received fair and impartial judgment or have been put out because of incidents or situations that have occurred outside of the school's authority.

9. WE WANT ALL STUDENTS WHEN BROUGHT TO TRIAL TO BE TRIED IN STUDENT COURT BY A JURY OF THEIR PEER GROUP OR STUDENTS OF THEIR SCHOOL.

We believe that the student courts should follow the United States Constitution so that students can receive a fair trial. The 14th Amendment of the U.S. Constitution gives a man a right to be tried by a jury of his peer group. A peer is a person from a similar economical, social, religious, geographical, environmental, historical and racial background. To do this the court would be forced to select a jury of students from the community from which the defendant came. We have been and are being tried by a white principal, vice-principal, and white students that have no understanding of the "average reasoning man" of the Black Community.

10. WE WANT POWER, ENROLLMENT, EQUIPMENT, EDUCATION. TEACHERS, JUSTICE, AND PEACE.

As our major political objective, an assembly for the student body, in which only the students will be allowed to participate, for the purpose of determining the will of the students as to the school's destiny.

We hold these truths as being self-evident, that all men are created equal, that they are endowed by their creator with certain unalienable rights, that among these are life, liberty and the pursuit of happiness. To secure these rights within the schools, governments are instituted among the students, deriving their just powers from the consent of the governed, that whenever any form of student government becomes destructive to these ends, it is the right of the students to alter or abolish it and to institute new government, laying its foundation on such principles and organizing its power in such form as to them shall seem most likely to effect their safety and happiness.

Prudence, indeed, will dictate that governments long established should not be changed for light and transient causes, and accordingly all experiences have shown, that mankind are more liable to suffer, while evils are sufferable, than to right themselves by abolishing the forms to which they are accustomed. But when a long train of abuses and force, pursuing invariably the same object, reveals a design to reduce them to absolute destruction, it is their right, it is their duty, to throw off such a government and to provide new guards for their future security.

Appendix D

EXECUTIVE MANDATE NO. 3:
STATEMENT OF THE MINISTER OF DEFENSE

DELIVERED ON MARCH 1, 1968,

SO LET THIS BE HEARD:

Because of the St. Valentine's Day Massacre of February 14, 1929, in which outlaws donned the uniforms of Policemen, posed as such, and thereby gained entrance to locked doors controlled by rival outlaws with whom they were contending for control of the bootlegging industry in Chicago; and because these gangsters, gaining entry through their disguise as Policemen, proceeded to exterminate their rivals with machine-gun fire, we believe that prudence would dictate that one should be alert when opening one's door to strangers, late at night, in the wee hours of the morning—even when these strangers wear the uniform of Policemen. History teaches us that the man in the uniform may or may not be a Policeman authorized to enter the homes of the people.

AND

Taking notice of the fact that (1) on January 16, 1968, at 3:30 A.M., members of the San Francisco Police Department kicked down the door and made an illegal entry and search of the home of Eldridge Cleaver, Minister of Information. These Pigs had no search warrant, no arrest warrant, and were therefore not authorized to enter. They were not invited in. Permission for them to enter was explicitly denied by the Minister of Information. Present were Sister Kathleen Cleaver, our Communications Secretary and wife to our Minister of Information, and Brother Emory Douglas, our Revolutionary Artist.

Taking further notice of the fact that (2) on February 25, 1968,

294

several uniformed gestapos of the Berkeley Pig Department, accompanied by several other white men in plainclothes, bearing an assortment of shotguns, rifles, and service revolvers, made a forceful, unlawful entry and search of the home of Bobby Seale, Chairman of our Party, and his wife, Sister Artie Seale. These Pigs had no warrant either to search or to arrest. When asked by Chairman Bobby to produce a warrant, they arrogantly stated that they did not need one. They had no authority to enter—what they did have was the power of the gun. Thus we are confronted with a critical situation. Our organization has received serious threats from certain racist elements of White America, including the Oakland, Berkeley, and San Francisco Pig Departments. Threats to take our lives, to exterminate us. We cannot determine when any of these elements, or a combinaton of them, may move to implement these threats. We must be alert to the danger at all times. We will not fall victim to a St. Valentine's Massacre. Therefore, those who approach our doors in the manner of outlaws, who seek to enter our homes illegally, unlawfully and in a rowdy fashion, those who kick our doors down with no authority and seek to ransack our homes in violation of our HUMAN RIGHTS, will henceforth be treated as outlaws, as gangsters, as evildoers. We have no way of determining that a man in a uniform involved in a forced outlaw entry into our home is in fact a Guardian of the Law. He is acting like a lawbreaker and we must make an appropriate response.

We draw the line at the threshold of our doors. It is therefore mandated as a general order to all members of the Black Panther Party for Self Defense that all members must acquire the technical equipment to defend their homes and their dependents and shall do so. Any member of the Party having such technical equipment who fails to defend his threshold shall be expelled from the Party for Life.

. . . . SO LET THIS BE DONE.

—Huey P. Newton
  Minister of Defense   MARCH 1, 1968

Appendix E

CHRONOLOGY

October 1966	Black Panther Party for Self Defense formed.
Dec. 12, 1966	Eldridge Cleaver parolled to S.F.
Feb. 21, 1967	Panthers provide armed bodyguard for Malcolm X's widow.
Apr. 1, 1967	Denzil Dowell killed by Richmond, Calif., police.
Apr. 18, 1967	Uprising and shots exchanged between police and blacks in Pittsburg, Calif.
May 2, 1967	26 Panthers arrested in Sacramento in connection with Panther armed visit to Calif. State Legislature.
May 22, 1967	Bobby Seale arrested under 1887 law outlawing guns near jail.
June 23, 1967	Cleveland riot.
June 29, 1967	Stokely Carmichael drafted into Black Panther Party.
July 10, 1967	Newark riot.
July 29, 1967	L.A. Mosque raided, 5:30 A.M.
Oct. 16, 1967	Oakland Stop the Draft Week demonstrations begin.
Oct. 28, 1967	Huey Newton arrested in Oakland for murder, intent to commit murder and kidnapping.
Jan. 15, 1968	David Hilliard arrested for passing out leaflets in Oakland.
	Eldridge and Kathleen Cleaver's S.F. apartment raided.

Feb. 17, 1968   Huey Newton Birthday Rally. Panther-SNCC coalition announced.

Feb. 25, 1968   Bobby and Artie Seale arrested after raid on apartment. Charged with conspiracy to murder.

                   Four Panthers, including Bunchy Carter and David Hilliard, arrested. Hilliard charged with carrying a concealed weapon.

Apr. 1, 1968   Martin Luther King predicts fascism coming to U.S.

Apr. 3, 1968   St. Augustine's Church, Oakland, raided by police.

Apr. 4, 1968   Martin Luther King murdered in Memphis, Tenn.

Apr. 5, 1968   L.A. SNCC office raided by police while members attend Martin Luther King memorial service.

Apr. 6, 1968   Bobby Hutton killed, Eldridge Cleaver wounded and returned to prison after Oakland gun battle.

Apr. 11, 1968   Blacks Strike for Justice Committee boycott of downtown Oakland merchants begins.

Apr. 16, 1968   Chicago Mayor Daley gives shoot-to-kill order.

Apr. 19, 1968   Bobby Hutton funeral and arrest of four Panthers returning from funeral.

May 10, 1968   4 Bay Area Panthers call press conference to repudiate confessions made in connection with Apr. 6 gun battle.

June 8, 1968   Bobby Seale convicted of carrying weapon near jail, sentenced to 3 years probation.

June 12, 1968   Eldridge Cleaver released from jail, writ of *habeas corpus.*

June 25, 1968   Eldridge Cleaver takes Panther case to U.N.

July 1968   Seattle Panther office raided.

July 27, 1968   Eldridge Cleaver speaks in Syracuse.

August 1968	Newark Panther office fire-bombed.
	Detroit Panther-police shoot-out—no injuries.
Aug. 5, 1968	L.A. shoot-out between police and Panthers, 2 Panthers killed.
Aug. 15, 1968	David Hilliard, George Murray and Landon Williams in Mexico City prevented from traveling to Cuba.
Aug. 17, 1968	Kathleen Cleaver denied entrance from Hawaii to Japan.
Aug. 18, 1968	Eldridge Cleaver nominated for President on Peace and Freedom ticket.
Aug. 25, 1968	Beginning of 4-day riots at Chicago Democratic Convention.
Aug. 28, 1968	Carmichael ousted from SNCC.
Sept. 4, 1968	150 off-duty N.Y. police attack 12 Panthers in hallway of Brooklyn court.
Sept. 8, 1968	Huey Newton declared guilty of manslaughter.
Sept. 10, 1968	Oakland Panther headquarters shot up by 2 Oakland police officers.
Sept. 27, 1968	Huey Newton sentenced 2–15 years on manslaughter conviction.
	Court of Appeals orders Eldridge Cleaver returned to jail. Granted 60-day stay (until Nov. 26).
Sept. 29, 1968	Michael O'Brien, S.F. police officer, kills Otis Baskett. O'Brien same policeman who wore "Gas Huey" pin on duty.
October 1968	Denver Panther office shot up by police during racial disturbances.
	N.Y. Panther office raided—no arrests.
Oct. 8, 1968	Cleaver lectures at U.C. Berkeley.
Nov. 6, 1968	San Francisco State College Strike begins.
Nov. 19, 1968	William Brent and seven Panthers arrested in S.F. after service-station holdup and exchange of gunfire with police.

Nov. 24, 1968	Eldridge Cleaver disappears.
Dec. 1, 1968	Newark Panther office bombed.
Dec. 7, 1968	43 Denver police raid Panther office. Panthers claim $9000 damage.
Dec. 12, 1968	12 Chicago Panthers arrested on weapons charges.
Dec. 18, 1968	Indianapolis Panther office raided, tear-gassed and ransacked by federal and local police.
Dec. 21, 1968	Denver Panther office raided.
Dec. 27, 1968	Des Moines Panther office raided.
Dec. 28, 1968	San Francisco Panther office raided.
Jan. 17, 1969	Bunchy Carter and John Huggins murdered in L.A. 8 Panthers, including Ericka Huggins, arrested and charged with assault to commit murder. Berkeley Panther office heavily watched by police.
Jan. 24, 1969	George Murray arrested on gun charge.
Jan. 30, 1969	Richmond, Calif., black officers complain about racisim and organize.
Feb. 9, 1969	3 black women maced by police in S.F.
Feb. 11, 1969	S.F. Black Officers for Justice complain about racism and organize.
Feb. 14, 1969	Over 600 S.F. police and firemen rally and complain about city administration's response to black demands.
Feb. 21, 1969	AFL-CIO approve organizing police union.
Feb. 25, 1969	Goons attack pro-integration group at S.F. School Board meeting.
Mar. 30, 1969	New Republic of Africa in gun battle with Detroit police.
April 1969	L.A. Panther office attacked by police—2 arrests.
Apr. 2, 1969	New York 21 Panthers arrested and charged with conspiring to blow up botanical gardens and department stores.

Apr. 26, 1969	Des Moines Panther office totally destroyed by bombing. 2 Panthers injured in blast. State police arrive seconds after bombing and arrest several Panthers. Panthers charge police complicity.
May 1, 1969	L.A. Panther office raided. During a 2-week period L.A. officers made 56 arrests of 42 Panthers.
May 20, 1969	Black students killed at Greensboro (N.C.) Agricultural, Technical and Trade College.
May 22, 1969	New Haven 8, including Ericka Huggins, arrested in raid on Panther office.
May 26, 1969	Fred Hampton charged with stealing ice cream, later convicted and sentenced to 2–5 years. Released on appeal.
June 4, 1969	Detroit police raid Panther office looking for suspect in New Haven murder of Alex Rackley.
	Chicago Panther office raided, police looking for George Sams. About 30 Panthers arrested, some charged with harboring a fugitive who was not found. Most charges dropped.
June 5, 1969	Denver raid on Panther office nets Rory Hithe and Landon Williams, wanted in connection with New Haven murder.
June 6, 1969	Lonnie McLucas arrested in Salt Lake City in connection with New Haven murder. Later confesses complicity in Alex Rackley killing.
June 7, 1969	Indianapolis Panther office raided during disturbance in city.
June 15, 1969	J. Edgar Hoover declares ". . . the Black Panther Party, without question, represents the greatest threat to the internal security of the country."

San Diego Panther office raided.

Sacramento Panther office raided.

June 16, 1969	Indianapolis Panther office raided—16 arrested.
June 21, 1969	William Brent hijacks plane to Cuba.
June 26, 1969	Carmichael resigns from Panthers.
July 1969	Peekskill, N.Y., Panther office burns.
July 21, 1969	Pan-African Cultural Festival in Algeria. Cleaver surfaces.
July 23, 1969	Police force their way into Bronx Panther home to effect an arrest.
July 31, 1969	Chicago Panther office raided. 3 Panthers involved in 45-minute gun battle.
Aug. 4, 1969	NAACP Legal Defense Fund to aid Panther 21 defense.
Aug. 7, 1969	Charles Bursey convicted of attempted murder and assault with a deadly weapon in connection with Apr. 6, 1968, shootings. Sentenced Aug. 28, 1969, to 1–15 years.
Aug. 9, 1969	Richmond, Calif., Panther office surrounded by police. Police leave after 30 minutes—no raid, no arrests.
Aug. 11, 1969	June Hilliard, Assistant Chief of Staff, and "G," Deputy Minister of Defense, arrested on drug charges. Charges dropped.
Aug. 19, 1969	Bobby Seale arrested and charged with Alex Rackley murder.
Aug. 20, 1969	Bobby Seale released on $25,000 bail and immediately rearrested and moved secretly to Chicago.
September 1969	Robert Williams returns to U.S.
Sept. 2, 1969	Calif. Juvenile Court Judge, Gerald Chargin, makes racist attack on Chicanos.
Sept. 8, 1969	Watts Breakfast Program raided by armed police.

Sept. 23, 1969   FBI and Philadelphia police raid Panther office.

Sept. 24, 1969   Warren Wells found guilty in Apr. 6, 1968, shootings, after 2 previous trials resulted in hung juries. Sentenced to 1–15 years.

Chicago 8 trial begins.

Oct. 4, 1969   Chicago Panther office raided for third time.

Oct. 11, 1969   Rodney Williams, San Francisco head of Police Community Relations unit, witnesses holdup and is charged with cowardice.

Oct. 18, 1969   Los Angeles Panther office raided.

Oct. 29, 1969   Bobby Seale chained and gagged at Chicago 8 trial.

November 1969   Emory and Judi Douglas detained by French officials while en route to Algeria. They are accompanied by Donald Cox.

Nov. 5, 1969   Bobby Seale given 4 years for contempt; his case severed and Chicago 8 become 7.

Nov. 22, 1969   San Diego Panther office raided.

December 1969   David Hilliard charged with threatening the life of President of U.S.

"Big Man" refused entrance to West Germany.

Dec. 4, 1969   Fred Hampton and Mark Clark killed by Chicago police.

Dec. 8, 1969   L.A. gun battle between Panthers and police. 11 Panthers, including 3 women, held off police for 5 hours.

Mar. 16, 1970   Muslim cows poisoned in Ala.

Mar. 25, 1970   Stokely Carmichael testifies to Strom Thurmond.

Aug. 5, 1970   Huey Newton released on reversal of manslaughter conviction.

Oct. 19, 1970   Chicago conspiracy charges against Bobby Seale dropped; contempt citation stands.

INDEX

Afro-American Association, 68
Agnew, Vice President Spiro T., 87, 141
Algeria (Algiers), 136–139, 150
Ali, Muhammed, 82, 214
Alpert, Stew, 109–113, 115
ACLU, 211
American Medical Association, 274
Anderson, David, 230–232
Andriotti, Dante, 47, 48
Anthony, Earl, 130
Anticolonial revolution, 136
Anti-Semitism, 103, 174–176, 233, 245
April 6, 1968, Shootout, 11, 12, 97, 185–194
Axelrod, Beverly, 215

Bail, 204, 205, 242
Baskett, George, 227, 228, 230, 231
Baskett, Otis, 228, 229, 233
Basta Ya, 60
Bay, Robert, 86
Berkeley Barb, 112
Bernstein, Mr. and Mrs. Leonard, 136
Bickett, Judge William Y., 244
Black, Ron, 117
Black attorneys, 207, 212
Black capitalism, 102
Black consciousness, 155, 157, 158, 162, 195, 267
Black Guards, 109–111, 158

Black history, 170
Black identity, 96, 100, 106, 138, 143, 150, 160, 163, 183, 195
Black liberation, 66, 67, 142
Black middle class, 75, 156, 160
Black Panther, 65, 88, 122, 135
Black Panther Party for Self Defense, 68, 77, 80, 185
Black Panther Party of Northern California, 68, 70, 80
Black Police in police forces, 39, 40; organizations, 41–46; recruitment, 45
Black population, Alameda County, 20
Black Power, 68, 71
Black power, definition of, 104
Black Student Unions, 68, 82, 84, 131, 140, 154
Black studies, 68, 81, 82, 131, 154
Black United Front, 100, 161, 183
Blacks and organized labor, 91
Blacks Strike for Justice, 12, 14, 15
Blauner, Professor Robert, 216, 217
Blumstein, Dr. Alfred, 208
Bodi, Alexander, 36
Boycotts, 12, 15, 19, 87, 148
Boyle, Kay, 238
Breakfast for Children, 58, 85–88, 107
Brennan, Vincent J., 242

303

BLACK CLASSIC PRESS
titles about The Black Panther Party and Black Power Movements

The Black Panther Party: Reconsidered
Charles Jones, ed.

This pioneering collection of essays examines this unique organization in depth using a new approach that places the views of party members alongside those of historians and cultural commentators. The result is a vital dialogue between inside and outside perceptions and realities.

ISBN-10: 0-933121-97-0. ISBN-13: 978-0-933121-97-3. 1998*, 2005. 519 pp. Paper. $22.95.

Blood in My Eye
George L. Jackson

Blood in My Eye *captures the spirit of George Jackson's legendary resistance to unbridled oppression and racism. His unique and incisively critical perspective becomes the unifying thread that ties together this collection of letter and essays in which he presents his analysis of armed struggle, class war, fascism, communism, and a wide array of other topics.*

ISBN-10: 0-933121-23-7. ISBN-13: 978-0-933121-23-2. 1971*, 1990. 195 pp. Paper $14.95.

A Panther is a Black Cat
Reginald Major

Reginald Major provides a vivid eyewitness account of the conditions leading to the formation of the Black Panther Party: unemployment, poor housing, police brutality, and a Black community held in bondage by white business leaders and politicians. He also knew the young Black men and women of the Panthers who, armed with guns, challenged those conditions. Major captured events as the Panther challenge set the example for Black resistance across the country.

ISBN-13: 978-1-57478-037-6. 1971*, 2006. 310 pages. Paper. $16.95.

David Walker's Appeal
David Walker

More than just a petition against slavery, David Walker's Appeal *is a foundational document from which many contemporary themes in Black political philosophy have evolved. Walker asserted the right of Black people to defend themselves against a common enemy by any means necessary. His clear presentation of the problems confronting people of African descent is prophetic, and it assures the relevance of the* Appeal *to contemporary readers.*

ISBN-10: 0-933121-38-5. ISBN-13: 978-0-933121-38-6. 1830*, 1993. 101 pp. Paper. $8.95.

Seize the Time
Bobby Seale

Seize the Time is Bobby Seale's riveting first person account of the conditions leading to the formation of the Black Panther Party for Self-Defense as a national organization. Written mostly while Seale was a political prisoner in the San Francisco County Jail in 1969 and 1970, he recounts the concepts and details of the inner workings of one of the most revolutionary grass-roots organizations in America. In the Introduction, Seale describes Seize as continuing "to have universal appeal as an account of an oppressed people's struggle for human liberation."

ISBN-10: 0-933121-30-X. ISBN-13: 978-0-933121-30-0. 1970*, 1991. 429 pp. Paper $18.95.

Black Power and the Garvey Movement
Theodore G. Vincent

Vincent provides valuable insight into understanding Marcus Garvey, his influence and the origins of the Universal Negro Improvement Association (UNIA). Initially intended to explore black militancy in the 1920s from the point of view of the Black power struggles of the 1960s, Vincent now adds a new introduction, providing new perspective.

ISBN 978-157478-040-6. 1972*, 2006. 302 pp. Paper. $16.95

Black Fire: an Anthology of Afro-American Writing
Amiri Baraka and Larry Neal, eds.

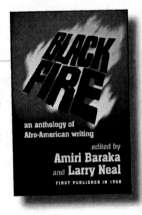

Black Fire, first published in 1968, is a seminal resource from the Black Arts movement. Editors Amiri Baraka and Larry Neal compiled over 180 selections from 77 cultural critics, literary artists and political leaders, including John Henrik Clarke, Sonia Sanchez, and Kwame Ture in this revolutionary anthology.

ISBN: 978-1-57478-039-0. 1968*, 2007. 670 pp. Paper. $24.95.

*Indicates first year published

To order these or other titles, please visit our website:
www.blackclassicbooks.com

Black Classic Press
P.O. Box 13414
Baltimore, MD 21203-3414